SOUTHAMPTON RECORDS SERIES

General Editors:
H. ROTHWELL: A. L. MERSON: A. T. PATTERSON

VOL. X

A SELECTION FROM
THE SOUTHAMPTON CORPORATION JOURNALS, 1815–35,
AND
BOROUGH COUNCIL MINUTES, 1835–47

A Selection from

The Southampton Corporation Journals, 1815–35,

AND

Borough Council Minutes, 1835–47,

edited, with an Introduction, by

A. TEMPLE PATTERSON,

Reader in Regional History in the University of Southampton

SOUTHAMPTON
AT THE UNIVERSITY PRESS
1965

© The University of Southampton, 1965

Printed in Great Britain by
The Camelot Press Ltd., London and Southampton

CONTENTS

MAPS

PREFACE AND ACKNOWLEDGEMENTS

Few towns, if any, can merit or repay more than Southampton does the increased attention to the more modern periods of their development which is a feature of the recent considerable growth of the systematic study of local history. It is virtually unique in being a southern town which grew in size and population during the industrial (or rather, in its case, commercial) revolution as fast as almost any of the smoke-grimed conurbations of the north and northern midlands. Moreover the previous phase of its history, when it was a spa and a place of fashionable resort, meant that this growth involved a physical, social and governmental transformation even greater and more interesting than most of theirs. And yet (which is perhaps the most interesting aspect of all) this change, while it could not take place without disputes and animosities, was achieved with less sustained bitterness than might have been expected. To anyone acquainted with the deep and abiding chasm which divided the people of Leicester, for example, at and after the reform of municipal government in 1835, the relative restraint and almost urbanity with which at least the main stages of the change were accomplished in Southampton form an intriguing contrast.

The selections and summaries from the Corporation Journals and Council Minute Books which follow, and the introduction and commentaries which accompany them, are therefore offered as a preliminary or as aids to the first part of that fuller study of nineteenth- and early twentieth-century Southampton which has yet to be made. I have taken for survey the period 1815-47 because, while including the last twenty years of the old unreformed Corporation's life, it embraces the first stage and closes with the second stage of the transformation of the town's government.

Considerations of space and interest have dictated a compromise in the selection of material. To reproduce in full the whole of four bulky manuscript volumes and parts of two others was obviously impossible. I have therefore quoted in full only the more important or illustrative entries, and have summarized (within square brackets) a great many more transactions, while omitting others of relatively little or no importance. Furthermore, in deciding what to include I have for the first five years inserted (usually in summary form) sufficient of the minor routine business which occupied most of the old Council's time to give what I hope will be an impression of how it was chiefly employed; and have subsequently omitted this and quoted or summarized only the more important or unusual matters. I have also added explanatory or amplifying matter (which will be found preceded by a paragraph mark and in smaller type)

vii

at the end of a number of the reports of meetings, preferring to do this rather than resort to footnotes which would have been so many and sometimes so extensive that they must have harassed the reader and ruined the pagination. The sources upon which these notes or commentaries are based have been given in the Bibliography; but to have inserted the very great number of detailed references involved would have cumbered this volume with an apparatus that would have increased its size and cost of production considerably. I have therefore to ask the reader's trust and indulgence for not having done so.

For the sake of conveying something of the flavour of the passages which are quoted in full, I have followed the Journals and Minute Books in the lavish use of capital letters which was then customary, and also in the contemporary spelling of certain words such as "honor", "controul" and "expence"; but where mere spelling mistakes have obviously occurred I have usually corrected them. On the other hand, in the matter of punctuation, which is sparse in the originals, I have felt constrained to insert an occasional comma or semi-colon where (but only where) the meaning might otherwise have been obscure.

An unavoidable handicap is that there is no map of Southampton in 1815 available to illustrate the opening of the period, and it has been necessary to fall back on that of 1802, while for the end of the period the map of the town in 1844 has been employed.

It is with great pleasure and gratitude that I express my warm thanks to the many people who have helped me: to Mr. C. E. Welch the City Archivist for his unfailing kindness and readiness to draw on his store of knowledge, to Mr. C. E. C. Burch the Assistant Archivist and their staff, whose helpfulness has lightened the work of consulting and transcribing the manuscripts involved; to Mr. R. Andrew the Editor of the *Southern Evening Echo* for allowing me to consult the ample files of local newspapers in the library of Southern Newspapers Limited, and to Mr. G. S. Raynes the Librarian of the *Echo* and his staff for so kindly and patiently facilitating my searches therein; to my colleagues Professor H. Rothwell and Mr. A. L. Merson for reading my typescript and giving me much valuable advice; to the staff of Southampton University Library, and in particular the indefatigable Mr. Alec Anderson and Mr. Maurice Line, for ready and rapid production of photostatic copies of many of the manuscripts and for much other help; and to Miss E. M. Sandell for the loan of valuable contemporary material and for helpful discussion.

The University of Southampton
December 1964.

INTRODUCTION

The central theme of Southampton's municipal history during this period is the transference of the government of the town from what was then called locally "the party of the gentlemen" to the business-men, or rather to the newer type of business-men who both created and were created by the railway and the docks.

The period opened when the Napoleonic Wars came to an end, with Southampton a third-class port which still enjoyed a considerable reputation as a watering-place "of elegant and fashionable resort". Its trade was largely regional, except for a coastal traffic in coal from Sunderland and Newcastle (in that order), the importation of wine and fruit from Portugal and Spain, of timber from the Baltic, and of oats, bacon, lard and flax from Ireland. Along the south coast its most regular commerce was with Poole, Swanage, Weymouth, Exeter, Dartmouth, Plymouth, Falmouth and Penzance in one direction, and Portsmouth, Chichester, Shoreham and Newhaven in the other, to all of which it re-exported some of this wine, fruit and timber. It had also maintained its old trading connection with the Channel Islands, from which came cattle, fruit, vegetables, pigs and occasionally oysters; and it dealt with London in a variety of goods and to a smaller extent with Bristol. Sufficient shipbuilding, too, was carried on, chiefly at Northam and Chapel on the banks of the Itchen, to enable most of the town's small vessels to be built locally, though building for the Navy had ceased with the return of peace. But it had had little share in the relatively rapid expansion of English overseas trade which began about the middle of the eighteenth century, since the main developments were in the more distant trades such as the East and West Indian and the American, which as yet scarcely concerned it.

On the other hand for sixty years or so it had experienced a rise to fashion and for a short time almost to fame as a seaside resort and spa, thanks originally to royal patronage by the three younger brothers of George III. This patronage had virtually ceased after the 1770's, but if the town had afterwards seen less of the cream of high society it had continued to be visited by many people of rank and note. Moreover its attractions and those of its immediate neighbourhood had brought some of the gentry and the well-to-do not merely to visit but to settle, so that a fringe of gentlemen's seats had developed to the north and north-west of the town and to the east across the Itchen; while nearer at hand "marine cottages" and villas had sprung up to meet the growing demand. In turn the prospects of employment or commercial profit opened up by the influx of visitors and new residents had drawn to the town numbers of people in all walks of life, so that it seems to have been as early as 1750 that an increase of population began which far preceded the age of railways and steamships and whose tempo was not so much accelerated as merely maintained by it. The French wars of 1793-1815 do not seem, at first at any rate, to have caused any interruption in this influx and increase, nor to have done much harm to Southampton's popularity as a resort; indeed they appear to have increased the number of naval and military officers, active or retired, who took up residence in or near the town. By the 1790's a number of the gentry and officers who lived locally, such as Sir Yelverton Peyton, Sir John Collins, Admiral Alexander Scott, General D'Auvergne and Colonel Heywood, were taking a leading part in the Corporation's activities and holding the highest civic offices.

In the closing stage of the Napoleonic War and for a few years afterwards (at the beginning of the period, that is, with which this volume is directly concerned) the town's social activities and popularity did indeed seem to be declining, though not its trade. As a watering-place and a resort for the leisured it was coming to have more competitors, some of them near at hand such as Cowes, with advantages which it did not possess. After all, it was hardly on the seaside, it had no sandy beach, and its waters contained comparatively little salt. But its commerce continued to advance, while still preserving its general pattern; and it was now developing a through passenger traffic to and from France, the Channel Islands and the Isle of Wight, to which the first cross-Channel packet-steamers gave a powerful stimulus. Yachting, too, which by then was all the rage among the fashionable world, and of which Cowes and Southampton Water were centres, began to draw more of that world again to and through the town. By about 1820, therefore, its reputation as a resort had somewhat revived, and this revival lasted for another ten or fifteen years.

Around 1815, however, the gentry and retired officers had temporarily ceased to be in evidence in the limited circle of the Corporation. At that period it was rather the older and more established merchant families, together with the bankers, lawyers, brewers, collectors of customs and the like—Rowcliffes, Eldridges, Lintotts, Durells, Taylors, Atherleys, Riddings, Moodys, Smiths, Le Feuvres—who presided decorously though a little sleepily over the civic affairs of the town. But presently the considerable post-war reduction of the armed forces brought many half-pay officers again to Southampton, some of whom in due course became members and then leading members of the Corporation. Their alliance with the older merchant families was assisted and strengthened by the fact that sons or younger brothers of several of the latter were now serving officers, so that a younger generation of Atherleys, Eldridges and Le Feuvres, home on leave, could talk across the dining-table of how things were going in the Services "since your time, Sir". Thus the governing municipal oligarchy came to be termed "the gentlemen's party", at least by those who were outside its circle though they might be rising men commercially.

Active membership of the Corporation was confined in 1815 and for twenty years afterwards to a bare score of "serving burgesses", nearly all of whom were also members of the Borough Council. This was composed of the Mayor, Sheriff, Senior and Junior Bailiffs, and all previous holders of these offices. If the Recorder, who must be a barrister, was also a burgess he too was a member. The Mayor and all former mayors were aldermen, the others common-councilmen. New councillors were admitted by election as Junior Bailiff, and if not already burgesses would be sworn in immediately before their election to this office. The usual though not invariable progression of office was from junior to senior bailiff and then to sheriff and mayor in successive years. Since the expense attending this last eminence caused some to evade it, however, and since a too rapid recruitment of the Council was not desired, the sequence was often broken by the re-election of a former mayor to the chair. The Mayor was formally chosen on the Friday before the feast of St. Matthew, but the process of election actually began a month earlier, on the Friday before St. Bartholomew's day, which was called private nomination day. The Mayor and aldermen then met and drew up a list of four persons who had served the office of sheriff, usually selecting the two senior aldermen who had been mayor only once and the two senior burgesses (if there were two) who had been sheriff but not mayor. On the day of formal election they met again and struck two names off this list, and also decided which of the remaining two they would recommend for election to the fuller meeting of common-councilmen and other serving (as well as honorary) burgesses which afterwards took place. Voting in this was by ballot, but there was no instance in this period of the person recommended by the Mayor and aldermen not being elected, although in 1830 six ballots were cast unavailingly for another.

The Mayor received no salary, but an allowance of 50 guineas at the end of his term of office, which was made up of £20 in lieu of the profits of the town soil and £32.10.0 in place of rents formerly received "for the support of his table", which had been surrendered in 1772 and 1774 respectively. This was intended to defray the expenses of the hospitality incumbent on him, and if his was a second term of office he was allotted £82.10.0. He also had an allowance of £30 for the dinners which he gave on quarter session days, another of £10 to enable him to provide a buck for the dinner on private nomination day, a compensation of 25 guineas in lieu of some wharfage dues which had also been surrendered, and fees of 6s. 8d. whenever the Corporation seal was affixed to a lease of Corporation property, 3s. 4d. when it was affixed to a licence to alienate or assign a lease, and 14s. on each private seal to the attestation of certificates. From these latter sources, which naturally varied considerably from year to year, he drew on an average £12. Together with the capon money reserved on the leases, 2 guineas allowed for postages, and one or two small donations from charities, his receipts were generally about £168, or £198 in a second mayoralty; but his expenses almost always exceeded this, sometimes by as much as £100, especially since he was expected to provide dinners for the Corporation not only on the quarter session days for which he received an (inadequate) allowance but also on the day when he was sworn into office and the day of electing his successor.

The Sheriff's main duties were to summon the juries for the sessions and assizes, at which he attended, and to hold a county court when necessary. He was also customarily the foreman of the court leet jury, and executed all writs directed to him from superior courts. He received no salary, and his principal functions were performed in practice by an under-sheriff, invariably an attorney, who was also appointed by the Corporation. The bailiffs, jointly with the mayor, were judges of the civil court of pleas, and sometimes held a court at one of the fairs, but received no salary or emoluments. The Recorder's main duty was to attend the quarter sessions, receiving 12 guineas for each attendance during the earlier part of the period, which was changed in 1830 to a salary of 50 guineas a year. He was also occasionally asked to give a legal opinion on some question affecting the Corporation. There were eleven justices of the peace for the borough: the Mayor, ex-Mayor, Recorder, Bishop of Winchester, five chosen from the aldermen and two from the other burgesses. The Bishop and the two last, however, never actually appeared on the bench. The Town Clerk, like the Recorder before 1836, was chosen by the Mayor, aldermen and councillors, and must be an attorney but not necessarily a burgess. He was also clerk of the peace, clerk of the quarter sessions, protonotary of the civil court of pleas, steward of the court leet, clerk to the justices of the petty sessions, attorney and solicitor to the Corporation, and in practice usually clerk to some of the boards of commissioners established by local acts of parliament. His salary as town clerk had remained at the antiquated figure of 30 guineas, but it was estimated that his various fees and other emoluments were worth another £400 a year to him. A town clerk before the Municipal Reform Act of 1835 was in fact the Pooh Bah of a corporation, and if he was a man like the notorious Thomas Burbidge of Leicester he might be its evil genius. If he was of the stamp of Thomas Ridding of Southampton he was likely to be its guide, philosopher and faithful servant.

Burgesses, serving and honorary, were nominated at a meeting of the Common Council and elected at the next meeting, which must be at least a week later. Serving burgesses, as already indicated, were few in number. Honorary burgesses were usually non-resident and after a resolution of October 1831 must be so, and were not eligible for any office. They were normally gentlemen living in Hampshire or the neighbouring counties, relatives or friends of members of the Council, persons temporarily connected with the town in some notable way, or occasionally people of national distinction. The number elected averaged from two to four a year, though there were some larger creations, as in 1829 when eighteen were added, apparently by allowing each member of the Council to make a nomination. By 1835 their number had risen to 160, so that they considerably outnumbered the serving burgesses; but (latterly at least) there does not seem to have been any very definite idea of creating them in order to sway the parliamentary elections for the borough (the franchise in which was vested in burgesses and scot-and-lot householders). The Corporation in fact differed from many others in having no exclusive party colour, though Tory opinions were inclined to predominate.

The subordinate officers of the Corporation included four sergeants at mace, or town sergeants, who received salaries of £15 a year for attending the Mayor and justices of the peace, serving summonses on the juries of the court of quarter sessions and court of pleas, and performing a variety of other functions. In addition, one was gaoler of the debtors' gaol at £35 a year and another of the felons' gaol at £30, while a third collected and retained for his own use the tolls of the poultry and vegetable market, averaging 6s. or 7s. a week, and the fourth was the water bailiff, in which capacity he collected and retained £8 or £9 a year as fish market tolls. Two unsalaried constables were annually elected by the Common Council from among the householders. They might produce substitutes, who need not be householders, but must pay them, usually about £10 a year. Petty constables or beadles of the wards were also chosen and also unsalaried, and might likewise produce paid substitutes. Even with the addition of three or four extra beadles or watchmen the policing of the town was ineffective, cases of neglect of duty or absence from duty being frequent. In April 1824, for example, the one and only "constable of the night" gave three casual tramps leave to make themselves comfortable in the "Cage" or lock-up at Bargate, joined them in drinking, fell into a drunken sleep, and was robbed by them. As was usual in the towns of that day, a private Society of Guardians existed, whose members subscribed to hire additional patrolmen and offer rewards to informers or for the discreet return of stolen property with no questions asked. There were three gaols, the two aforementioned and the Bridewell, all of which were accommodated in God's House Tower and Gate and the gallery between them, besides the temporary lock-up at Bargate referred to above.

The chief courts of jurisdiction within the borough were those of quarter and petty sessions, the court leet and the court of pleas. The court of quarter sessions took cognizance of all offences which could be tried at a county quarter sessions and of capital felonies, though its jurisdiction in the latter cases was not always exercised; indeed if it seemed from the depositions taken before the magistrates that the case was such that execution would follow in the event of conviction it was taken out of the quarter sessions' jurisdiction to the county assizes. Petty sessions, at which two justices attended, were held regularly every week. The antiquated machinery of the court leet was from time to time employed to make presentments, chiefly of nuisances and encroachments, which were sometimes drawn to the Common Council's attention by the Sheriff. The civil court of pleas, usually called the common court of the town, was held on each Tuesday for the first three weeks after a new mayor came into office and on alternate Tuesdays afterwards, for the recovery of debts and similar pleas. Although it was supposed to be held by the Mayor and Bailiffs, the Junior Bailiff alone normally attended, and even he contributed merely the authority of his presence, while the Town Clerk, as the officer of the court, took the evidence, summed up and directed the jury, which was drawn from the tradespeople of the town.

The Corporation's chief sources of revenue were quit-rents and fines from its property, market rents and a bi-annual payment from the Harbour Board. The said property was mostly let at small rents on leases for forty years, renewed every fourteen years for fines which usually represented one and a quarter years' rack rent. The market rents were sums paid for the use of small shops in or near the Market, the soil of which was the Corporation's property. It had formerly been entitled to certain dues on shipping called groundage, wharfage, storeage, cranage and anchorage, as well as petty customs; but the act of parliament which had created the Harbour Commissioners in 1803 had put an end to these and directed that the Corporation should receive instead one-fifth of the port dues collected by the Commissioners, after the Collector's poundage had been deducted. The chief recurrent items of expenditure were salaries; the repair and insurance of Corporation property such as the Guildhall, the Audit House in the High Street where the Council normally met, and the gaols; the costs of dinners and entertainments other than those furnished by the Mayor; the interest on a debt incurred chiefly through the building of the Audit House and the expense of unwise litigation; fee-farm rents and other permanent outgoings in which the Town Clerk's bills were a noticeable item; and gifts from the Corporation's charity fund. These last, which were specific, irregular and usually small, must be distinguished from the payments and loans, averaging about £320 a year, made on account of various charitable endowments for which the Corporation were trustees. The chief of these were: Steptoe's Charity, of late seventeenth-century origin, from which interest-free loans of £20 each were made to young people just setting up in trade and money was annually distributed to the poor; the town's share, along with twenty-three others, in the similar but sixteenth-century Sir Thomas White's Charity; Alderman Taunton's bequest, dating from 1752, which was devoted chiefly to the education of poor but promising boys, the provision of marriage-portions for deserving servant-girls, and the maintenance of aldermen or their widows who had fallen into poverty; Mrs. Fifield's Gift, established in 1772 for the supply of clothes to the poor who were not in receipt of parish relief, the purchase of coal for the inmates of God's House Hospital, and the proper maintenance of her family tomb; and Alderman William Freeman's, of 1780, which was also given to poor persons not receiving alms.

A corporation of the old "unreformed" sort that existed before 1835 was hardly aware that a problem of local government existed at all. Some of its former functions had disappeared or declined with the passing of the centuries, and it was usually slow to grasp or even incapable of grasping that new needs had arisen and new activities were called for. Little was left of that regulation of the town's economic life which had bulked large in medieval and Tudor times except the formal registration of apprenticeships. The maintenance of local defences had ceased to be a municipal matter; though in a walled town like Southampton it was necessary from time to time to decide whether a gateway should be pulled down or widened, or if some crumbling tower should be shored up or left to collapse. The antiquated machinery of police continued to function, though more and more inadequately. Justice was administered, usually conscientiously and with moderate competence, by magistrates whose office made them normally the busiest and most active members of a corporation. In addition there remained the management of its property and revenues, which thus became the chief concern of a borough council. For the provision of the amenities and services which the growth of population and the progress of civilization made necessary the eighteenth century had developed the practice of creating by local acts of parliament special boards of commissioners which were separate from the Council. Thus in Southampton a Waterworks Board had been established in 1747, a Paving and Lighting Board in 1770 and a Harbour Board in 1803. There was also the Board of Poor Law Guardians set up by an act of 1773 which had empowered the several parishes (of Holy Rhood, St. Michael's, St. Lawrence's-with-St. John's, All Saints and St. Mary's) to unite for the purpose of poor relief and the maintenance of a single poorhouse; and there were the Southampton–Winchester and Southampton–Romsey turnpike trusts. Not only did these last have under their care the main highways into the town (the former controlling that through Swaythling and Portswood as well as that from Winchester *via* the Avenue), but they were also responsible for several important thoroughfares within it. The rest of the streets were untidily divided between the Pavement Commissioners and the Borough Council, with the result that the four bodies concerned came into occasionally acrimonious contact over such questions as the laying of drains, water-pipes, sewers and presently gaspipes; as well as over encroachments, parking and the restriction of anything that might cause a public nuisance on the highways, such as the holding of fairs and markets. It is true that a modicum of co-operation between the Council and all these boards and other bodies was provided in practice by the fact that some or all of its members were *ex officio* members of them as well; but they were usually the least conscientious in attendance, and at its best this apparatus was a clumsy, cumbersome and creaking set of machinery.

The Southampton Corporation of 1815-35 thus vegetated rather somnolently through the even tenor of an existence that consisted chiefly of granting leases and licences; making loans from Steptoe's or White's Charities, together with subscriptions to worthy causes and small gifts to distressed and deserving persons; administering with fairness but not with absolute punctuality the other charitable endowments with which it had been entrusted; and enjoying dinners on regular and frequent occasions which included not only those already mentioned but quit-rent day and the bi-annual audit of accounts. The attendance at its meetings ranged from two (on one occasion) or three to a dozen, and it was never considered that the number present was too small to discharge business, except that for the election of new burgesses a quorum of nine was required. On the other hand there were several meetings of which it was recorded that there was nothing to transact—formally and officially at least. On audit days the dinners seem to have been regarded as the really important business, for the auditing was perfunctory, at least until the closing years of this period. By then the Council's unbusinesslike habits and frequent financial difficulties (which culminated in 1824-5 after a visit from the Charity Commissioners in its being obliged to mortgage the Audit House and Market House to ensure the punctual and proper payment of the town charities) had led to the setting up of a Finance Committee that recommended some economies. But if the Council was unbusinesslike it was not corrupt, even though there is a suggestion of previous easy-going laxity in the resolution passed on 22 March 1822 that "any Member of the Common Council who has a Lease in course of Renewal shall not be present at the Council when the Terms of such Renewal are discussed and settled". The gravamen of the criticism that came to be levelled against it, however, was that in addition to being unrepresentative—or rather, because it was unrepresentative—it did not move with the times. The town's increasing needs, in what was becoming a new age, largely escaped its notice; and the progress of the town mainly took place independently of it. Hence when the Municipal Corporation Commissioners visited Southampton in 1833 to hold their inquiry they reported that "no great interest seems to have been taken in late years in the proceedings of the Governing Body; when questions have arisen in which the inhabitants took any interest, a want of confidence in that body has frequently shown itself".

Southampton in fact, after the Napoleonic Wars and more particularly after 1820, was entering a transitional period in which, while its social and recreational attractions on the one hand had revived rather more and for a little longer than has perhaps always been recognized, its modern expansion as a port was beginning to get under way. In this conjunction surely lies the chief explanation why it was now, and not twenty years later, that the growth of its population accelerated further. It is possible indeed that in view of the natural but perhaps excessive attention which has been concentrated on the liners of later years the importance of the part played in its development by the through passenger traffic and the steam-packets of the 1820's has been rather overlooked. It was in this decade that Southampton began to vaunt itself as a gateway to the Continent, and in the last three years of the 1820's these local steamboats were carrying more than 100,000 people a year, even though they did not yet run in the winter months. In the 1830's a change that was still relatively gradual but was nevertheless completely altering the character of the town came over Southampton. On the one hand it was now that the tide of fashion began to ebb definitely and finally from it as a resort. But this involved no pause in its overall progress, since the very factors—steam transport and the through traffic—which were bringing this phase of its history to an end were also the strongest forces stimulating its further development and transformation. If more people were going elsewhere they were often doing so by way of Southampton and its steamers, and so still bringing profit to the town. It was the steamer interests which were prominent in the rising demand for improved landing facilities which led to the construction of the Royal Pier in 1833; and to increase the through passenger traffic was one of the motives of the group of local men who formed the London and Southampton Railway Company in 1831, though they also had hopes of making Southampton a great cargo port which were not to be fulfilled. When after its initial difficulties in attracting capital the Company had established itself securely, its natural sequel and indeed almost offshoot was the Dock Company which was set up in 1836. By this time, however, the old Corporation was defunct.

To say that this stream of progress largely by-passed the Corporation does not mean of course that the latter was entirely oblivious of it. There were members like W. J. Le Feuvre who had steam-packet interests, and at least one, Captain Ward, who played a leading part in the early history of the Dock Company. As a body, however, it gave no lead but merely bestowed its blessing when these proposed developments, in their initial form, were brought to its notice.

But though the Corporation was criticized as unrepresentative and oligarchic as well as for its *fainéant* tendencies, there was never directed against it anything like the degree of party and sectarian bitterness which a corporation like that of Leicester aroused.[1] It contained both Whig and Tory members (though Tories predominated and there were no Radicals) and Whigs like J. R. Keele and P. C. Fall were elected to mayoral and other offices in their proper turn, though men of both parties joined in the condemnation of ultra-radicalism expressed in the loyal address voted in 1820. It is true that there was enough of the contemporary Anglican feeling against nonconformists for them to be excluded from the Council, but the town was not such a stronghold of dissent (despite the eminence of the Reverend Thomas Adkins and the respectability of the leading members of his Above Bar congregation) as could cause this to arouse strong passions. When Messrs. Ellis and Maude of the Commission of Enquiry into

[1] See A. Temple Patterson, *Radical Leicester*, chaps. IV, VI, VIII and X-XIII.

Municipal Corporations (on whose report the subsequent Municipal Reform Act was based) visited Southampton in the course of their circuit in 1833, the Corporation did not put obstacles in their way as Leicester's did but treated them with due courtesy and gave them every possible help in their investigations. For this it was praised even by pronounced Radicals like Joseph Lankester and Dr. Francis Cooper, who were also at pains to emphasize, when they were invited by the Commissioners to give evidence, that they did not impute the least shadow of corruption to the Corporation but only complained of its apathy towards improvements. It could almost be said in fact that the old Corporation, like the House of Lords in *Iolanthe*, had done nothing in particular but done it very well; and one is tempted to add that its members made their exit like gentlemen for the very simple reason that that, in the widest sense of the word, is what they were. In 1835 the passing of the Municipal Reform Act naturally aroused some resentment on one side and enthusiasm on the other; and Le Feuvre, the last mayor of the old dispensation, made two unsuccessful attempts to carry a motion in the Council that a brief should be sent to Sir Charles Wetherell, the most uncompromising opponent of the measure in the House of Commons, on behalf of the Corporation. Even then, however, leading Radicals declared at a public meeting in support of the bill that though the Corporation had been put on trial by the late inquiry it had been honorably acquitted. At the same time they complained that its merits were negative and it had done too little for the improvement of the town. Surely, declaimed William Lankester after paying personal compliments to individual members, a new gaol should have been built, or a hospital endowed, or schools established, or an efficient police constituted, or marshes and ditches drained? But when the end came at the close of the year it was in contrast again to the violent decease of the Corporation of Leicester, whose Journal still bears the blots and stains and rents that show where Burbidge the outgoing Town Clerk dashed his pen into the page in fury after making his last entry. Here the Corporation, having arranged its affairs to the best of its ability, quietly closed its books and decorously expired.

The Municipal Reform Act of 1835 divided Southampton into five wards, corresponding in name though not entirely in boundaries to the five parishes. For these wards 30 councillors were to be elected by the ratepaying householders—12 for All Saints, 9 for St. Mary's, and 3 each for Holy Rhood, St. Michael's and St. Lawrence's—and were to hold office for three years, one-third retiring annually. In addition ten aldermen were to be elected by the councillors (though not necessarily from among their own number) and were to hold office for six years, five retiring every three years. The mayor was to be elected annually by the aldermen and councillors. The Council was empowered to levy a borough rate, but its accounts must be regularly and publicly audited. Justices of the peace would henceforth be appointed by the Home Office, and would therefore not necessarily be members of the Council, though its recommendations would have weight; and the control of the charities would be transferred to trustees similarly appointed.

The outcome of the first municipal elections provided yet another contrast to towns like Leicester, where the change to a more democratic system was accompanied by a complete turnover in the personnel and party colour of the town government. It was, however, quite in keeping with the moderation of Southampton's municipal politics before 1835 and the relatively restrained nature of the recent criticisms that the elections should leave the Tories (or, as they were beginning to call themselves, Conservatives) in control. The old Corporation had been mainly though not exclusively nor aggressively Tory; and after a brief attempt to conduct the election on a non-party basis of common concern for the interests of the town had broken down, a majority of the same party was returned to the Council. There it enlarged itself by electing as aldermen ten more Conservatives who were not already councillors. The new Council included most of the more enterprising Conservative leaders of the old one (of whom one was promptly elected Mayor) and about half its members; while another element of continuity was supplied by the equally prompt reappointment of Ridding as Town Clerk. "Gentlemen" mayors, too, were chosen as often as not in the thirteen years of Conservative government that followed, and several newcomers of that stamp were included in the infusion of new blood which the Council now received. Addressing itself in businesslike fashion to its task of coping with a changing town, it set up standing committees for particular departments of administration. The Watch Committee introduced a modern police force on the metropolitan model; the Finance Committee embarked on the levying of borough rates which presently produced complaints of over-taxation that were not confined entirely to the Liberal-Radical opposition; the Lease Committee occupied itself with much of the business which had formed the staple work of the old Corporation; and the transfer of the administration of the town charities to the new trustees was made in due course.

If the old Corporation had survived even it would have been compelled by the progress of the Railway Company and the formation of the Dock Company to pay more attention to these harbingers of the new age, since both were now applying to buy portions of the Marsh and mudlands. But the amount of time and interest which the new Council devoted to these matters showed that it was much better attuned to its time and circumstances. Even those of its members whom for convenience we may call the gentlemen were men of business too. Nevertheless its attitude to these new enterprises was not one of unanimous approval, for the spokesmen and supporters of the Dock Company had to overcome an opposition which became increasingly a party and Radical one.

Indeed, one of the most interesting features of Southampton's local politics in this period is the fact that it was after and not before the reform of the corporations that strong party, sectarian and even personal divisions arose in the Council and stormy debates became frequent (though in contrasting its atmosphere with that of its predecessor some discount must be allowed for the fact that the latter's debates were not reported in the press, as these were). Several reasons may be adduced for this development of bitterness. Nonconformity in religion and radicalism in politics were then very closely linked; and under the new dispensation a small group of nonconformist business-men like the Lankesters, divided from their opponents by sectarian issues on which they felt deeply, had entered the Council. Another factor probably was that in Southampton as in some other towns advantage was now taken of the reduction of the newspaper stamp duty to establish a Radical journal. The Conservative *Hampshire Advertiser*, which had come into existence in 1822 under the title of *Southampton Herald* and changed its name in 1827, was now confronted by the *Hampshire Independent*; and the two papers banged and slanged away at each other over national, local and very often personal matters, and no doubt heated the passions of their respective readers in the process. Again, the growth of the town which the docks and railway stimulated was mainly in St. Mary's Ward and emphasized its working-class and petit-bourgeois character, so that it became a solid Radical stronghold. Its Radicalism was intensified by the grievance that All Saints, the "gentlemen's" or well-to-do ward and the only other one with room to expand, had more representation on the Council though it was less populous and not growing so fast.

For some years from 1836 onwards, therefore, the municipal elections were fiercely fought and soon produced an alignment in the Council which changed little until 1846. A small but persistent and very vocal phalanx of St. Mary's Radical councillors confronted a solid Conservative majority holding the other wards. In view of the smallness and proportionately limited representation of three of these, the key positions were All Saints and St. Mary's. If the Conservatives could win the latter, as for a moment in 1841-2 they seemed to be beginning to do, their grip on the government of the town would become virtually unchallengeable; if the Radicals could carry a substantial part of All Saints, as they eventually did in 1847, they would come into power.

By 1836 or soon afterwards, too, the line of policy dividing the parties in local government had taken shape. The Conservatives on the whole favoured the railway, docks and other enterprises which they considered likely to promote the trade and prosperity of the town. To this, however, an important reservation must be made, arising from the strong regional element in the politics of Southampton. Proposals even of this sort which came from, or were thought likely to favour, the developing Itchen area and the so-called "Itchen Interest" in which some of the St. Mary's Radicals were prominent were liable to meet with strong Conservative opposition. The Radicals for their part sought in general to promote public improvements such as better streets, houses and water-supply, which would benefit particularly the poorer inhabitants. Nor were they without means of doing so, since for part of the period after 1836 they had an intermittent and precarious control of the Pavement and Waterworks Boards and the Board of Guardians, chiefly by virtue of attending more regularly than their opponents. The result, however, was that the Borough Council inclined to block the proposals of the Boards, while the latter (if more indirectly) did what they could to retaliate in kind. Thus at a moment when Southampton's population was growing relatively as fast as that of almost any northern industrial town, when its character was changing and its needs were correspondingly urgent, its municipal government was handicapped and developments were delayed by this tendency to dead-lock.

Matters reached their worst point in 1841-2. A particularly corrupt and hard-fought parliamentary election in 1841, in which the Conservative candidates were successful, was followed by their being unseated on petition on the ground of bribery practised by their agents. The hearing by a Committee of the Commons in 1842 of evidence in support of these petitions involved the washing in public of a great deal of the dirty linen of both local parties, to the accompaniment of violent accusations and counter-accusations and even a challenge to a duel, involving the fiery-tempered Le Feuvre. In the midst of all this a Conservative or Conservative-led mob broke up an anti-Corn-Law meeting organized by the Liberals, and a Conservative mayor refused them police protection for a second one. In such an atmosphere it is small wonder that both the improvement projects of the Pavement Commissioners and a plan brought forward by the Council for the enclosure of the Marsh were frustrated (though there were cross-currents in each case and neither was a straight-forward party issue).

Fortunately this situation did not last very long. Tempers cooled, and in 1843 the obvious and terrible need of increased burial accommodation enabled the Council to carry through a proposal, and obtain a local act, for the building of a town cemetery on the Common. This was followed by the successful revival of its Marsh enclosure scheme, and by an act of 1844 it was empowered to enclose the Marsh for building purposes and thus obtain the means of buying out the interests which certain individuals still possessed in the common lands of the East and West Magdalens (Marlands), Houndwell, Hoglands and Porters Meadow. These could then be laid out subsequently as parks and public spaces. At the same time the Pavement Commissioners brought forward an improvements bill with ultimately equal success, though the Council still opposed it until substantial concessions were made to its point of view and requirements. By the Improvement Act of 1844 the maintenance of all the streets of the town was concentrated in the hands of a reorganized Board of Commissioners, who were also given power to build new ones and to undertake an extensive scheme of sewerage and drainage.

In the next two years the political temperature was lowered further and a measure of inter-party co-operation was achieved, chiefly as a result of the impact of the railway boom of 1845-6 on the local railway situation. Dissatisfaction with the London and South-Western Railway (as the London and Southampton had renamed itself in 1839) was now widely felt in Southampton; and the Council as a united body took the lead in successive attempts to break its monopoly by taking advantage of the sudden spate of railway projection to attract some rival line to the town. The South-Western, however, was too strongly placed, and succeeded in absorbing or driving off all potential rivals. The same fear of monopoly prompted the Council to oppose a bill which the Dock Company was promoting to enlarge its powers, primarily for the purpose of building a graving dock, since some of its clauses aroused fear that the Company might be enabled ultimately to buy up the Royal Pier and the town quays. In this case, however, the Council was more successful and secured the deletion of the offending clauses.

By this time the Conservative hold on the municipal administration was weakening. The nation-wide divisions in the party which culminated in the deep and bitter schism caused by Sir Robert Peel's *volte-face* (or apostasy) over the repeal of the Corn Laws were fully reproduced in Southampton. The town's two Conservative members of parliament took different sides in this schism, each with his local following, and the split reacted on the municipal elections. Those of 1846 were feebly contested, and the Liberals gained ground in the smaller wards. A year later their opponents were, if anything, even more divided and apathetic, and almost resigned in advance to the defeat which they now suffered when the Liberals broke their grasp on All Saints. Partly or largely because the fires of party strife had sunk lower of late, they accepted this defeat gracefully and with a commendable display of public spirit. The leaders of both parties met around the dining-table of the retiring mayor (who by a coincidence was again Le Feuvre) and exchanged compliments and good wishes; so that what may be regarded as the second stage of the transition of Southampton's municipal government was achieved almost as smoothly and painlessly as the first, though in the sequel this era of good feeling proved to be comparatively brief.

I

The Corporation Journals, 1815–35

Friday the 27th day of January 1815

[Present: Richard Eldridge, Mayor; John Rowcliffe, late Mayor; Thomas Durell, George Atherley, Samuel Silver Taylor, John Rushworth Keele, William Lintott.

Several leases of Corporation property were ordered to be granted and two licences to alienate property held on lease from the Corporation sealed.]

Subscription for the Relief of the Poor at this Season   £26.5.0

STEPTOE'S BOND CHARITY

Resolved that William Mitchell of Southampton Bookbinder be advanced the sum of twenty pounds and that Thomas Baker of Southampton printer and Isaac Fletcher of Southampton Stationer be accepted as his Sureties.

BILLS ORDERED FOR PAYMENT

Messrs. Lintotts' Bill for coals at the Audit House		£10.16.0
Do.	Do. Godshouse	10.19.0
Do	for Shrub in the years 1812–14	19.8.0
Thomas Holder one Quarter's Salary due St. Thomas Day		3.15.0
The Town Sergeants	Do.	15.0.0

CORPORATION ACCOUNTS

A statement of the Accounts was laid before this Council by the Treasurer to the 31st day of December last and it appears that there was then a Balance in the Treasurer's hands of £232.14.10.

¶ Of the members present, Eldridge was a well-to-do timber merchant, Rowcliffe a merchant who later fell into reduced circumstances, Durell and Atherley were both bankers, Durell being also a wine and coal merchant, as was Lintott; Taylor had succeeded his father Walter as proprietor of the block works at Wood Mill which supplied the Navy with that article for many years until steam-works were built in the dockyards, and Keele was a surgeon and incidentally the maternal grandfather of Admiral of the Fleet Lord Jellicoe, the commander of the British Grand Fleet in the first world war. Thomas Holder was the Keeper of the "Cage" or lock-up at the Bargate.

Shrub was a drink made with the juice of oranges or lemons, sugar, and rum or other spirit.

Friday the 3rd day of March 1815

[Present: the Mayor, Arthur Atherley, Durell, Rowcliffe, Lintott, Keele, Taylor.

One licence to alienate and several leases were sealed].

BILLS ORDERED FOR PAYMENT

Thomas Skelton's Bill for Stationery	£10.11.4
William Sheldon's Bill for Smith's Work at the Audit House and Market House	1.11.3
John Hookey's Bill for Stone Mason's work at the Market	2.0.6
Cornelius Stark's Bill for the Markets	13.7.9

STEPTOE'S MONEY

Resolved that James Burbank Fryer of Southampton Bookbinder be advanced the sum of twenty pounds and that Edward Baker of Southampton Merchant and John Lock of Southampton Victualler be accepted as his Sureties.

¶ Arthur Atherley, like George, was a member of an old Southampton family which had latterly become prominent as bankers. They were connected by marriage and political affiliations with the Carters who had dominated the Whig borough of Portsmouth for many years, and their bank [Atherley & Fall's] was regarded as the Whig house in Southampton, while the other leading banking establishment, Maddison's, was the Tory house. Arthur Atherley represented the town in Parliament in 1806-7, 1812-18 and 1831-5, after which he retired to Arundel, where he died in 1844 aged 74.

Friday the 10th day of March 1815

[Fifteen members were present, but the attendance bore no relation to the importance of the business in hand, since only two or three very minor matters were transacted.]

Tuesday the 4th day of April 1815

[Five members were present, and again only minor business such as the payment of the salaries of Thomas Holder and the town sergeants to Lady Day was dealt with.]

Friday the 6th day of May 1815

[Four members—the Mayor, Durell, Lintott and Keele—were present. Two leases were sealed.]

At this Council the Mayor brought up an account of the Quit Rents received the first day of May Instant amounting to the sum of £108.11.7.

At this Council the Treasurer brought up an Account of the sums paid for Interest on Bonds amounting to the sum of fifty two pounds ten shillings.

SUMS PAID BY THE TREASURER

... The Town Clerk's allowance pursuant to the order of the 30th day of November 1814 [by which he was allowed 30 guineas a year for his attendance on the Mayor and justices of the peace at various times for which he could not properly make any charge, to be paid in two instalments at the bi-annual audits] £15.15.0

Friday the 30th day of June 1815

[Seven members were present. Two leases and four licences to alienate were sealed, an award of £20 was made from Steptoe's Charity, the Treasurer was instructed to pay the Town Clerk certain bills and sums of money, and four bonds were sealed to "Thomas Ridding of Southampton, gentleman", three being for £100 each and one for £50.]

At this Council the Mayor brought up an Account of the Market Rents received the 20th day of May last amounting to £32.19.0.

It was resolved that John Rumbold the younger be apprenticed to George Stone of Southampton whitesmith with the usual fee of five pounds.

¶ Thomas Ridding was the Town Clerk. His father of the same name had held the office from 1787 until his death in 1804. The son had gained much insight into its duties while working under his father during the latter part of this time, and after a brief interval while the post was held by William Curry had in turn been appointed when the latter died in 1810. In his private capacity he was now lending money to the Corporation, which was normally accustomed to approach the wealthier of its own members when it required a loan.

Friday the 14th day of July 1815

[Eleven members were present, including the Recorder, Charles Hilgrove Hammond.]

WATERLOO SUBSCRIPTION

Resolved that this Corporation do subscribe Ten Guineas to the Subscription for the benefit of the families of the slain and of the numerous wounded of the British Army under the command of the illustrious Wellington in the signal victory of Waterloo and in the several Battles which have been or may be fought in the present campaign.

Friday the 18th day of August 1815

[Eleven members were present. One lease and one licence were sealed and one bill paid.]

PRIVATE NOMINATION

This day being the Friday before the Feast of St. Bartholomew the Mayor and other officers of this town were nominated by the Mayor and Aldermen . . . according to the ancient customs and usages of this Town the rest of the Members of the Common Council having withdrawn.

Friday the 1st day of September 1815

[Five members present.]

At this Council the following Gentlemen were proposed as Honorary Burgesses of this Corporation:

William Jolliffe Eldridge Esquire a Major in the Bombay European Regiment and

Sir Leonard Thomas Worsley Holmes Baronet of Westover House in the Isle of Wight . . .

and this day week is fixed for putting the question.

¶ Major Eldridge was presumably related both to the Mayor and to the Jolliffe family, who were mercers and drapers and belonged to the Corporation circle, William Edward Jolliffe being a member at this time. The family of Holmes had for generations been one of the most distinguished in the Isle of Wight and in the parliamentary representation of local boroughs.

Friday the 8th day of September 1815

[Eight members were present. Major Eldridge and Sir Leonard Holmes were unanimously elected honorary burgesses.]

MESSRS TRIM AND TOOMER'S BOND

Application having been made to this Council by Messrs Trim & Toomer for payment of the bond of £580 entered into to them on the 13th day of August 1813 and there not being sufficient cash in the Treasurer's hands for that Purpose

Resolved that a Common Council be held on the 22nd. Instant to consider of selling the lower piece of Land on the South Side of the Road at the bottom of Bridge Street to raise some money to enable the Corporation to discharge the said Bond.

¶ Cornelius Trim and Edward Toomer of Southampton were bankers, to whom the Corporation had given £420 and this bond in discharge of a debt of £1000.

Friday the 22nd day of September 1815

[Seven members present.]

So few members attending at this Council it is Resolved that the Sale of the Land at the bottom of Bridge Street be considered at the next Council.

[Two bills were ordered for payment.]

Friday the 29th day of September 1815

[Eleven members present.]

MESSRS TRIM AND TOOMER'S BOND

The discharging of this Bond being further considered and Messrs Trim & Toomer having consented not to press for more than half of the Principal Money for the present upon the Interest being paid and one Moiety of the Principal being shortly discharged and it appearing to this Council that they may shortly be enabled by the payment of some Fines on Renewals [sc., of leases] and other sources to raise sufficient money to discharge such Moiety without selling the Land . . . at the bottom of Bridge Street It is Resolved not to sell such Land at present.

Ordered that the Treasurer do pay Messrs Trim & Toomer the Interest on such Bond.

William Lintott Esquire was this day sworn Mayor. . . .

Tuesday the 3rd day of October 1815

[Seven members present.]

At this Council John Sadleir Moody Esquire was sworn Sheriff for the year ensuing . . .

John Rushworth Keele was sworn on this day Senior Bailiff for the year ensuing . . .

Richard Price Lintott Esquire was sworn on this day Junior Bailiff for the year ensuing . . .

This day Richard Price Lintott was sworn a member of the Common Council of this Corporation.

This day William Colson, as a substitute for James Newman, and William Argyle were sworn Constables for this Town and County for the year ensuing. . . .

[One lease and one licence were sealed.]

Tuesday the 10th day of October 1815

[Eleven members present.]

This day the Common Council proceeded to the election of a Coroner in the place of Mr. Charles Smith deceased . . . when Mr. John Barney attorney at law was elected to the office. . . .

BILLS ORDERED FOR PAYMENTS

The late Mayor's allowance	£52.10.0
Do. in lieu of Dues	26.5.0
Do. for postage	2.2.0
Do. for Fyfield's Gift	1.1.0
Do. for a Buck for Private Nomination Dinner	7.17.6

The Cryer's Bill for posting Handbills, crying notices, allowance for Sundays and cleaning rooms	£7.8.6
The Sergeants, one Quarter's Salary at Michaelmas last	15.0.0
Thomas Holder's Quarter's Salary	3.15.0
Thomas Sheldon's Bill for repairs at the Audit House	1.10.11
Thomas Masters for cleaning the Fish Market for one year	5.0.0

MARKET RENTS

The Mayor brought up an Account of the Monies received the seventh instant amounting to £30.10.2½.

¶ Thomas Masters was the town sergeant who was also Water Bailiff and had the oversight of the Fish Market.

Tuesday the 24th day of October 1815

[Ten members present, including the Recorder.]

At this Council Arthur Atherley . . . Esquire who was on the 16th day of July 1814 elected a Justice of the Peace took the Oath of Office . . .

The Mayor reported to this Council the Death of Sir Yelverton Peyton Baronet a Justice of the Peace for this Town and County and one of the Members of this Corporation. Resolved that a Common Council be held on Friday the 27th day of October . . . to elect and nominate one of the Aldermen and Burgesses . . . a Justice of the Peace . . . in the Room of the said Sir Yelverton Peyton.

MRS. FIFIELD'S TOMB

Warren and Beavis bills for repairing the Tomb and two years' cleaning
£2.1.5

¶ Sir Yelverton Peyton had been mayor in 1791-2 and 1799-1800.

Friday the 27th day of October 1815

[Nine members present, including the Recorder.]

At this Common Council John Butler Harrison Esquire was unanimously elected a Justice of the Peace in the Room of Sir Yelverton Peyton . . .

At this Council the Certificate of Duties in lieu of Petty Customs to . . . the Lords Commissioners of the Treasury and also the Barons of His Majesty's Exchequer was sealed certifying that the amount of Duties in lieu of Petty Customs came to the sum of £94.16.2 from the Feast of St. Michael the Archangel 1814 to the Feast of St. Michael . . . 1815.

This day Mrs. Fifield's Charity was ordered to be distributed by Messrs. Jolliffe.

GREAT COATS AND GOWNS

Ordered that this Charity be distributed by Messrs. Jolliffe for the year ensuing and in case the gentlemen shall not have disposed of the coats and gowns according to the lists of Messrs. Jolliffe's now delivered to them on the first day of January next that the Mayor do give away such as shall then remain undisposed of.

¶ In 1552 the town's annual fee-farm payment to the Crown had been reduced, in consideration of its diminished trade, from £200 to £50, so long as the amount collected for petty customs in any year did not reach £200, and no carracks of Genoa or galleys of Venice had entered the port during the year—i.e. so long as the once lucrative trade with these Italian republics had not been resumed. Although the fee-farm had ceased to be paid to the Crown the certificate continued to be made out; though after 1803 the sum reported represented that part of the Corporation's fifth of the port dues which was in lieu of petty customs—see 10 December below—and the antiquated clause concerning the carracks and galleys had been omitted for some years.

Friday the 10th day of November 1815

[Five members present.]

At this Council the Mayor brought up an Account of the Quit Rents received the sixth day of November amounting to . . . £115.0.4.

This day the interest on bonds was paid amounting to . . . £130.

The Town Clerk's allowance of . . . fifteen guineas was paid to him.

At this Council the Treasurer delivered in the following Account—

Amount of Dues collected under the Act for improving the port . . .

Six months ending Michaelmas 1815

Boomage		£65. 6. 6	
Tonnage		92. 7. 0	
Wharfage		589. 5. 5	
Wharfage and Storage of Goods Coastwise received			
	£364.11. 6		
Due 29 December	498. 1. 6		
	862.13. 0		
Due 25 March	592.12. 8	270. 0. 4	
		£1016.19. 3	
Collector's Poundage	£37. 6.11		
Mr. Watson's Salary	50. 0. 0		
Half Year's Fee Farm	25. 0. 0	112. 6.11	
		£904.12. 4	
One fifth due to the Corporation is	£181. 2. 7		
In lieu of Petty Customs	45. 5. 7		
Do. of Wharfage, etc.	135.17. 0	£181. 2. 7	

¶ The above calculation is that by which the sum due from the Harbour Commissioners to the Corporation for the previous half-year, under the Act of 1803 which provided that it should receive one-fifth of the port dues less certain deductions, was arrived at. William Watson was the wharfinger and Collector of Dues, as well as Harbour Master.

Friday the 8th day of December 1815

[Five members present. One lease and one licence were sealed, a subscription of ten guineas was voted to "the Society establishing in this Town for the investing Monies of Poor Persons at Interest", and four bills were ordered for payment, including £23.12.3 for the last four quit rent dinners and £17.10.6 and £16.14.0 respectively for the expenses of Chapel Fair in 1814 and 1815.]

¶ Of the four annual fairs held in Southampton until late in the eighteenth century only two now survived: Above Bar Fair, held on May 6 and 7, and Chapel or Trinity Fair, held near the Chapel Mill on the bank of the Itchen, which lasted from the Saturday in Whit week till the following Wednesday. It was opened by the Mayor and Bailiffs with much ceremony, followed by a feast. This last, however, was discontinued as one of the measures of economy adopted by the Corporation on 16 September 1830 (q.v. below).

Tuesday the 19th day of December 1815

[Ten members present. The only entry records a gift of ten guineas to a poor widow and her family.]

Friday the 9th day of January 1816

The Mayor brought up an Account of the Market Rents received the 6th day of January last amounting to £30.10.1½.

Resolved that the thanks of this Common Council be unanimously given to the Reverend Thomas Mears the Chaplain to this Corporation for his very excellent and admirable and appropriate Sermon preached before this Corporation at Saint Lawrence's Church yesterday, being the day appointed for a public Thanksgiving . . . upon the Conclusion of the late Treaty of Peace and also that [he] be requested to print his sermon and to permit it to be done at the expence of this Corporation . . .

Resolved that this Corporation do pay the difference between the cost of twenty-two tons of potatoes and the Money to be received by the Sale of them to the Poor at twenty-one Pounds for sixpence.

¶ The difference amounted to £17.16.3.
The Rev. Thomas Mears, a former pupil of the Free Grammar School, was the active, benevolent and highly respected incumbent of the united parishes of St. Lawrence and St. John from 1794 till his death in 1835, and also of St. Michael's from 1793 to 1817 and then of All Saints from 1817 to 1835. It must be remembered that some parishes, like the first three of these, were too poorly endowed to be the sole support of a parish priest. The peace referred to was that which brought the Napoleonic War to a formal close.

Friday the 16th day of February 1816

[A subscription of ten guineas was voted to "the Fund raising for the Relief of Sufferers at the late Fire in French Street"; a bill was ordered for payment; and Thomas Masters, being no longer able through old age and illness to attend to his duties as Water Bailiff and a town sergeant, was pensioned off with £30 a year.]

Friday the 23rd day of February 1816

FREE SCHOOL

At this Council the Mayor laid a letter before the Corporation from the Reverend C. T. Griffith wishing to make some alteration regarding the Free School if not incompatible with the Rules and Statutes of the School and the Town Clerk is directed to call upon him to . . . confer with him thereon and report thereon to the next Council.

¶ The Free Grammar School, founded in Edward VI's reign, was beginning to decline, like almost all similar foundations in other towns providing chiefly a classical education which was no longer in much demand. It had flourished in the late eighteenth century under the headship of Dr. Richard Mant, but had now less than twenty pupils. The premises, West Hall, situated between Bugle and French Streets, were old and in bad repair, and the present headmaster, Mr. Griffith, who was also the Vicar of St. Michael's, formed a plan for removing the School to a site Above Bar, which however he failed to secure. See 21 November 1817 and 29 May 1818.

Friday the 15th day of March 1816

At this Council a letter was received from the Commissioners of the Waterworks requesting permission . . . to take up and remove any young plants or bushes in the Common which grow in the way of and hinder the cutting of the Lines of the Waterworks thereon. Resolved that this Council do give leave for the same to be done if Mr. John D. Doswell shall be of opinion that the same be necessary for the compleating [*sic*] of the Waterworks Reservoir and pipes and drains leading thereto.

STEPTOE'S AND SIR THOMAS WHITE'S BONDS

Ordered that letters be written to the several Defaulters in payment of the Bonds upon the above Charities and if the same be not forthwith paid that they be proceeded against for Recovery.

[Seven leases were renewed.]

¶ The Waterworks Commissioners had begun some years earlier to make a reservoir on the Common which was not yet finished. Doswell was the Corporation Engineer.

Friday the 5th day of April 1816

[Three leases were sealed, four bills ordered for payment, and two youths apprenticed, both to shoemakers.]

Friday the 3rd day of May 1816

[Stephen Lintott was elected Junior Bailiff to replace Richard Price Lintott, who had died in office.]

Wednesday the 8th day of May 1816

At this Council the Mayor brought up an Account of the Market Rents received the 6th day of April last amounting to £31.2.3.

At this Council a Letter was received from . . . the Town Clerk of Bristol requesting the Corporation will support them [*sic*] in opposing the Bristol Gaol Bill now in progress through the House of Commons by which it is intended to provide for its maintenance out of the Corporation Funds, stating that all Corporation property is involved in the Question.

Resolved that the Town Clerk do write to Mr. Atherley and to the Right Honorable Sir George Rose in the absence of his son Mr. George Henry Rose to request they will oppose the Bristol Gaol Bill as it appears . . . to involve a principle highly injurious to the Rights of every Corporate Body.

¶ The veteran Tory politician Sir George Rose, whose country house Cuffnalls was at Lyndhurst, had possessed much influence over the borough of Southampton for many years; and his son had represented it since 1794, with various partners. Atherley, however, had made a breach in the family's domination by winning one seat in 1806; and the representation of the town had subsequently been divided between Whigs and Tories, since between 1807 and 1812 another Whig, Josias Jackson of Bellevue House, had temporarily replaced Atherley.

Friday the 10th day of May 1816

[£117.3.0 was received for quit rents on 6 May, £66.5.0 was paid as interest on bonds, and the Town Clerk's allowance of 15 guineas was also paid. The Corporation's fifth of the port dues collected between 29 September 1815 and 25 May 1816 amounted to £128.17.4½. Durell's bill of £13.15.0 for wine consumed by the Corporation was ordered for payment.]

Friday the 2nd day of August 1816

[Two leases and a licence to alienate were sealed and seven bills ordered for payment, the market rents received to 6 July were reported as amounting to £31.2.3, and a loan of £20 from Steptoe's Charity was made to a hairdresser.]

Friday the 9th day of August 1816

No order was made.

¶ The same entry occurred again on 23 August and on a few subsequent occasions which will not be recorded.

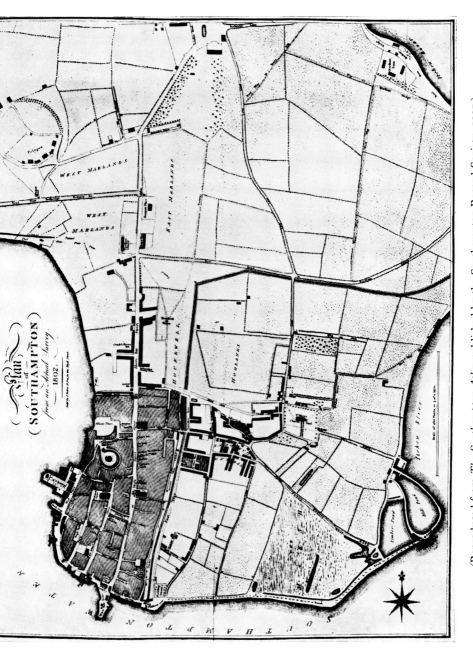

(Reproduced from *The Southampton Atlas* published by the Southampton Record Society, 1907.)

Friday the 16th day of August 1816

[Ordered that defaulters in repayment of loans from Steptoe's and White's Charities and their sureties were to be written to for payment.]

Friday the 30th day of August 1816

At this Council the following Gentlemen were proposed as Honorary Burgesses:

The Revd. Samuel Heathcote of Hursley in the County of Southampton.

Thomas Hayward Budd of Bedford Row in the County of Middlesex Esquire.

Frederick Jennings Thomas Esquire a Captain in the Royal Navy.

Sir Alexander Inglis Cochrane K.G.C.B. [*sic*], Vice-Admiral of the Red.

The Revd. William Austen, Rector of Horsted Keynes in the County of Sussex.

James Croft Esquire of Greenham Lodge in the County of Berkshire.

Sir Herbert Sawyer, K.C.B., Vice-Admiral of the White.

Joseph Lomer of Newgate Street in the City of London, Draper.

Thomas Castle of Cornhill in the City of London, Haberdasher.

James Gauntlett Esquire of Winchester, a Captain in His Majesty's Army.

George Tarbutt Esquire of Millbrook in the County of Southampton.

Henry Riddle Moody Esquire of Oriel College Oxford.

Gilbert Heathcote Esquire a Captain in the Royal Navy.

Edward James Foote Esquire, Rear-Admiral of the White.

Thomas Alston Brandreth Esquire a Captain in the Royal Artillery . . .

Sir John Pollen of Redenham in the County of Southampton.

George Ward of Bellevue House in the Isle of Wight Esquire.

Arthur Atherley the youngest of Southampton Esquire and of Trinity College Cambridge, Master of Arts.

Thomas Pipon Esquire a Major of the 7th Regiment of Hussars.

George Pitt Rose Esquire of Saint John's College Cambridge.

John Lintott the younger, Gentleman, a Lieutenant in His Majesty's 51st Regiment of Foot.

¶ The Heathcotes of Hursley Park were prominent Tory political figures in Hampshire. Admiral Cochrane, later Commander-in-Chief at Portsmouth, should not be confused with his more famous nephew, the hero of a score of brilliant exploits in the late war. Rose and Atherley were of course fledglings of the families of the borough M.P.s; while the names of several others—Lomer, Moody, Lintott—suggest membership of or kinship with families belonging to the Corporation circle. All were unanimously elected at the next meeting of the Council on 6 September, at which two leases were renewed, a youth was apprenticed to a stonemason, and £20 lent from Steptoe's Charity to a cooper.

Sunday the 29th day of September 1816

George Atherley Esquire was this day sworn Mayor . . .

Tuesday the 1st day of October 1816

[John Rushworth Keele was sworn Sheriff and Samuel Le Feuvre a Common Councilman and then Junior Bailiff. Stephen Lintott was sworn Senior Bailiff on 8 October.]

Friday the 25th day of October 1816

[The market rents received on 5 October were reported as £29.17.2; one lease was sealed, four bills were ordered for payment, and Mrs. Fifield's Charity and the greatcoats and gowns for the poor ordered (as annually) to be distributed by Messrs. Jolliffe.]

William Babbidge having contrary to the orders of the late Mayor persisted in frequenting the Poultry Market with worsted and articles of woollen It is Ordered that the Town Clerk do draw a case for the Opinion of Counsel whether the Corporation can forbid him from frequenting the Market in that way.

Ordered that the Town Clerk do make Inquiry as to the Encroachments made by William Rolph in the Common . . . and report to the next Council.

Friday the 8th day of November 1816

[The quit rents received on 4 November were reported as £111.5.9; £90 interest on bonds and the Town Clerk's allowance were paid; a certificate to the Treasury and the Exchequer that the dues in lieu of petty customs had amounted between Michaelmas 1815 and Michaelmas 1816 to £68.15.6 was sealed; the Corporation's fifth of the port dues for the past half-year was declared to be £146.4.11; five bills were ordered for payment and £20 from Steptoe's Charity was lent to a gardener.]

It being represented to this Council that Mr. Henry Roe has been carrying his Buildings upon the Town Wall adjoining his Premises . . . near unto Orchard Street and it appearing that such Town Wall is not included in his Lease

Ordered that the Town Clerk do write to Mr. Roe to remove such Building and not to carry up any Thing upon the Town Wall there.

Tuesday the 12th day of November 1816

At this Council Mr. Henry Roe attended in consequence of the letter written to him . . . and stated his having made such Incroachments by

Mistake and his Readiness to make Amends for any Damage done to any of the Corporation Tenants in Orchard Street. . . .

Friday the 29th day of November 1816

[An honorary burgess on the list of recent creations was admitted and sworn, a youth apprenticed to his father (a shoemaker), £20 lent from Steptoe's Charity to a schoolmistress, 25 guineas subscribed "for the Relief of the Poor at this Season", and two leases were sealed, one being "a lease of the Ground for the Use of Bathing Machines near Itchen Ferry".]

Friday the 20th day of December 1816

CHRISTMAS MONEY TAKEN OUT 1816

The Gifts are: Mr. Pemberton's	£2.10.0
Mr. Parkinson's	10.0
Mr. Sandys' [*sic*]	5.0
Do. to the Minister of Saint Lawrence	1.18.4
Mr. Rose's	5. 0.0
Mr. Jacomine's	2.10.0
Mr. Sadleir's Gift to the Pensioners at God's House	2.13.4
	£15. 6.8

Which Gifts are disposed of as follows:	
To Mr. Saml. S. Taylor for All Saints	£2.15.8
„ Mr. Durell for Holy Rhood	1.15.4
„ Mr. W. E. Jolliffe for Saint Michael's	1.12.0
„ Mr. Hilgrove for Saint Lawrence's	10.8
„ Mr. S. Lintott for Saint John's	10.8
„ Mr. J. B. Harrison for Saint Mary's	10.8
„ the Revd. Dr. Mant for Christmas Eve Sermon	10.0
„ Hampton at the Old Almshouses	10.0
„ the Churchwardens of Saint Lawrence's for Sandys' Sermon and the Poor	1.18.4
„ the Revd. Mr. Griffith, Free School	2. 0.0
„ the Pensioners at God's House	2.13.4
	£15. 6.8

At this Council the Case respecting Babbidge's standing with Worsteds in the Poultry Market which was stated for the Opinion of Mr. Serjeant Letts was received from him and the Opinion was read advising that the means of removing him should be by Act of Trespass and it is thereupon ordered that the Town Clerk do look into the title Deeds of the present Market and report thereon at the next Council.

[Two apprentices were bound, to a cabinet-maker and a whitesmith respectively; the Mayor's allowances and town sergeants' salaries were paid; £20 from Steptoe's Charity was lent to a printer; six bills were ordered to be paid; and the Town Clerk was instructed to write to several persons who had not paid their fines on the renewal of their leases.]

¶ "Sandy's" should no doubt be "Sendy's", under which spelling modern reference is usually made to a charity established in 1583 which provided an endowment for the almshouses, gifts to the poor and annual sermons. These "old" almshouses, as by now they were commonly called, had been built in 1565 near St. Mary's Church in order to house at what was then a safe distance from the town any who might fall victims to pestilence. From pest-houses they became almshouses, and in 1806 the Corporation had granted a lease of the premises to the then occupier at £2 a year. Dr. Richard Mant was Rector of All Saints from 1793 to 1817, when Mears succeeded him. In God's House Hospital four old men and four old women were maintained, who also received occasional gifts from charities such as these.

Tuesday the 24th day of December 1816

[Two of the recent list of honorary burgesses were admitted and sworn, but no other business was transacted.]

Friday the 24th day of January 1817

[The market rents received on 11 January were reported as £531.3.4½, five bills ordered for payment (including £5.16.0 for the audit dinner in November last and £1.11.4 for the repair of Mrs. Fifield's tomb), two youths apprenticed to a brickmaker and a cordwainer respectively, and leave was given to the lessee of the brick-kiln on the Common "to put up a Gate where a style lately stood on the north Side of the Common near the Brick Kiln . . .".]

Friday the 7th day of March 1817

The case of William Babbidge standing in the Market with Mr. Serjeant Letts' Opinion thereon being taken into further consideration It is Resolved to proceed according to such Advice. Ordered that [he] be written to acquainting him that if he still persists in standing in the Market an action will be commenced against him accordingly without further notice.

Ordered that William Rolph be written to acquainting him that if he does not immediately throw open the Ditch between the Common and the Field belonging to him an action of Trespass will be commenced against him.

[Three licences were sealed, four leases ordered for renewal, a bill was ordered for payment, a tailor advanced £20 from Steptoe's Charity and a youth apprenticed to a cordwainer.]

Friday the 28th day of March 1817

[Easter gifts totalling £32.16.8 were distributed to the poor from Sendy's, Reynolds's, Mrs. Parkinson's, De la Motte's, Pemberton's, Paul Mercer's and Sadleir's Charities; bills ordered for payment; a licence and four leases sealed; £20 was advanced to a "mariner" from Steptoe's Charity; and a lease was ordered to be granted to Samuel Silver Taylor, John Sadleir Moody and Thomas Sloane Moody, brewers, of the South-ampton Arms on the Common for fourteen years at a rent of £30 a year.]

¶ The Southampton Arms was alternatively known then, and is much better known now, as The Cowherd's Inn.

Thursday the 17th day of April 1817

[A lease and two licences were sealed, and market rents amounting to £32.1.9 reported as received; the Corporation's fifth of the port dues for the past half-year was declared to amount to £103.2.5, a loan of £20 made from Steptoe's Charity, and a youth apprenticed to a tailor.]

Friday the 9th day of May 1817

[The quit rents received on 5 May were reported as £122.18.8, the Town Clerk's allowance and £65 interest on bonds paid, six bills ordered for payment, two leases sealed and one ordered for renewal, and a youth was apprenticed to a tailor.]

A letter was received from Mrs. Scott desiring Payment of her Bond and it is Ordered that the Town Clerk do inform her that the Corporation cannot pay it not having Money in their Treasurer's hands.

The Mayor reported that he had received the following letter from the Guardians of the Poor . . .

> Sir,
>   The Guardians have it in contemplation to afford Relief to the Poor by employing them in repairing roads and other public works. We are directed to express to yourself and the other Members of the Corporation the Request of the Court of Guardians to be permitted to dig Gravel in Southampton Common, and to employ it in such manner as they may judge most conducive to the Object they have in view . . .

Ordered that the Town Clerk do acquaint the Guardians of the Poor that this Corporation are willing to grant permission for the digging Gravel for the above purpose provided the Mayor be from time to time consulted from what part of the Common the Gravel shall be taken . . .

Friday the 20th day of June 1817

The Town Clerk reported to this Council that pursuant to their order of the 7th day of March last he wrote to William Babbidge respecting his standing in the Market and receiving no answer thereto had commenced an action against him . . .

[The Town Clerk also reported that he had followed the same procedure with regard to William Rolph's trespass on the Common. Three youths were apprenticed, to a stonemason, a wheelwright and a builder respectively; five bills were paid, a lease was sealed, sums of £25 each were advanced from Sir Thomas White's Charity to three of the town porters, and £20 from Steptoe's Charity to a shopkeeper.]

¶ At one time the Company of the Town Porters had had a monopoly of employment to carry heavy goods, and particularly wine, from the wharves to merchants' warehouses. They were still frequently employed, being paid by those who engaged them, but their monopoly no longer existed.

Friday the 4th day of July 1817

[Three licences and a lease were sealed; the Rev. C. T. Griffith's annual salary of 25 guineas as Headmaster of the Free Grammar School was paid; and an application received from William Rolph through his solicitor Charles Marett that the suit concerning his alleged trespass should be submitted to a referee, which was agreed to.]

¶ The Headmaster of the Grammar School, in addition to his salary, held the School-house virtually rent-free on a lease from the Corporation. He also augmented his remuneration by fees from the pupils, except in the extremely rare cases when poor men's sons were admitted to free tuition (see 8 February 1819), and for boarding.

Tuesday the 29th day of July 1817

[At this meeting, at which only three members were present, the sole business transacted was the swearing-in of an honorary burgess.]

Wednesday the 20th day of August 1817

[The half-year's market rents were reported as £30.10.3. A licence was sealed and a lease ordered for renewal, a loan of £20 was made from Steptoe's Charity and two bills were ordered for payment]

Friday the 5th day of September 1817

At this Council the following Gentlemen were proposed as Honorary Burgesses:

> Thomas Wren Carter, Esquire, of Portsmouth . . . a Commander in the Royal Navy and
> James Bandinel Esquire, of the Secretary of State's Office, London . . .

[Three leases were sealed and two bills ordered for payment, one being for 10 guineas for two years' subscription to "the School upon the Principles of the Established Church".]

¶ The Home Secretary was still frequently referred to as the Secretary of State.

The two rival organizations for developing primary education, the National Schools Society, which was an offshoot of the Church of England, and the nonconformist British and Foreign Schools Society, founded in 1811 and 1814 respectively, had both begun to set up schools in Southampton. The school referred to above, in St. Michael's Square, was the first of the National Schools—to employ the term commonly used.

Friday the 12th day of September 1817

[A lease was sealed and another ordered for renewal, a loan of £20 made from Steptoe's Charity and a bill ordered for payment.]

Friday the 19th day of September 1817

[A licence was sealed and two loans were made, of £25 from White's Charity and £20 from Steptoe's Charity respectively.]

Monday the 29th day of September 1817

[William Edward Jolliffe was sworn Mayor.]

Tuesday the 30th day of September 1817

[Stephen Lintott was sworn Sheriff and Samuel Le Feuvre and T. S. Moody Senior and Junior Bailiffs respectively, the latter having previously been sworn a Common Councilman at the same meeting.]

Resolved unanimously that the thanks of this Corporation be given to George Atherley Esquire late Mayor for his very great Attention and Exertion in the various and arduous duties of his office as Mayor . . . for the year past which has been a year of very unusual trouble.

¶ The trouble was probably financial (see e.g. 9 May above and 5 December below) and perhaps also the defence of the Corporation's rights and claims against encroachments.

Friday the 31st day of October 1817

[The market rents received on 18 October were reported as £30.10.3, and the Corporation's fifth of the port dues for the past half-year as £127.1.10½; a certificate to the Treasury and the Exchequer that the duties collected in lieu of petty customs during the past year amounted to £57.11.0 was sealed; various bills were ordered for payment, two loans from Steptoe's Charity and three smaller payments of charity money made; the annual distribution of Mrs. Fifield's Charity and of greatcoats and gowns for the poor was ordered to be carried out by Messrs. Jolliffe; and a licence was sealed.]

Wednesday the 5th day of November 1817

[Three bills from Messrs. W. Lintott & Sons were ordered for payment, for shrub for the years 1815-17 (£18.8.0) and coal for the Audit House and God's House respectively.]

Friday the 7th day of November 1817

[The quit rents received on 3 November were reported as £127.4.3, the Town Clerk's allowance and £122.10.0 interest on bonds paid, and six bills ordered for payment.]

Friday the 21st day of November 1817

At this Council a report was received from Mr. Griffith that he was desirous of purchasing a House Above Bar to exchange the same for the present School House And it is ordered that the Town Clerk do see Mr. Griffiths . . . thereon and if the Exchange appear at all practicable that he do take the opinion of Counsel thereon . . .

Friday the 5th day of December 1817

It appearing to this Council that for some Years past the Mayors have discontinued keeping the Corporation Cash Book as was formerly done . . . Resolved that the Mayor be requested to keep such Book . . . and that all Receipts and Payments be entered thereon at each Common Council and that the Receipt and Expenditure be particularly attended to by the Mayor in future.

Tuesday the 23rd day of December 1817

[The annual distribution of Christmas gifts from various charities, amounting to £15.6.8 (see 20 December 1816), was made to the poor, the pensioners at God's House, the Rev. Mr. Mears for his Christmas Eve sermon at All Saints, the churchwardens of St. Lawrence's for Sendy's sermon, and the Rev. C. T. Griffith of the Free School. In addition "Woolston's Charity to apprentice boys" was also distributed, to the amount of £72.10.2 to cover the three years 1815-17. This was presumably Nathaniel Mills's Bequest, dating from 1636, of an annual rent-charge on the manor of Woolston for the purpose of apprenticing poor boys. The Corporation furthermore subscribed 25 guineas "for the Relief of the Poor at this Season". Three bills were ordered for payment and a licence was sealed.]

Friday the 9th day of January 1818

At this Council a further application was made by the Revd. Charles Tapp Griffith respecting his changing the situation of the Free School. . . .

[A loan of £20 from Steptoe's Charity was made to a widow; four bills were ordered for payment and five awards made from the charity fund.]

Friday the 30th day of January 1818

At this Council the Accounts for the last year were examined with their several Vouchers to the 31st day of December last and it appears that there was a balance due to the Treasurer of £275.12.11.

¶ The unbusinesslike habits into which the Corporation appears to have fallen seem to have included the omission since January 1815 to draw up a proper statement of accounts. Another reflection of them (see 23 December above) may be that instead of an annual distribution of the Woolston Charity being made it was apparently overlooked for two years and a lump payment was then made to cover three years at a time.

Friday the 13th day of February 1818

THE CORPORATION AGAINST ROLPH

At this Council the Town Clerk reported that he had conferred with Mr. Marett . . . respecting the Arbitrators or Umpire to whom the Cause should be opened and that Mr. Thomas King of Eling was named as a proper person and this Council do approve of Mr. King as the Umpire.

At this Council the Town Seal was affixed to a Bond to William Rolph in the penal sum of £100 to abide by the award of Mr. Thomas King.

This day Richard Cozens was elected Cowherd of Southampton Common in the room of William Timms who has quitted the Office To hold and enjoy that Office during the pleasure of the Corporation with the right to occupy such part of the Southampton Arms public house as is restored for the use of the Cowherd and with all Emoluments Profits and Perquisites to the same Office belonging, Subject nevertheless to such Conditions Stipulations and Regulations as are set forth in a Bond executed by the said Richard Cozens and one surety in the penal sum of £100.

Saturday the 21st day of March 1818

[The annual distribution of Easter gifts from various charities, amounting to £32.16.8, was made to the poor; a loan of £20 was advanced from Steptoe's Charity and five bills were ordered for payment.]

Friday the 10th day of April 1818

CHARITY FUND

Mr. Bond a decayed surgeon   £1.1.0

[The market rents for the past half-year were reported as £30.8.9; a licence and three leases were sealed.]

Friday the 8th day of May 1818

MR. WILLIAM ROLPH'S ENCROACHMENT

At this Council the award of Mr. Thomas King was brought up and read Whereby he awarded that the Boundary Line which he had staked out between the land of William Rolph and the Southampton Common was the proper and true Boundary and that the Fencing thereof belonged to the said William Rolph and that within three Months he should make a Wall or Timber Fence there. . . .

[A bill of £6.5.0 for the last audit dinner was ordered for payment, two small awards were made from the charity fund, and instructions given that the Town Clerk should be repaid the 12-guinea fee which he had paid the Recorder for attending the last Quarter Sessions.]

Friday the 15th day of May 1818

[The Corporation's fifth of the port dues for the half-year ending at Lady Day 1818 was reported as £120.3.5; a licence was sealed, two leases were ordered for renewal, and instructions given for William Rolph to be served with a copy of Thomas King's award.]

Friday the 29th day of May 1818

Mr. Griffith applied to this Council stating that he had found that . . . a very considerable Expence would be incurred by continuing the Application for the Exchange and that he was therefore desirous of having Leave to underlet West Hall demised to him by the Corporation for a School House. . . .

Resolved that a licence be granted to Mr. Griffith for that purpose, he entering into a Bond for keeping a School in some proper House in the Town with a fit and proper School Room to the satisfaction of the Mayor Bailiffs and Burgesses for the time being for the use of any Scholars upon the Foundation, and also for the immediate delivering up of West Hall in good Repair and in a fit and convenient State for a Schoolhouse upon Mr. Griffith's Death or Quitting the School or leaving the Town.

Friday the 12th day of June 1818

At this Council the Town Seal was affixed to a licence to enable the Reverend Charles Tapp Griffith to remove the School from West Hall to Bugle Hall and to underlet West Hall. . . .

[Another licence and a lease were sealed, and two loans made from Steptoe's Charity.]

¶ The original Bugle Hall had been destroyed by fire in 1791, but the name had been given to a smaller house built on part of the same site to which the School was now transferred until after Griffith's departure and the rebuilding of the old premises in 1819-20. (See 28 August and 2 October 1819.)

Friday the 31st day of July 1818

[Five bills were ordered for payment, two loans made from Steptoe's Charity, a licence was sealed and a youth apprenticed to a whitesmith.]

Friday the 21st day of August 1818

[A lease was sealed, a loan made from Steptoe's Charity and a gift from the charity fund, instructions were given that a new pound should be built for the Common, and the private nomination of the Mayor and other officers for the ensuing year took place.]

Friday the 4th day of September 1818

[Eleven leases were ordered for renewal and four bills for payment, including a subscription of 5 guineas to the National School in St. Michael's Square; a payment of £1 was made from the charity fund; Edward Deal Bridger of North Stoneham, gentleman, and John Castle, "of Bermondsey Street in the County of Surrey", surgeon, were proposed as honorary burgesses; and Joseph Lomer, grocer, Wilson Lomer, Esquire, and James Boville, merchant, all of Southampton, as serving burgesses. All were unanimously elected on 11 September.]

Tuesday the 29th day of September 1818

[Walter Raleigh Smith was sworn Mayor.]

Tuesday the 6th day of October 1818

[Samuel Le Feuvre was sworn Sheriff and John Jolliffe Junior Bailiff, being previously sworn a Common Councilman on the same day; but Thomas Sloane Moody, the Junior Bailiff of the previous year, refused to serve the office of Senior Bailiff to which he had been privately nominated, for which he was fined £50 at the next meeting of the Council on 9 October, the fine to be remitted if he resigned his burgess-ship within one month, which he did.]

Tuesday the 13th day of October 1818

[Joseph Lomer, who had been elected a burgess only on 11 September was sworn a Common Councilman and then Junior Bailiff.]

Friday the 6th day of November 1818

[The quit rents received on 2 November were reported as £140.19.1, and the Corporation's fifth of the port dues collected during the past half-year as £128.14.2; two leases were sealed; the Town Clerk's allowance, the Recorder's fees of 24 guineas for attending the Michaelmas Sessions and the swearing-in of the Mayor, and various bills were paid; the annual distribution of Mrs. Fifield's Charity and of greatcoats and gowns to the poor was directed to be made as usual; a loan was made from Steptoe's Charity, £60 advanced to the Town Clerk to enable him to have twenty stamps affixed to the Burgess Book (which had evidently also been negligently kept), and the annual certificate to the Treasury and Exchequer sealed, stating that the duties received in lieu of petty customs during the twelve months ending at Michaelmas 1818 amounted to £62.4.7, and adding this time that "no carracks of Genoa nor Gallies of Venice had arrived at this port within that period".]

¶ The Corporation had received a sharp reminder from the Exchequer that in making out the annual statement it must not omit this ancient clause.

Friday the 11th day of December 1818

Resolved that the thanks of this Common Council be unanimously given to the Reverend Thomas Mears the Chaplain to this Corporation for his excellent sermon preached before [it] on the 29th day of November last upon the Death of our most gracious Queen Charlotte, the consort of George III . . . and that he be requested to print his Sermon. . . .

Friday the 18th day of December 1818

[Directions were given for the annual distribution of Christmas gifts to the poor from the charities; three leases were sealed and three bills ordered for payment.]

Friday the 22nd day of January 1819

[The accounts for 1818 were examined and showed that the previous adverse balance of £275.12.11 had been reduced to one of £65.3.6; a bill was ordered for payment, two youths were apprenticed, two loans from Steptoe's Charity and three gifts from the charity fund were made, and the Recorder's fee of 12 guineas for attending the Epiphany Sessions was paid.]

Monday the 8th day of February 1819

[Two children of poor parents were chosen scholars upon the foundation of the Free Grammar School, "to be admitted and taught by the

Schoolmaster, Gratis, according to the Rules of the School"; a licence was sealed, a loan made from Steptoe's Charity, three bills were ordered for payment, and the Town Clerk was instructed to write to the sureties of defaulters on eight loans from Steptoe's Charity and two from White's, requiring repayment on pain of legal proceedings. Three had paid up before the next meeting of the Council, but it is not recorded that any of the others did so.]

Friday the 12th day of March 1819

[A licence to alienate was sealed, three leases were ordered for renewal and three bills for payment, a loan was made from Steptoe's Charity, two youths were apprenticed, and directions issued that the town sergeants' uniforms be obtained from Messrs. Jolliffe as usual.]

Friday the 2nd day of April 1819

[Two leases were ordered for renewal and various bills and charity monies ordered to be paid.]

Tuesday the 7th day of April 1819

It being resolved to ride the bounds of . . . this Town on Tuesday next being Cut thorn day with the Court Leet

It is also Resolved that Mr. Le Feuvre the Sheriff be allowed the sum of Thirty five pounds for the Expenses attending that day. . . .

¶ The Court Leet, of which the Mayor and aldermen were the "Lords", the Sheriff the foreman and the Town Clerk the steward, had three main surviving functions, which however it had exercised only intermittently since the end of the eighteenth century—the making of presentments for encroachments on the highways and common fields, the inspection of weights and measures used in the markets and shops, and the perambulation of the bounds of the borough to the accompaniment of a cold collation at Cut Thorn and a subsequent supper.

Friday the 7th day of May 1819

[The quit rents received on 3 May were reported as £138.5.1, and the Corporation's fifth of the port dues for the past half-year as £132.5.1; the Town Clerk's allowance, £110 interest on bonds, and four bills were paid.]

Tuesday the 27th day of July 1819

[Market rents amounting to £31.4.0 were reported as received; the Town Clerk was reimbursed 24 guineas paid to the Recorder as his fees for attending the Easter and Midsummer Quarter Sessions; a loan from Steptoe's Charity and a payment of two guineas from the charity fund were made.]

Tuesday the 17th day of August 1819

At this Council a letter was received . . . on the part of Messrs. Barlow Brothers, who have contracted to light the Town with Gas, applying for a grant of some Mud Land to the Northward of the West Quay . . . but it not appearing that the Commissioners of the Pavement are satisfied that the situation is a proper one and It being doubtful whether it be not too near the Town

Resolved that the Town Clerk do acquaint the Commissioners of the Pavement that such application has been made and do learn their Ideas respecting the Situation. . . .

¶ The Paving Commissioners were also Lighting Commissioners as well.

Friday the 20th day of August 1819

The Town Clerk reported to this Council that the Commissioners of the Pavement were satisfied that if the proper Precautions . . . are taken the situation proposed will be a desirable one and therefore wish the same to be granted.

Resolved that . . . a Lease be granted to Messrs. Barlow's of a piece of Mud Land containing Half an Acre lying at the North End of the Long Rooms . . . to hold from Michaelmas next for Forty Years at a Fine of one Guinea, Quit Rent ten Guineas and five shillings for Capons under the usual Covenants.

BILLS ORDERED FOR PAYMENT

Mr. Samuel Le Feuvre the Sheriff—for Attendance as below at the Cut Thorn

Paid for Horses for the Serjeants		£2.12.6
Do.	for the Trumpeters	1. 1.0
Do.	for the Constables	1. 1.0
Paid Trumpeters		1. 1.0
Ringers		10.6
		£6. 6.0

At this Council the Court Leet presentments were considered and Directions given respecting the same and the Presentments respecting the Scales, Weights and a proposed Boundary Stone to be placed in Burgess Street are to be further considered at the next Council.

[This was also private nomination day.]

¶ Gas lighting, which had been invented independently in France and England towards the close of the eighteenth century, had begun to be introduced in this country from 1800 onwards. The early gasometers were regarded by many people with considerable alarm, least they should explode, and in fact Southampton's was erected in 1820 not on the site discussed above but in the Northam district.

Saturday the 28th day of August 1819

At this Council a letter was received from the Reverend Griffith Master of the Free Grammar School signifying his desire to resign the Mastership of the School at the first day of January next. . . .

¶ He had been offered the headmastership of Lord Weymouth's School, Warminster, which had previously been held by his father and his brother.

Friday the 3rd day of September 1819

At this Council the following Gentlemen were proposed as Honorary Burgesses:

John Dyke Alexander of Freemantle House in the parish of Milbrooke [His name, which was really Josias Dupré Alexander, was incorrectly rendered and he had to be proposed again under the latter designation on 12 October.]

William Hornby Esquire, son of John Hornby Esquire of Hook House near Titchfield.

Arthur Carter Esquire a Lieutenant of the Royal Artillery.

John Lee of Colworth House in the County of Bedford Esquire.

Henry Minchin of Clayfield Lodge in that part of the parish of Milbrooke which lieth in the liberties of the Town . . . of Southampton

Thomas Evans of Hatton Garden London Esquire and

Edward Bridger of Angel Court Throgmorton Street London Esquire.

[A licence was sealed, a loan made from Steptoe's Charity, seven leases were ordered for renewal and some bills to be paid.]

Friday the 7th day of September 1819

At this Council the following Gentlemen were proposed as Honorary Burgesses:

Augustus Champion de Crespigny Esquire eldest son of Sir William Champion de Crespigny Baronet M.P. for Southampton.

John Guitton of Little Park in the County of Southampton Esquire.

Benedict John Angell Angell of Rumsey House near Calne in the County of Wilts. and

The Reverend Alexander Scott of West Tarring in the County of Sussex.

¶ Sir William de Crespigny had replaced his fellow-Whig Atherley at the general election of 1818. Since another Whig country gentleman, William Chamberlayne of Weston Grove, had just previously succeeded to Rose's seat when he vacated it through his appointment as Clerk of Parliament earlier in that year, and had held it at the general election, the parliamentary representation of the town, previously divided, was now entirely in Whig hands till 1826.

Tuesday the 14th day of September 1819

[All the gentlemen proposed as honorary burgesses on 3 and 7 September were unanimously elected and the following additional nominations were made:

John Scard of Totton;

Henry Bunbery Minchin, eldest son of the Henry Minchin nominated on 3 September;

Major-General Samuel Wilson of the East India Company's army;

William Alexander Mackinnon of Portswood House;

Major George Humphrey of the 73rd Regiment.]

Friday the 24th day of September 1819

[The election of the gentlemen proposed as honorary burgesses on 14 September took place.]

The State of the Free School being taken into Consideration

Resolved that the Gentlemen now present together with Mr. Richard Eldridge and Mr. Stephen Lintott be a Committee to confer . . . on the best mode of compleating [sic] a School House fit for the purpose.

Wednesday the 29th day of September 1819

[Richard Eldridge was sworn Mayor.]

Friday the 2nd day of October 1819

[The committee appointed on 24 September reported in favour of pulling down the existing Free School buildings, selling "the Eastern part of the land fronting French Street" in lots upon leases for forty years and building a new school house with the proceeds and the money raised by the sale or conversion of the materials.]

Ordered that an advertisement be inserted in the Salisbury and Winchester Journal Oxford [omission] and the Times Newspapers for holding a Common Council on Thursday the 21st day of October Instant for the Election of a Master of the Free Grammar School and that the Testimonials of any Candidate be sent to the Town Clerk's Office on or before the 14th Instant. . . .

At this Council Charles Henry Rich of Bossington in the County of Southampton Esquire Eldest Son of the Reverend Sir Charles Rich Baronet . . . of Shirley in the County of Southampton was proposed as an Honorary Burgess. . . .

¶ The "Free School buildings" referred to were not the temporary accommodation at Bugle Hall, but the previous premises.

Tuesday the 5th day of October 1819

[John Jolliffe was sworn Sheriff and Joseph and Wilson Lomer Senior and Junior Bailiffs respectively, Wilson Lomer having been previously sworn a Common Councilman.]

Thursday the 21st day of October 1819

This being the Day appointed for the Choice of a Master of the Free Grammar School. . . . The Common Council now assembled elected the Reverend Thomas Lawes Shapcott B.A. of Saint Albans Hall Oxford now residing at Marlboro' in the County of Wilts. . . .

Thursday the 18th day of November 1819

[The half-year's quit rents were reported as £86.5.0 and the Corporation's fifth of the port dues as £203.6.4. A certificate to the Treasury and the Exchequer was sealed that the dues in lieu of petty customs for the past year had amounted to £87.17.1 and that no carracks of Genoa nor galleys of Venice had visited the port during the period. The Town Clerk's allowance was paid.]

Friday the 18th day of December 1819

[Two leases and two licences were sealed, some bills ordered for payment, a youth was apprenticed, a loan made from Steptoe's Charity and the Christmas charity money distributed.]

> NOTE: From this point the routine business which occupied much of the Council's time—the granting, sealing or renewal of leases and licences, payment of bills, making of apprentices and of loans and gifts from the Charities and so forth—will no longer be recorded; the periodical statements of fifths of port dues will be set out in Appendix A; and only relatively important or unusual entries will be quoted for the remainder of the old Corporation's life.

Friday the 28th day of January 1820

At this Council the Accounts for the last year were examined . . . and it appears that there is a Balance due to the Treasurer of £272.19.9.

Resolved that [five named] gentlemen be a Committee to examine the State of the Income and Expenditure of the Corporation and that they be desired to make a special Report thereof and of all the Corporation Property and Revenue and whether any means can be devised of improving the source and of liquidating the existing Debts and also to state an Account of all the Debts and Charges upon the Property.

Ordered that a letter be written to Mr. Griffith desiring him to deliver up the Possession of the Free School's premises and to name some person to value the Dilapidations on his part.

D

¶ Mr. Griffith continued to be Vicar of St. Michael's until 1825, when he was succeeded here also by Mr. Shapcott, who held the living till he died in 1854.

Friday the 4th day of February 1820

His late Majesty King George the Third having departed this life on Saturday . . . last, His Majesty King George the Fourth was on Wednesday . . . proclaimed at the Balcony at the Audithouse at the Outside of Bargate and at the Customhouse with the usual Solemnities. . . .

Tuesday the 4th day of April 1820

[Two honorary burgesses were proposed:
    John Vignoles of Cornahir in the county of West Meath in Ireland,
        a lieutenant in the Royal Navy, and
    Abel Rouse Dottin of Southampton, Esquire.]

¶ Dottin was a newcomer to Southampton who failed by one vote to win one of the town seats at the general election following George III's death, at which the sitting members, Chamberlayne and De Crespigny, were again returned. He purchased Bugle Hall for his residence and soon became distinguished for his benefactions and his support of railway and other undertakings which promoted prosperity; and represented the town in Parliament as a Tory from 1826 to 1831 and again from 1835 to 1841.

[The meetings of the Council from May to August inclusive were occupied, apart from routine business of the kind referred to above, in overseeing the pulling down of the old Free School premises, the (unsuccessful) attempt to dispose of part of the ground by lease, and the building of a new school house.]

Friday the 1st day of September 1820

[The Bishop of Winchester was elected an honorary burgess, and William Browne Angell of Binfield in Berkshire and the Rev. Roger Hall, Rector of Ellingham in Norfolk, were nominated as such, being subsequently elected on 8 September.]

Friday the 29th day of September 1820

[Stephen Lintott was sworn Mayor.]

Tuesday the 3rd day of October 1820

[Joseph Lomer was sworn Sheriff and Wilson Lomer and James Bovill Senior and Junior Bailiffs respectively, the latter being previously sworn a Common Councilman.]

Friday the 13th day of October 1820

[The Sheriff reported that as a result of correspondence regarding the custom by which the Lord Warden of the New Forest used annually to present a buck to the Corporation he had been assured that this would continue to take place in future.]

Friday the 23rd day of November 1820

Resolved that an Address to His Majesty be sent expressive of the Attachment of this Corporation to His Person and Government [and]
The Mayor having brought forward the following Address
Resolved that the same be adopted. . . .

Most Gracious Sovereign,

We your Majesty's most Dutiful and Loyal Subjects . . . humbly beg Leave to renew our Assurances of the firmest Attachment to your Royal person and Government; at a moment in which Wicked and Factious Men are striving by every Art of Malice and Falsehood to pervert the Minds and alienate the Hearts of your faithful People.

Impressed as we are with the utmost Conviction, that we cannot hope for Happiness or Safety as a Nation, but by Obedience to that divine Law which enjoins Submission to the constituted Authorities under which we live, We solemnly assure Your Majesty of our Determination to support by every means in our Power the Religion, Laws and Government of our Country. . . .

¶ Radical political feeling was then very strong, especially among the working classes, and was viewed by both Tories and Whigs with an alarm which had recently been increased by the Cato Street Conspiracy. In this a band of desperate extremists had planned to attack and murder the members of the Cabinet while they were assembled at dinner at Lord Harrowby's, but their design had been discovered and they were arrested and their leaders sentenced to execution.

Friday the 19th day of January 1821

At this Council the Town Seal was affixed to a licence to enable Mr. W. N. Martin Administrator of Mrs. Mary Martin, Mesdames Baker, Forsyth and Martin to assign the Long Rooms and premises . . . to Sir William Champion de Crespigny.

¶ The Long Rooms near the West Quay had been opened as assembly rooms in 1761, when Southampton was first blossoming out as a spa of elegance and distinction. They had remained in the hands of the Martin family for half a century, but had suffered latterly from the relative decline of the town's popularity as a resort and watering-place. A revival was now taking place, however, one feature of which was that the widow and daughters of the late John Martin were replaced as Corporation tenants by a succession of others of whom Sir William was only the first and under whom the Rooms were again much used throughout the 1820's for balls, concerts and other entertainments. They were eventually thrust into a second and more lasting decline by the opening of the New Assembly Rooms (afterwards named the Royal Victoria Rooms) in the Spa Gardens in 1830.

Friday the 16th day of February 1821

[The examination of the last year's accounts showed that the adverse balance had been further reduced to £34.12.2.]

Friday the 30th day of March 1821

. . . Resolved that the undermentioned leases be renewed . . .

To Messrs. Maxfield, Kelly and Court, otherwise Collins, of a Messuage adjoining the Theatre in Saint John's Parish devised to the late Thomas Court, otherwise Collins, on the 6th day of November last and since assigned to them.

¶ Between them, the three families referred to here conducted not only Southampton's Theatre Royal in French Street but also the theatres of Winchester, Portsmouth and for a time Chichester during nearly three-quarters of a century. John Court, who assumed the name of Collins, began his theatrical career in Edinburgh in the middle of the eighteenth century, and by the 1770's had become the manager of the Southampton theatre, the others named coming into his hands or those of his talented son Thomas before the close of the century. Only one was normally open at a time, however, the order of the company's seasons being Southampton–Portsmouth–Chichester–Winchester, Southampton being visited during the autumn and early winter. Kelly, the son of a London carver and gilder, to which trade he was apprenticed, took to the stage about this time and after successes on the Warminster–Devizes–Salisbury circuit was engaged by Collins, married his daughter and became a favourite at Southampton. During Collins's old age and after his death in 1807 Kelly was associated with the latter's sons Thomas, whose early death had just taken place when this entry was made, and Stephen, and with Maxfield another prominent member of the company, in the management of the usually struggling enterprise. Stephen Collins, who may just conceivably have been the model for Dickens's Vincent Crummles, died in very embarrassed circumstances in 1830, after which Kelly and Maxfield battled on till 1837, when they retired.

Friday the 27th day of April 1821

TEMPORARY MARKET AT THE EAST END OF BRIDGE STREET

Resolved that the terms on which the Corporation are willing to let the piece of Land belonging to them lately paved by Subscription near the End of Bridge Street to be used for a Market are that each Butcher do pay each Market day for his standing the ancient and accustomed Market Toll of fourpence. . . .

¶ In 1773 the Corporation, at the cost of saddling itself with debt for the remaining sixty-two years of its existence, had built a Market and Audit House in the lower part of the High Street. The upper part of this contained a council chamber and other rooms which were used for meetings and administrative purposes; while the ground floor was occupied by the market, divided into four compartments. Of these the outer two were entirely covered, the one facing High Street being used for the sale—on Tuesdays, Thursdays and Saturdays—of poultry, butter and other farm produce, and the other, which faced French Street, for the sale of fish. The intervening space was open except that sheds ran laterally on each side, devoted to the sale of vegetables and butcher's meat respectively. By now this Market House had become too small for the increased amount of trade, and a butchers' market was built at the far end of Bridge Street. In the following year a vegetable or green market was added (see 6 and 21 September 1822). Neither, however, proved to be much frequented, since by now the butchers and fruiterers were preferring to sell their wares in shops at their own residences.

Thursday the 3rd day of May 1821

At this Council the following Gentlemen were proposed as Serving Burgesses:

Philip Cartaret Fall	of the Town of Southampton		Esquire
William Oke	,,	,, ,,	Merchant
Richard Davison Pritchard	,,	,, ,,	Esquire
Martin Maddison the Younger	,,	,, ,,	Esquire and
William Le Feuvre	,,	,, ,,	Merchant.

¶ All were unanimously elected and sworn in on 11 May, at which time Stephen Judd of Southampton, surgeon, was also proposed, being elected and sworn in a week later. Fall was a partner in the bank of Messrs. Atherley & Fall and Maddison in that of his family, while Le Feuvre was a wine merchant with increasing shipping and other commercial interests.

Friday the 18th day of May 1821

At this Council Samuel Silver Taylor Esquire one of the Executors of the Will of Elizabeth Bird late of this Town Spinster ... produced a copy of such part of her Will as related to a Bequest of 1400 three per cent Consolidated Bank Annuities to be under the Guardianship of the Mayor for the time being together with the other Gentlemen of the Corporation and the Minister of All Saints Southampton for the time being, the interest whereof is to be paid to her servant Jane Cash for her Life and after her death to be disposed of in annuities of five pounds each to six poor single women for their lives.

Saturday the 16th day of June 1821

A proclamation having been issued for His Majesty's Coronation on the 19th of July next and this Corporation being desirous of testifying their

Loyalty. . . . Resolved that the Mayor be authorized to propose a Subscription of Fifty Guineas towards a Ball and Supper to celebrate the same.

Friday the 3rd day of August 1821

Thursday the 19th day of July last being the Day of the Coronation of His Majesty . . . the same was celebrated in this Town by a public Ball and Supper in the Long Rooms . . . at which near 400 persons attended, by a large Party of the Mayor and Corporation with their Friends dining together at the Audit House at the Individual Expense of the Corporation except some Gentlemen holding public Situations in the Town who were invited at the Corporation's Expense, and by an Entertainment of the poor Inhabitants on the Marsh at which above 6000 persons were regaled, the Expences of which were defrayed by a Subscription raised by the Town at large amounting to £475.

Ordered that . . . the sum of Twenty four pounds thirteen shillings and sixpence be paid for the Dinners of the above mentioned public Gentlemen invited

That the sum of Ten guineas be paid, the Subscription entered into by the Mayor on behalf of the Corporation towards the Entertainment for the poor Inhabitants.

Thursday the 30th day of August 1821

This day His Royal Highness Prince Augustus Frederick Duke of Sussex . . . fourth surviving brother of His present Majesty was unanimously elected a Burgess of this Corporation.

His Royal Highness having honoured this Corporation with his presence a loyal Address was made to him . . . and he then took the oath . . . and was enrolled.

¶ All the Duke's brothers had previously been made honorary burgesses, but his politics were Whig whereas theirs were Tory.

Thursday the 29th day of September 1821

[George Atherley was sworn Mayor.]

Tuesday the 2nd day of October 1821

[Wilson Lomer was sworn Sheriff and James Bovill and P. C. Fall Senior and Junior Bailiffs respectively, the latter having previously been sworn in as a member of the Council.]

Saturday the 10th day of November 1821

Resolved that the sum of two hundred pounds be borrowed of Mr. Richard Eldridge on two Bonds of one hundred pounds each at five per cent. . . .

Friday the 25th day of January 1822

[An examination of the accounts for the previous year showed that the adverse balance had risen to £821.2.2.]

Friday the 22nd day of March 1822

At this Council the Report of the Committee appointed [on 28 January 1820] to consider the State of the Income and Expenditure of the Corporation and of the Property belonging to them and the Charge thereon ... being read and taken into ... Consideration and pursuant to their Recommendations

It is resolved that the monies to arise by the Sale of Timber in the Common be applied wholly in discharge of the Bond Debts in future.

That the Corporation do in future attend to Economy in the Management of their affairs so as to reduce their present Debt and enable them to leave a larger Fund at command to be employed as Occasion may offer to benefit the Town at large to the utmost of their Power.

That the fluctuating Debt now due to the Bankers and Bonds to the amount of £600 be paid off as soon as possible.

Resolved that the Mayor's allowance of Twenty one pounds ... towards the Expence of his Quarter Sessions Dinner be wholly discontinued immediately and that the Corporation do allow that sum in addition to their other allowances for the Current Year and that in future Years the Mayor's Allowances be as follows:

His annual allowance	£52.10.0
For Dues	26. 5.0
For Sessions Dinners	30. 0.0
For Postages	2. 2.0
For a Buck	10. 0.0
	£122.17.0
On serving the office a second time the additional sum of	30. 0.0
	£152.17.0

That the Town Clerk be allowed in his annual Bill the sum of five Guineas as a Remuneration for his Loss on the Non Renewal of Leases and Non Granting of Licences to alienate the several Leasehold Properties ageed to be sold by the Corporation to the Commissioners for improving this Port.

That any Member of the Common Council who has a lease in course of Renewal shall not be present at the Common Council when the Terms of such Renewal are discussed or settled.

Friday the 10th day of May 1822

At this Council three persons who hold Oyster Coves upon the Shore off the Platform attended and agreed to pay a rent of two shillings and sixpence . . . annually. . . .

Friday the 24th day of May 1822

Resolved that the Corporation will subscribe Ten Guineas towards the Fund now raising for the distressed Irish poor in the southern parts of Ireland.

Friday the 14th day of June 1822

The Mayor laid before this Council a letter from . . . the Stewards for the present Year of the Races intended to be established in this Town requesting permission to have the Ground marked out in the Southampton Common for such Races.

Resolved that Leave be given . . . and that this Corporation do subscribe Ten Guineas towards the Racing Fund.

¶ The Town Races, which had been one of Southampton's attractions before the French Wars, had lapsed during them, so that this establishment of a two-day race-meeting, with a ball at the Long Rooms, a Race Night at the Theatre and ordinaries each day at the Dolphin Hotel, was another feature of the town's partial and temporary revival as a fashionable resort. A similar application and subscription figured annually in the Journals afterwards and then for some years in the minute books of its successor the reformed Borough Council. The Races suffered, however, from the Committee's inability to find and keep to a regular date which did not clash with that of other meetings in the neighbourhood or with functions such as Cowes Regatta. After a time it became difficult to raise sufficient funds and to prevail upon local gentlemen to act as stewards, and there were repeated doubts as to whether the meeting could be kept going. It eventually lapsed in 1849.

Friday the 6th day of September 1822

Mr. Eldridge having built a place for an additional Green Market in the Town Ditches adjoining the new Butchers Market near the Bridge at the Bottom of Bridge Street, and it being very desirable that the Market people should be removed out of the Public High Street to prevent the Annoyances occasioned thereby to the Inhabitants and persons passing through the same,

Resolved that the said new Building or place in the Town Ditches be appointed to be used as an additional Market and that in consideration of Mr. Eldridge having so erected such Buildings he be allowed to receive and take the legal Market Tolls thereof for his own use till some further order is made respecting the same.

Ordered that the Town Clerk do draw up previous to the next Council a Notice to be published declaring the said removal of the Market from the said High Street and appointing the said Building or place so erected . . . in the Town Ditches for an additional Market for Fruit, Garden Stuff, Herbs, Roots or other Vegetables and also for persons frequenting the Market with any Goods or Wares for Sale not being victuals or provisions.

¶ For the new Butchers' Market in Bridge Street see the entry for 27 April 1821 above.

Friday the 21st day of September 1822

At this Council it is ordered that a lease for 28 years be granted to Mr. Richard Eldridge of the Tolls of the new Butchers' Market near the Bridge at the End of Bridge Street at a Rent of one shilling and four shillings for Capons, Mr. Eldridge covenanting to erect a substantial Timber and Slate covering and to keep and leave the same in repair.

Sunday the 29th day of September 1822

[John Rushworth Keele was sworn Mayor.]

Tuesday the 1st day of October 1822

[James Bovill was sworn Sheriff and P. C. Fall and William Oke Senior and Junior Bailiffs respectively, Oke having previously been sworn a member of the Council.]

Friday the 8th day of November 1822

[Captain William Bowles, R.N., was proposed as an honorary burgess, and elected on 15 November.]

Friday the 24th day of January 1823

[The examination of the previous year's accounts showed that the adverse balance had been reduced again to £276.0.5.]

Friday the 6th day of June 1823

The Town Clerk reported to this Council that the Reverend Dr. Hill had signified to him that the Warden and Fellows of Queen's College were willing to renew their property in French Street (being part of the Fish Market) and the Fish and Kettle public house, held by this Corporation by lease from them, at the undermentioned sums of money

Fine £23.2.6

Leases £6.2.6

. . . and also to renew their property in Bugle Street . . . likewise held by the Corporation by Lease from them . . . upon the following Terms

Fine £56.17.6

Leases £6.2.6

Ordered that the Town Clerk do write to Dr. Hill desiring that such leases may be made out as the Corporation are desirous of renewing upon those Terms.

Thursday the 17th day of July 1823

Ordered that Mr. Edward Toomer be paid the sum of Three hundred and Fifty pounds due to him on Bond dated the 29th day of August 1820 with the Interest due thereon to this day.

The Committee appointed to superintend the Erection of a Column to Mr. Chamberlayne, one of the Members in Parliament for this Town, for his Munificent Gift of the Iron Pillars for putting up the Gas Lamps, having presented this Corporation with a Model of the Coat of Arms of this Town which was made for the purpose of casting the Arms upon the Column

Ordered that the thanks of this Corporation be given to the Committee and that this Corporation do subscribe Twenty Guineas to the Fund for erecting the said Column. . . .

¶ The Chamberlayne Monument, described in the contemporary *Guide to Southampton* as "a splendid cast-iron column surmounted by an urn bearing a large gas-light, which is useful to the mariner", was originally erected at the corner of Northam Bridge Road, subsequently transferred to the Town Quay as a seamark (see 10 April 1829 below), and finally removed in the 1860's to its present position at the southern extremity of the Parks.

Friday the 5th day of September 1823

At this Council the following Gentlemen were proposed as Honorary Burgesses . . .

William Wyon of His Majesty's Mint London Esquire

The Reverend Charles Tapp Griffith of Warminster in the County of Wilts. Clerk and

Charles Keele of Hythe in the County of Southampton Esquire a Lieutenant in the Royal Navy.

¶ Mr. Wyon had just presented the Corporation with the dies of a medal to commemorate "the Event of his Majesty's coming within the Limits of this Port in his Yatcht [*sic*], which His Majesty had intended to do but was prevented by his indisposition and the unfavourable state of the Weather".

Monday the 29th day of September 1823

The Mayor reported to this Council the Death of Samuel Silver Taylor Esqre, an Alderman, Justice of the Peace for this Town . . . and one of the Members of this Corporation. . . .

Richard Eldridge Esquire was this day sworn Mayor. . . .

¶ William Edward Jolliffe was subsequently elected a justice of the peace to replace Taylor.

Tuesday the 30th day of September 1823

[P. C. Fall was sworn Sheriff and William Oke and R. D. Pritchard Senior and Junior Bailiffs respectively, Pritchard having previously been sworn a member of the Common Council.]

Friday the 30th day of January 1824

[The annual examination of accounts showed that the adverse balance had been further reduced to £123.11.0. It must be borne in mind, however, that this did not include the sums owed by the Corporation on bond.]

Resolved that the Interest on the several sums owing by the Corporation on Bond be reduced to four per cent from Lady Day next and It is ordered that the Town Clerk do inform the Holders of the several Bonds thereof by letter.

¶ Several bondholders elected to be paid off rather than accept the lower rate of interest.

Friday the 5th day of March 1824

Resolved that this Corporation will subscribe to the new Church intended to be built in All Saints Parish the sum of One hundred Guineas. . . .

¶ The church alluded to was St. Paul's. The subscriptions hung fire somewhat for a time, but it was completed and opened in 1828.

Friday the 9th day of July 1824

Ordered that . . . [12 persons] be sued on their several Bonds due on . . . Charities [two on White's and ten on Steptoe's] and their sureties.

Friday the 30th day of July 1824

Mr. Fall the Sheriff having stated to this Council that the Court Leet of which he is the Foreman appear to have been very remiss in their Duty and it appearing desirable to ascertain the precise Duty of the Leet and the mode of enforcing the Law respecting it

Resolved that the following five Gentlemen be a Committee to examine into the Custom and Usages of the Court Leet and make a Report thereon. . . .

Certain persons having subscribed for the Erection of Hot and Cold Baths near the Platform . . . application was made on their behalf for a lease of the Land or Shore lying between the Platform and the Bridewell for that purpose.

Resolved that a Lease thereof be granted to them for forty years from Michaelmas next at a Rent of One Guinea, Quit Rent one Guinea and Capons four shillings.

¶ This entry foreshadows the construction of the Royal Gloucester Baths and Promenade Rooms, opened in 1829 and constituting another manifestation of the town's partial recovery as a resort. They contained, according to an advertisement, "hot baths of solid marble . . . shower baths on a new and improved principle, medicated, vapour and shampooing baths . . . for inveterate scrofula and skin diseases, rashes, eruptions, gouty and rheumatic afflictions, stiff joints and all those disorders dependent on a morbid circulation of the blood". The Subscription Room was "regularly supplied with the London and provincial papers and the Weekly Court Journal", and refreshments could be obtained at the bar. "Select Quadrille and Card Parties" were held there during the winter season, and for a few years the Royal Gloucester Baths, which had entirely thrown into the shade the "Original Warm and Cold Baths" at the Long Rooms, almost rivalled the New Assembly Rooms as a centre of entertainment and fashion.

Friday the 10th day of September 1824

At this Council the following Gentlemen were proposed as Honorary Burgesses:

> The Very Reverend Hugh Nicholas Pearson . . . Dean of Salisbury and Michael Hoy of Midanbury House in the County of Southampton Esqre.

¶ Hoy, a local man who by his industry had acquired an ample fortune and extensive estates, adopted as his heir his nephew James Barlow, a surgeon in the Navy who took the additional name of Hoy and became, together with Dottin, a leader of the Tory party in Southampton. He was a member of parliament for the town between 1829 and 1831 and again from 1835 to 1837.

Wednesday the 29th day of September 1824

[Stephen Lintott was sworn Mayor.]

Tuesday the 5th day of October 1824

[William Oke was sworn Sheriff and R. D. Pritchard and Martin Maddison Senior and Junior Bailiffs respectively, the latter being previously sworn a member of the Council.]

Friday the 3rd day of December 1824

Mr. Eldridge the late Mayor reported to this Council that he attended the Commissioners for enquiring into Charities respecting the Charities under this Corporation when they came to this Town in the months of August and September last and Mr. Durell and Mr. Atherley reported that they also attended, . . . when they recommended that the sums due from this Corporation upon the several Charities of Mrs. Fifield Mr. Alderman Freeman and Mr. Alderman Sadleir and also of Mr. Alderman Taunton should be secured by some Mortgages pursuant to the Wills of the Testators, and the Commissioners seeing no objection to such security being made upon the Corporation property if made to Trustees It was proposed that the Market house and Audithouse should be mortgaged to four Trustees for the purpose of securing the several sums due to the several Charities of Mrs. Fifield Mr. Freeman and Mr. Sadleir and the Payment of the annual Interest thereof or produce which has arisen therefrom and that the one fifth of the Rates Dues and Duties payable to this Corporation under the Acts for Improving the Port of this Town should be likewise mortgaged to four Trustees to secure the Payment of the Money due upon Mr. Alderman Taunton's Charity and Interest thereon at four per cent . . . and the same being now taken into Consideration It is Resolved that such securities be given for the several Charity Monies and that the Town Clerk do prepare the Deeds necessary. . . .

Tuesday the 14th day of December 1824

The Corporation having made a Statement of their Charity Accounts for the inspection of the Commissioners for inquiring concerning Charities . . . the following is the present General State of Alderman Steptoe's Account [a balance of £1009.4.6 in hand and £1351.10.0 due on bonds to the Corporation.]

Tuesday the 11th day of January 1825

Resolved that the following Gentlemen having consented to be Trustees in the Deeds prepared for the Security of the several undermentioned Charities be appointed and nominated . . . accordingly

The Reverend William Waring of Itchen
The Reverend Thomas Lawes Shapcott
William Henry Lintott of . . . Romsey . . . Merchant and
Thomas Ridding Gentleman.
Mortgage Deeds sealed
Mrs. Silena Fifield's Charity
Mr. Alderman William Freeman's Charity
Mr. Alderman Richard Vernon Sadleir's Charity
At this Council the Town Seal was affixed to a Deed of Mortgage for

the term of two thousand years to the said William Waring [etc. . . .] their Executors Administrators and Assigns of all that capital Messuage or Mansion House called the Audit or Council house situate on the West Side of the High Street in the parish of Holy Rhood . . . with the open Poultry and Butter Market and Shops occupied by Butchers and Poulterers under the same And also all those several Shops or Sheds and Tenements situate on the West Side of the said Audit or Council House in the parishes of Holy Rhood and Saint Michael . . . in the several occupations of the Town Cryer and the Gardeners Butchers and Poulterers frequenting the said Market and the Tolls and Rents of all the said Markets In order to secure the Payment of The several sums following under the several Wills following

> The Will of Mrs. Silena Fifield, spinster[1]
>> The Capital Sum of   £1300
>> Interest on the above, £44.4.0 on the 1st of November
> The Will of Mr. Alderman Freeman
>> The Capital Sum of   £100
>> Interest or Proceeds on the above, £5.3.2
> The Will of Alderman Mr. Richard Vernon Sadleir
>> The Capital Sum of   £350
>> Interest on the above . . . £17.17.0

£1750

At this Council the Town Seal was also affixed to a Deed of Mortgage for the term of two thousand years to the said William Waring [etc. . . .] of All that One fifth Part of the several Rates and Duties on Goods and Vessels payable under the two Acts of 43 George III and 50 George III for improving the Port . . . to the Mayor and Common Council of the said Town, In order to secure the Payment of the Capital Sum of £3229 and Interest thereon at four per centum . . . under the Will of Mr. Alderman Taunton, Such Interest to be paid as follows, £21, part thereof, quarterly for daily Morning and Evening Prayers to the Ministers who shall have read the same or in default thereof for the other purposes of his Will, and the Residue of such Interest to be paid to the decayed Aldermen of the said Town or their Widows in the manner in the said Will mentioned, and in case of no such Objects of the said Charity to be laid out and invested at Interest to accumulate according to the Directions contained in the said Will.

Resolved that as long as there shall be no Objects of the Charity of Mr. Alderman Taunton for decayed Aldermen and their Widows and whenever hereafter it shall happen The surplus of the said Interest shall be

[1] The prefix "Mrs." or "Mistress" was at that time still not infrequently used of an unmarried woman.

laid out annually in the purchase of some of the publick Stocks or Funds at the Bank of England to accumulate for the purposes of this Charity, And in order to insure regular Investment thereof and to acquaint the Corporation in future that such Money is held upon such Trusts It is further

Resolved that at the time of the annual Examination of the Accounts of the Corporation in January A Report shall be made of such Investment and of the Total Amount which shall then stand in the Names of this Corporation in the Stocks at the Bank of England for this Charity.

Friday the 28th day of January 1825

[The examination of the last year's accounts showed a balance of £527.1.4 in the hands of the Treasurer. It was resolved that £108 surplus of interest received by or payable to the Corporation for Taunton's Charity should be laid out in the purchase of 3% Consols.]

Thursday the 11th day of August 1825

[Sir William Heathcote of Hursley and Henry Dobree the Younger of Beau Sejour in Guernsey, Merchant, were proposed as honorary burgesses, and elected on 19 August.]

Thursday the 29th day of September 1825

[Samuel Le Feuvre was sworn Mayor.]

¶ Le Feuvre was at that time the Collector of Customs. Later he held that post in Barbados, dying in 1836.

Tuesday the 4th day of October 1825

[R. D. Pritchard was sworn Sheriff and Martin Maddison and Stephen Judd Senior and Junior Bailiffs respectively, the latter having previously been sworn a member of the Council.]

Friday the 3rd day of March 1826

This day the Mayor laid before the Council a Letter he had received from Thomas Durell Esqre. stating that in consequence of his having retired to Jersey for the Remainder of his Life he begged to resign his office of a Justice of the Peace . . . and his Resignation is accepted

The Mayor reported to this Council that on the 21st day of February last he had been served with a notice from the Reverend Henry Riddell Moody as executor of the Will of the late Robert Sadleir Moody Esqre for Payment of the following Bonds from this Corporation [five dated 27 February 1792 and one dated 12 October 1792, for £50 each] at the expiry of six months from the service of this Notice . . . making together £300 and interest.

¶ At a meeting of the Council on 18 August following the Treasurer was directed to pay off these bonds.

Wednesday the 8th day of March 1826

Application having been made to this Council on behalf of Mr. Thomas Durell for Payment of the Interest of the Residue of Mr. Taunton's Charity [he] having now by reason of unfortunate Embarrassments become a decayed Alderman, Resolved that a Common Council be held . . . on the 22nd day of March . . . to consider such Application.

[On 22 March the Town Clerk was directed to write to Mr. Durell enquiring the amount of his present income, and on 31 March, after an answer had been received, it was resolved to consider his application further at a meeting on 10 April.]

Monday the 10th day of April 1826

It is Ordered . . . pursuant to the Will of Mr. Alderman Taunton That the whole of the Residuary Interest to be henceforth received be paid to Mr. Thomas Durell at Midsummer and Christmas until it shall be otherwise ordered at a Common Council. . . .

Friday the 21st day of July 1826

At this Council the Book of Dr. Speed's called the History and Antiquity of Southampton which had been missing was received from Mr. Durell and it is Resolved that in future no Book be taken out of the Mayor's closet without the permission of the Common Council and a Receipt given for the same

And the same Book was deposited in the Mayor's Strong Closet. . . .

The Mayor laid before this Council two Letters received by him from Mr. John Rowcliffe one of the Aldermen of this Corporation dated at Caen in France applying for payment to him of Interest of Monies under the Trusts of Mr. Taunton's Charity for decayed Aldermen stating his Circumstances to be such that he is become a decayed Alderman under the true Intent and Meaning of Mr. Alderman Taunton's Will.

¶ It may have been pure coincidence that so soon after the finances of Alderman Taunton's Charity had been placed on a better basis by the mortgage of the Corporation's fifth of the port dues a little crop of applications to benefit by it sprang up.

Friday the 4th day of August 1826

[It was resolved that the residue of the interest of Taunton's Charity should henceforth be divided between Durell and Rowcliffe.]

Friday the first day of September 1826

[The following were proposed as serving burgesses:
Captain Peter Rainier, R.N.
Charles Day, Esq., of the Tithing of Portswood.
John Storey Penleaze, Esq.
Captain Peter Breton of the Polygon.
Captain (later Rear-Admiral) William Ward, R.N.]

¶ The three retired officers here named, who reinforced the "gentlemen" element in the Council, were all subsequently active and prominent members. Ward also played a leading part in the development of the Docks and in local Tory politics. Breton was a Southampton man by birth who had retired to his native town about 1820 after military service in the East. Charles Day, who resigned his burgess-ship two years later on the ground of ill-health, was a former East India Company merchant who in 1814 had established himself at Spear Hall, a long-vanished mansion standing about where Alma Road is now. From there he appears to have moved to Bevois Mount a few years afterwards. His son Charles Arthur Day was later associated with the engineer William Summers in the important iron-works of Day and Summers at Millbrook and then at Northam.

Friday the 8th day of September 1826

[The above five gentlemen were unanimously elected serving burgesses; George Alexander Fullerton of Westwood in the tithing of Portswood was proposed as such; and the Honorable Peter Boyle de Blaquière of Bartley Lodge and Lt.-Col. Philip Le Feuvre, commanding the 36th Native Infantry in the East India Company's army, as honorary burgesses.]

Friday the 29th day of September 1826

[John Jolliffe was sworn Mayor.]

Tuesday the 3rd day of October 1826

[Martin Maddison was sworn Sheriff and Stephen James and W. J. Le Feuvre Senior and Junior Bailiffs respectively, the latter having been previously sworn a member of the Council.]

Friday the 13th day of October 1826

At this Council the Town Seal was affixed to two Bonds for One hundred pounds each with interest at four per cent. . . .
Viz. No. 132 to Charles Hilgrove Hammond Esqre
No. 133 to The Reverend Arthur Atherley Hammond Clerk
and the sum of two hundred Pounds was paid into the Chest.

Friday the 26th day of January 1827

[The annual examination of accounts showed an adverse balance of £148.2.3. Vice-Admiral Sir Thomas Byam Martin, Comptroller of the Navy, was proposed as an honorary burgess and elected on 2 February.]

Friday the 6th day of May 1827

Resolved that this Corporation will subscribe towards the Fund of the Regatta for the present year the sum of Ten Guineas.

¶ The Regatta, which had been an annual event for a time during Southampton's heyday as a spa and resort of fashion, had been revived in 1826 in a rather small and half-hearted way. It was now being organized on a larger scale, accompanied by a ball, and was very successful for a couple of years, after which it began to decline again.

Friday the 27th day of July 1827

This day His Grace The Duke of Buckingham and Chandos . . . was proposed and unanimously elected an Honorary Burgess. . . .

Friday the 10th day of August 1827

[Lieutenant Matthew Barton Bradby, R.N., of Hamble, and Henry Beverley Mitford of Exbury House were proposed as honorary burgesses and elected on 17 August.]

Friday the 7th day of September 1827

A licence was sealed to enable Sir William Champion de Crespigny to assign the Long Rooms, Baths and other premises near the West Quay to Jonathan Webb of Southampton, confectioner, and Thomas Clarke of Salisbury, corn merchant, for the remainder of the term of his lease.

¶ During Sir William's tenancy and under the management of a Mr. and Mrs. Chilton the Rooms had latterly fallen into disrepair. Webb and Clarke repaired them and made a determined effort to develop them again, and also the Baths, for which they claimed a "superior mode" of obtaining water; but the competition of the Royal Gloucester Baths and presently the New Assembly Rooms was too formidable.

Saturday the 29th day of September 1827

[Joseph Lomer was sworn Mayor.]

Thursday the 2nd day of October 1827

[Stephen Judd was sworn Sheriff and W. J. Le Feuvre and Captain Peter Rainier Senior and Junior Bailiffs respectively, the latter having previously been sworn a member of the Common Council.]

Friday the 9th day of November 1827

At this Council Mr. William Lomer resigned his Office of a Serving Burgess with the Consent of the Mayor and Common Council assembled . . . and having stated to this Council his extreme poverty and great Distress and having solicited some Assistance from this Corporation under his present Situation

Resolved that he be paid the sum of fifty pounds to aid him under his distressing circumstances.

Friday the 25th day of January 1828

[The examination of the accounts showed a favourable balance of £604.1.6. It was ordered that the Town Clerk should be paid the sum of £200 with the interest thereon in partial reimbursement of the £500 which he had lent the Corporation on 3 March 1826. Bishop C. R. Sumner of Winchester was proposed as and elected an honorary burgess.]

Tuesday the 29th day of January 1828

It appearing that this Port has been classed at a late Classification of Ports by the . . . Treasury in the third Class of Ports when by comparison of the foreign Trade with other ports It appears entitled to be classed in the second Class.

Resolved that this Corporation will present a Memorial to the . . . Treasury requesting that they will be pleased to reconsider such Classification and to place Southampton in the second Class.

Friday the 25th day of April 1828

The Mayor laid before this Council a Letter . . . received by him from Mrs. Ann Durell Widow of the late Mr. Alderman Thomas Durell who died at Jersey, applying for a Share of the Dividends and yearly Interest of Mr. Alderman Taunton's Funds applicable for the Relief of decayed Aldermen and of Aldermen's Widows . . . and application was also made to this Council on behalf of Mr. Alderman Rowcliffe . . . now receiving one Moiety of the said Dividends and Interest that Mr. Durell being now dead an order may be made for the Payment of the whole of such Dividends and Interest to him and the same having been taken into consideration it is

Resolved that a Common Council be held . . . on the 9th day of May next . . . to consider the several Applications of Mrs. Durell and Mr. Rowcliffe.

¶ It was decided on 9 May to take counsel's opinion as to whether, since both applicants were living outside England, they were proper objects of Taunton's Charity, but the opinion of Mr. Pepys of the Chancery Bar being favourable to them the Council resolved to divide the residuary interest of the Charity equally between them.

Monday the 22nd day of September 1828

Ordered that the Corporation do subscribe to Mr. Graham [a celebrated balloonist] towards his Expences of ascending in a Balloon from Mr. Baker's Saw Mill Yard on Friday last the sum of Two Guineas.

Friday the 29th day of September 1828

[James Bovill was sworn Mayor.]

Tuesday the 30th day of September 1828

[W. J. Le Feuvre was sworn Sheriff and J. S. Penleaze Junior Bailiff, the latter having previously been sworn a member of the Council.]

¶ Captain Rainier presumably became Senior Bailiff, since he was Junior Bailiff in the previous year and Sheriff in the following one, but there is no entry to that effect.

Friday the 31st day of October 1828

At this Council It is Resolved . . . That no pork (except sucking pigs and dairy pork to be exposed for sale and sold only in Quarters not exceeding twenty pounds Weight per Quarter) nor any Bacon be hung up nor exposed for sale in the open Market appointed for Poultry Eggs and Butter under the Audithouse in this Town And it is appointed and directed and ordered to be proclaimed that the Market for selling pork and Bacon shall from henceforth be held and kept in the new Butchers' Market called Saint George's Market being part of the additional Market some time since erected in the Town Ditches. . . .

¶ See 6 September 1822.

Friday the 23rd day of January 1829

[The examination of the accounts for 1828 showed that the favourable balance had dropped to £48.14.8. Sir Joseph Sidney Yorke of Sidney Lodge, Hamble, was proposed as an honorary burgess, and elected on 30 January. The report of the committee appointed on 30 July 1824 to inquire into the customs and usages of the Court Leet and the expediency of continuing to hold the Leet was received and ordered to be considered at the next meeting—which was not done.]

¶ It will be noticed that this committee had taken four and a half years over making its report.

Friday the 30th day of January 1829

At this Council it was resolved that each Common Councilman who has attended during the last twelve months shall be allowed to nominate an Honorary Burgess. . . .

Friday the 6th day of March 1829

At this Council the Report of the Court Leet Committee was read and taken into Consideration. . . .

[The Report of the Court Leet Committee, which is in the Page and Moody Papers in the Southampton City Archives, was to the effect that it was not expedient to give up holding the Court, "though from the various alterations in the Law and the great Population of the Town. . . . It does not seem expedient . . . to put in execution the whole of their ancient Powers". There would be no advantage, it continued, in summoning all residents between the ages of 16 and 60 to attend and do suit and service, but before this was discontinued it recommended that legal advice should be taken. It seemed proper to the Committee, however, that a jury should be summoned and sworn to make presentments, which might be laid before the Grand Jury if they were for offences cognizable at Quarter Sessions, but concerning other offences advice should also be sought as to how far the Court could or should enforce its ancient right of fining, and whether it could impose fines on jurors who did not attend. The Court's most onerous function and also that which it performed most ineffectively, the report added, was the inspection of weights and measures, and it urged that application should be made to the justices to appoint an inspector of weights and measures by virtue of the powers conferred on them by recent legislation. Finally it recommended that the bounds of the town should be perambulated by the Court more frequently than of late, and that not more than three or four years should be allowed to pass without this being done; but that the expensive feasting with which this had previously been accompanied should be discontinued.]

. . . It was thereupon Resolved that the opinion of Counsel be taken upon the necessity of summoning all Residents to do suit and service [and] upon the Power and Expediency of punishing petty offences in the Leet and the levying of Fines on jurors and others. . . .

That Application be made to the Justices to appoint an Inspector of Weights and Measures. . . .

That the Lords of the Leet and their Jury will perambulate the Bounds of this Town . . . on Hock Tuesday in the present year. . . .

And the further Consideration of the Report is deferred to a future Council.

¶ An Inspector of Weights and Measures was appointed in due course. The Court Leet duly perambulated the boundaries and afterwards—despite the report—dined at the Audit House, the usual £35 being allowed to the Sheriff for the expenses of the occasion.

[About this time the following honorary burgesses were proposed and subsequently elected, presumably as a result of the resolution passed on the previous 30 January:

6 March.	Captain Jenkin Jones, R.N., of Purbrook near Portsmouth.
	William J. Spurrier of High Hall near Wimborne.
	The Rev. Edward T. Richards, Rector of Farlington near Portsmouth.
	Vice-Admiral Sir John P. Beresford, Bart., of Harley Street, London.
	George Buck of Lyndhurst.
20 March	Vice-Admiral Sir George Cockburn, Bart.
	William Henry Tilston of London.
27 March.	Henry Fox Atherley of Arundel.
10 April	The Marquis Chandos.
	John Le Feuvre, Lieutenant R.N.
24 April.	William Charleton of London, merchant.
	Captain J. G. Willim (East India Company's army) of Hereford.
8 May.	Sir Arthur Paget of Hamble Cliff.
10 July.	Major-General Sir Richard Hussey Vivian of Beechwood, Eling.]

Friday the 10th day of April 1829

Resolved that this Corporation do subscribe towards the Removal of Mr. Chamberlayne's Gas Column from the Corner of Northam Bridge Road to the Quay

£2.2.0

Friday the 24th day of July 1829

Ordered that the several persons from whom any money is remaining due upon those Bonds of Steptoe's Charity lent above ten years be immediately applied to for payment of the Money due thereon and that they be acquainted that if not paid they will be sued for the amount.

Friday the 7th day of August 1829

At this Council the Right Honorable Lord Yarborough Baron of Yarborough in the County of Lincoln and of Appuldurcombe in the Isle of Wight . . . was unanimously elected an Honorary Burgess. . . .

Wednesday the 29th day of August 1829

[At this Council and another on 11 September the opinions of two counsel on the duties of the Court Leet and the benefits arising from it were read and considered.]

Tuesday the 29th day of September 1829

[Philip Cartaret Fall was sworn Mayor.]

Tuesday the 6th day of October 1829

[Captain Rainier was sworn Sheriff and J. S. Penleaze and Captain Breton Senior and Junior Bailiffs respectively, the latter having previously been sworn a member of the Council.]

¶ Penleaze applied to the Council on 11 December for leave to resign the office of Senior Bailiff, which was granted him. Captain Breton then became Senior Bailiff and on 21 December Captain Ward was elected and sworn Junior Bailiff, having previously been elected a Common Councilman. On 5 March 1830 Penleaze applied for and secured leave to resign his burgess-ship also, giving as his reason that he intended to leave the town. Between the last two dates he had come forward as a Whig to contest the by-election caused by the death of William Chamberlayne, but had been defeated by the long purse of the Tory James Barlow Hoy (see 10 September 1824). Nevertheless he returned to the town and to the fray to take a double revenge on Hoy in the Reform Bill elections of 1831 and 1832, but withdrew without contesting that of 1835.

Friday the 29th day of January 1830

[The examination of the accounts for 1829 showed an adverse balance of £83.7.7. Three honorary burgesses were proposed: Lt.-Col. Henry John Bowler of the East India Company's service, Captain (half-pay) James Goddard Doran of the 14th Regiment, and James Barlow Hoy the victor in the recent by-election.]

Friday the 5th day of February 1830

[Captain Benjamin Clement, R.N., and John Frederick Breton of Landford House, Wilts., were proposed as honorary burgesses and elected on 12 February.]

Friday the 9th day of July 1830

His late Majesty King George the Fourth having departed this life . . . His Majesty King William the Fourth was on Tuesday the 29th day of June proclaimed at the Balcony of the Audithouse at the Outside of Bargate and at the Custom House with the usual Solemnities. . . .

Friday the 30th day of July 1830

At this Council an Application was made from the Commissioners of the Waterworks for five acres of land marked out in the Common at the upper part including the present Brickkiln to make Reservoirs for water to be brought from Woodmill, to supply the Town with water—and Mr. Doswell the Town Engineer having stated to this Council that it is practicable to obtain ten times the Quantity of Water (or even more) beyond the present supply from the springs that pass through the Common, It is

Resolved that Mr. Ridding do write to Mr. Amor the Clerk to the Commissioners of the Waterworks acquainting him that the Corporation decline complying with the Application of the Commissioners . . . unless they can satisfy the Common Council that Mr. Doswell's opinion is erroneous At the same time the Corporation desire it may be understood that they are anxious to afford the Commissioners . . . every facility in obtaining a more ample provision of water than is now brought into the Town.

Ordered that the Town Clerk do commence Actions against [7] persons who have not paid . . . sums due on Bonds under Mr. Alderman Steptoe's Charity to this Corporation. . . .

Monday the 16th day of August 1830

It appearing to this Council by a conference with the Commissioners of the Waterworks and Re-examination of Mr. Doswell that it is possible that a sufficient Quantity of Water cannot be obtained [sc. from the springs] in the Common, and the Commissioners . . . having renewed their Application for Lands and Reservoirs as follows

For one acre and a half of Ground on the Common for the purpose of forming a Reservoir to be connected with the present Waterworks

And, after stating that they are in treaty for a larger supply of Water, for six acres of Land on the East side of the Common for two Reservoirs

Resolved that this Corporation will grant to the Commissioners . . . the Acre and a half of Ground for a Reservoir North side of the present Reservoir at a Rent of fifteen shillings a year and that if the Treaty is effected for a larger supply of water this Corporation will grant to the Commissioners six acres of land on the East side of the Common for two Reservoirs at a Rent of three pounds a year.

The immediate scite [sic] of the several Reservoirs to be approved of by the Corporation.

¶ Two more reservoirs were accordingly built, in 1830 and 1831 respectively, but the problem of an adequate water-supply for the fast-growing town was not solved thereby (see 19 January 1838).

Friday the 20th day of August 1830

Resolved that a Finance Committee be appointed to look into the accounts of the Corporation to see what Expences can be saved and to report thereon. . . .

George Frederick Pitt Esqre having very handsomely offered the Corporation a valuable Library of Books to be kept and preserved by them for the Benefit of this Town and to be read under certain Rules and Regulations to be made by the Corporation

Ordered that the Town Clerk do prepare a Deed of Gift from Mr. Pitt. . . .

¶ The library of 1100 books now presented to the Corporation had been accumulated by William Molyneux [1656-98], his son Samuel [1689-1723] and Nathaniel St. André [1680-1776], the last of whom lived latterly in Southampton, built Bellevue House, and bequeathed the collection and the greater part of his property to Pitt and his brother William, who were the children of St. André's former maidservant. The history of the collection is fully described in the introduction to the catalogue of it recently published by the Southampton Public Libraries Committee.

Thursday the 16th day of September 1830

The Report of the Finance Committee being taken into Consideration at this Council and the several Recommendations of the Committee having been proposed

It is Resolved that all Expences attending the Chapel Fair both the Dinner at the Opening of the Fair and the Entertainment at the Bailiff's Booth . . . be discontinued

That the luncheon on the Mayor's first Court Day at the Audithouse be discontinued

That the Daily Newspaper allowed to the Mayor . . . be discontinued at Michaelmas next

That the Stamps upon the Entry of the Admission of 2 Burgesses by the Mayor after Michaelmas next shall be paid for by the Burgesses so nominated as well as by all others [who already did so, by a resolution of 27 February 1829].

That the allowance of faggots for a Bon Fire in the Marsh on the 5th day of November and to Constables and Beadles for Refreshments be discontinued

That the Audit Dinners on the first Monday in May and . . . in November be discontinued and that the Audit for the Receipt of the Quit Rents be held at eleven o'clock in the forenoon instead of four o'clock in the afternoon as hitherto

Resolved that there be no Dinner on the Day of privately nominating the Mayor and other Officers on the Friday before the Feast of Saint Bartholomew but that the Mayor do give a public Dinner to the Corporation and such other Gentlemen of the Town and Neighbourhood as he may choose to invite on The King's Birthday

That there be no wine given at the Audithouse on the King's Birthday . . . at Noon as hitherto. . . .

[Dr. Edwin Godden Jones of Swathling and William Henry Gater of West End were proposed as honorary burgesses, and elected on 24 September.]

¶ The change of spelling to Swaythling apparently took place in 1895, and is ascribed to the wishes of Sir Samuel Montague who had just been made a baronet and later became Lord Swaythling.

Wednesday the 29th day of September 1830

[John Rushworth Keele was sworn Mayor.]

Tuesday the 5th day of October 1830

[Captain Peter Breton was sworn Sheriff and Captain Ward and R. D. Pritchard Senior and Junior Bailiffs respectively. In this case the Junior Bailiff was already a member of the Council.]

Friday the 29th day of October 1830

At this Council Charles Hilgrove Hammond Esqre the Recorder resigned his office. . . .

Resolved unanimously that the thanks of this Corporation be given to Mr. Hammond for his constant and faithful Services as Recorder for the long period of thirty years

That a handsome Piece of Plate of the Value of Seventy five Guineas be presented to Mr. Hammond as a Mark of their Respect and Esteem

Resolved that the Recorder be allowed a Salary of Fifty Guineas a Year [instead of fees].

Friday the 5th day of November 1830

This day at a Common Council . . . the Mayor Aldermen and the Rest of the Members (whereof the Mayor and two of the Senior Aldermen were three) . . . have unanimously elected . . . Peregrine Bingham Esqre of the Middle Temple London Barrister-at-Law Recorder. . . .

Friday the 19th day of November 1830

At this Council a Letter was read from Captain Stephens Honorary Secretary to the Subscribers enclosing Notes of the Subscribers respecting the intended Railway and Docks requesting the Common Council would appoint an early day to receive a Deputation from the Subscribers on the Business

Resolved that a Common Council be held on Monday next . . . for the Purpose. . . .

¶ At this meeting the first breath of a new Southampton may be said to have penetrated the Council Chamber.

A project for a London, Portsmouth and Southampton Railway had been formed, largely by London and Portsmouth interests, as early as 1825 (a year of premature and over-optimistic railway speculation), but though a company had been set up the scheme had come to nothing. The bursting of many such bubble projects in that year had then delayed for some time any further definite attempt to form a railway company, though the advantages of a connection with London by rail continued to be discussed in Southampton. In 1830, however, the construction of the Manchester and Liverpool Railway provided a stimulus, and on 6 October A. R. Dottin presided at his home Bugle Hall over a meeting of persons interested, who formed a committee and opened a subscription to enable a survey to be made. The committee included, besides Dottin, his fellow-M.P. Hoy, John Fleming the active and benevolent squire of South Stoneham, De Blaquière, Samuel Le Feuvre, R. D. Pritchard and Lt.-Col. Henderson, a retired officer of Engineers who like several others of his kind became prominent in railway promotion. It came quickly to the conclusion that the plan must be extended to include the building of docks, without which a railway would not be sufficiently profitable, and that the support of influential and moneyed people in London and other towns must be enlisted.

The name of Captain Stephens, R.N., the Honorary Secretary, deserves to be rescued from oblivion. Like many other naval officers without much means or influence, he had attained captain's rank relatively late in life. In addition to being one of the earliest (some claimed that he was the very first) of the local advocates of a railway and docks, he had already played a leading part in the revival of the Regatta and in the scheme for the construction of a landing pier (the future Royal Pier referred to in the entry for 3 February 1831 below). Having ruined himself financially by his experiments and activities, he was in due course elbowed into the background when the railway project had gained momentum and was showing good prospects of success.

Monday the 22nd day of November 1830

At this Council a Deputation from the Subscribers to the intended Railway and Docks attended.

Resolved that in consequence of the Representation made by the said Deputation, the Corporation are willing to treat with the Committee or any respectable Company that may be established for making liberal arrangements with a view to the Extension of the Port.

Friday the 28th day of January 1831

[The examination of the accounts for 1830 showed a balance of £404.9.8 due to the Corporation.]

Thursday the 8th day of February 1831

Resolved that this Corporation do subscribe one hundred Pounds to raise a Fund for defraying the Expenses of applying to Parliament to obtain a Bill for the intended Landing Pier, either to be repaid out of the first Monies to be borrowed or to be secured by Mortgages under the intended Act.

¶ The growth of steam-packet traffic during the past decade had led to increasing criticism of the delays and inconvenience caused to passengers landing or embarking at low tide by the lack of a pier. Several private projects for building one had already come to nothing, when at a town meeting on 4 December 1828 a committee was set up, including Samuel and W. J. Le Feuvre and others with packet interests, as well as Colonel Henderson, to explore the best means of attaining this object. Acting as a pressure group, the committee succeeded after rather prolonged negotiations in prevailing upon the Harbour Commissioners to approach Parliament for leave to bring in a bill for the erection of a pier. This was introduced and passed later in 1831, and the Pier was opened on 8 July 1833 (see the entry for that date below).

Friday the 18th day of February 1831

Application was made to this Council on the Behalf of the Owners and Occupiers of Houses built on the Lands on each side of the Turnpike Roads adjoining East and West Magdalens Common Fields and of the Persons having Rights of Common on those Fields to inspect the Books Documents and papers of this Corporation to see if any Evidence can be obtained therefrom of the Original Grant or Conveyence of the Public Rights on those Fields and what the Rights of the Owners of them are; and several of the Books and Documents from which such Evidence may probably be obtained being in ancient character of Handwriting which the Gentlemen of this Corporation who are desirous of obtaining this Evidence cannot decypher, Application was also made that Mr. William Turner Allchin, Attorney at Law, who is versed in ancient Writings, be permitted to inspect such Books and Documents for the above Purpose.

Resolved that Leave be given to Mr. Allchin to inspect such Deeds and Writings and Documents and to make therefrom any Extracts or Minutes which may tend to explain or elucidate the Rights upon and over Magdalen Common Field both of the Commoners and of the Owners but on the express Condition that no Communication of any such Extracts Minutes or Documents be made by Mr. Allchin until the same shall have been laid before the Corporation in Common Council assembled and their approval thereof obtained and that Mr. Allchin be now sworn to keep the secrets of this Corporation and not to communicate any information he may so obtain without the consent of this Corporation and

The said William Turner Allchin was at this Council [so] sworn.

¶ By long-established custom whose origins had been lost from sight the common or lammas lands of the East and West Magdalens, Houndwell and Hoglands were held from Lady Day to Michaelmas by individuals living on their fringes or in houses built on former encroachments on them, and then given up to common pasture for the other half of the year. Not unnaturally this had led to disputes; especially since, whereas after the holders or owners had taken one crop of hay or grain they were supposed to allow the herbage to grow again until the fields were thrown open to the commoners, some of them had lately begun to dig gravel-pits or re-plough the land for late crops, thus destroying the after-grass and infringing the commoners' six months. Both parties to the dispute were now appealing to the Corporation to settle it by reference to its records, but (despite Mr. Allchin's palaeographic skill) without any immediate result.

Friday the 4th day of March 1831

At this Council copies of the several Entries made in the Court Leet and other Books examined by Mr. Allchin pursuant to the Council's order . . . were received and ordered to be considered at the next Council.

Monday the 28th day of March 1831

At this Council the Extracts made by Mr. Allchin were perused . . . and Mr. Ridding is directed carefully to peruse the same and to mark with Red Ink such parts as related to other property not under the present Circumstances of Magdalens and any thing which may appear inadvisable to lay before the Public, and [it is resolved] that Mr. Allchin be desired to copy the same omitting such parts in order that they may be delivered to the Committee.

¶ The committee referred to was one which had been set up by a meeting of commoners to defend their rights.

Friday the 17th day of June 1831

Resolved that this Corporation do subscribe towards the Relief of the distressed Irish the sum of Ten Guineas.

Wednesday the 6th day of July 1831

Resolved that this Corporation do lend . . . to the Commissioners of the Pier the sum of five hundred Pounds at five pounds per centum . . . on Security of the Mortgage of their Tolls.

¶ The Pier Act created a body of commissioners who were in fact identical with the existing Harbour Commissioners and who proceeded to borrow money from the Corporation and a number of individuals on mortgages of their prospective tolls. They were henceforth styled the Pier and Harbour Commissioners.

Friday the 22nd day of July 1831

At this Council a Letter was received from Colonel Henderson as Chairman of the Southampton and London Railway Company communicating a Resolution of the Company . . . that the Directors should be at Liberty to appoint the Mayor to be a Director by virtue of his Office and for the next following Year and desiring the approbation of this Corporation to the intended Undertaking

Resolved that the Common Council entertain a full Sense of the great public Advantages which must arise from a Rail Road from London to Southampton and therefore approve the Mayor's Acceptance of the Office of a Director. . . .

Tuesday the 6th day of September 1831

[The Mayor reported that at a public meeting of the inhabitants which he had been requested to convene for the purpose of considering how the coronation of William IV should be celebrated, a committee had been elected and had subsequently come to the conclusion that in view of the increased population it was no longer practicable to give a public dinner to the poor, as had been done at the last coronation. It was therefore resolved that in addition to a firework display on the Marsh the church bells should be rung and a salute fired from the guns on the Platform.]

Monday the 12th day of September 1831

At this Council the Town Seal was affixed to a Deed of Exchange of the Old Alms House near the Poor House at Saint Mary's to the Guardians of the Poor for seven new houses now erected by them on Land they have lately purchased . . . in a street called Grove Street in Saint Mary's parish.

Thursday the 29th day of September 1831

[William Oke was sworn Mayor.]

Tuesday the 4th day of October 1831

[Captain Ward was sworn Sheriff and Martin Maddison and Stephen Judd Senior and Junior Bailiffs respectively.]

Friday the 28th day of October 1831

Resolved that in future no Gentleman be named as an Honorary Burgess of this Corporation who is resident within any of the united parishes of this Town.

¶ An exception was shortly afterwards made in favour of George Frederick Pitt in view of his recent gift of a library to the Corporation.

Friday the 18th day of November 1831

At this Council the Corporation offered to assign to Mr. Ridding Three of the Mortgages of the Tolls of the Port granted by the Port Commissioners to this Corporation on the 6th day of July last with the Interest due thereon in discharge of the Debt of Three hundred Pounds lent by him to the Corporation March 3rd 1826, which Mr. Ridding is willing to accept. . . .

Thursday the 26th day of January 1832

[The examination of the accounts for 1831 showed a balance due to the Corporation of £221.17.7.]

Thursday the 2nd day of February 1832

At this Council a Letter was received from Colonel Henderson applying for the Consent of this Corporation that the Railway may pass across the Marsh and over such other Property belonging to the Corporation as may appear by the Plans to be affected by the proposed Measure. . . .

Resolved that this Corporation do consent . . . the Corporation Rights and Pier Commissioners' Dues being to be saved by the Act of Parliament.

Friday the 17th day of August 1832

An Application was made to this Council by the Commissioners of the Pavement that this Corporation will allow a proper Place for a Pig Market several of the Inhabitants having complained to them of the Pigs being permitted to stand in the High Street near Holy Rhood Church where the ancient Market was And the following Gentlemen are appointed to be a Committee to view Saint George's Market [the Butchers' Market in the Town Ditches] and any other place they may think proper to see if any part of it or some proper Place can be found for a Pig Market. . . .

Saturday the 29th day of September 1832

[John Jolliffe was sworn Mayor.]

Tuesday the 2nd day of October 1832

[J. R. Keele was sworn Sheriff and Stephen Judd and W. J. Le Feuvre Senior and Junior Bailiffs respectively.]

Friday the 12th day of October 1832

At this Council the Committee appointed . . . to view Saint George's Market to see whether there or elsewhere a proper Place could be found for removing the Pig Market . . . reported that the Upper or Southern part of the Market is a proper Place. . . .

Ordered that the necessary Steps be taken and Notices given for holding the Pig Market in that part of Saint George's Market. . . .

Friday the 16th day of November 1832

A Letter was received at this Council from . . . the Guardians of the Poor requesting that they may be permitted to form and lay down a Ride or Drive entirely round the Common by employing the Labour of the unemployed Poor under the Direction of some Surveyor of the Corporation

Resolved that the Mayor be directed to see Mr. Page [the Clerk to the Guardians] thereon and direct him to draw out a plan of such Ride or Drive to be laid before the next Council and that in the mean time Mr. Page do occupy the Poor in levelling or draining any part of the Common which may appear to him most necessary to be done with a View to such Ride or Drive being compleated.

¶ The Guardians had a few months previously adopted the policy of granting relief to the able-bodied only in return for work.

Friday the 11th day of January 1833

At this Council a Plan of the intended Drive round the Common drawn by Mr. Page . . . was produced and inspected and the same is approved of and the Gentlemen present at this Council are appointed a Committee to superintend the making such Road. . . .

Friday the 25th day of January 1833

[The examination of the accounts for 1832 showed a balance due to the Corporation of £697.13.3.]

Friday the 15th day of February 1833

At this Council a Letter was received from Mr. S. M. Phillipps [the under-secretary of the Home Office] . . . desiring a Return to be made of the Charitable Funds and Property, the manner acquired and purpose for which given and how distributed and applied. . . .

Ordered that the Town Clerk do prepare and make out such Returns.

Thursday the 4th day of April 1833

Resolved that this Corporation will subscribe the sum of Fifty Pounds towards the Repairs and Enlargement of Saint Mary's Church. . . .

Friday the 10th day of May 1833

At this Council a Mortgage of one hundred pounds was received from the Commissioners for building a new Landing Pier . . . at five per cent . . . being the sum advanced by this Corporation on the 3rd day of February 1831 towards obtaining the Act of Parliament.

Friday the 17th day of May 1833

At this Council a letter was received from James Spearing resigning his Office of Town Cryer on account of his Age and Infirmities.

This Corporation taking into Consideration the long and faithful Services of James Spearing who was elected Town Cryer the 11th day of

October 1796 and his great age being now upwards of 87 years old and that he is become incapacitated principally from a Fracture met with whilst in his Duty. . . . It is Resolved that he be allowed a Superannuation Salary of Twenty five Pounds per annum. . . .

Friday the 21st day of June 1833

Resolved that the Duchess of Kent and Princess Victoria be invited to come to Southampton on their way to the Isle of Wight and to grace the Opening of the New . . . Pier with their Presence. . . .

[The Corporation subscribed 25 guineas on 28 June towards the expenses of the opening of the Pier.]

Monday the 8th day of July 1833

The Commissioners for building a new . . . Pier . . . having applied to the Corporation to attend in their Robes the Procession for opening the same And the Corporation having robed at the Town Hall proceeded accompanied by the Commissioners . . . and several Gentlemen of the Town and a Band of Music to the New Landing Pier and being arrived thereat a Deputation . . . of seven Gentlemen accompanied by the Town Clerk proceeded on board the Emerald Royal Yatch [sic] to invite their Royal Highnesses The Duchess of Kent and the Princess Victoria who were then just arrived in the River to land at the Pier.

Afterwards the Deputation returned to the New Pier and their Royal Highnesses in their Barge steered by Admiral Tinling deputed by the Mayor as Admiral of the Port were graciously pleased to land upon the New Pier and were received at the Foot of the Stairs by the Mayor and Corporation and conducted to a Marquee pitched upon the Head of the New Pier where refreshments were provided for them—and their Royal Highnesses being seated they were addressed by the Town Clerk . . . [who expressed the Corporation's gratitude for their attendance and requested the Duchess to name the Pier, whereupon she christened it "The Royal Pier".]

¶ Rear-Admiral Charles Tinling was probably the senior of the retired naval officers living in the town. As a member of the reformed Corporation he later combined Toryism with very vocal championship of the poor and defence of the common lands against what he regarded as encroachments and some others considered improvements.

Friday the 19th day of July 1833

At this Council John Rushworth Keele Esqre the Foreman of the Court Leet brought in their Presentments and It is Ordered that such Presentments will be taken into consideration [at the next Council.]

Friday the 26th day of July 1833

At this Council it is ordered that the following persons be written to stating that the Court Leet have made Presentments of the following Nuisances

The Trustees of the Winchester Turnpike and Mr. Fitzhugh [William Fitzhugh of Bannisters] respecting their burying the soil of the surface in digging Gravel in West Magdalens Field

Mr. Fitzhugh and Mr. Weld [James Weld of Archers Lodge, a relative of Lord Petre] respecting their drains emptying into the waste land by the side of the avenue above Belle Vue . . .

[Eight owners and/or occupiers]—for making a Nuisance on part of Bernard's Field in Saint Mary's Parish by running out their drains there. . . .

Friday the 20th day of September 1833

[Vice-Admiral Sir John Gore, K.C.B., and Robert Stratton of Dibden Lodge were proposed as honorary burgesses, and elected on 27 September.]

Saturday the 29th day of September 1833

[Stephen Judd was sworn Mayor.]

Tuesday the 1st day of October 1833

[W. J. Le Feuvre and Captain Breton were sworn Bailiffs. James Lomer was sworn Sheriff on 8 October.]

Friday the 1st day of November 1833

The Commissioners appointed . . . for enquiring into Municipal Corporations, Messrs. Ellis and Maude, arrived in this town on Saturday the 12th day of October last and proceeded to a public Examination of several Members of the Corporation and their Town Clerk and inferior Officers on Tuesday the 15th . . . and three following days . . . and afterwards continued at the Dolphins Inn examining several of the Charters and various Books of the Corporation till Saturday the 26th. . . .

Resolved that the Town Clerk be presented with the sum of Ten Guineas for his great Trouble and Attention in searching out Books and Papers for the Commissioners and his Attendance upon them not only during their public sitting but during their Continuance here. . . .

Saturday the 16th day of November 1833

The Common Council having ascertained with much satisfaction that the preliminary forms are now in due Course of Execution for the Introduction of a Bill into Parliament at the earliest period of the ensuing session for the construction of the London and Southampton Railway feel that the Opportunity has arrived for the Expression of their marked Opinion of the great Importance of the Undertaking.

Resolved that placed in a prominent Situation as regards the Interests of their fellow Townsmen and desirous to promote to the utmost of their Power the Prosperity of the Town and Port of Southampton as well as the general Advantage of the Community with which this Corporation is so intimately blended They cannot but view the Establishment of the intended Railway as a national Measure calculated to realise the most important advantages to the Public and more especially to the local Interests of this Town and Neighbourhood and are desirous . . . to afford every facility in their Power towards its accomplishment. . . .

¶ The original railway company had not succeeded in attracting sufficient backing either in Southampton or at first in London, so that the plans for bringing into Parliament a bill for the construction of the line had had to be suspended. But meanwhile Colonel Henderson had removed to London and managed to win the support of moneyed interests there, after which he had toured the principal northern and Scottish cities and recruited further capital. It thus became possible to take up the interrupted project again, though the idea of building docks as well was now dropped from it.

Friday the 6th day of December 1833

[The Mayor reported that as one of the executors of the will of the late Mrs. Sarah Spinks he had received from her estate the sum of £236.18.6, the produce of £300 worth of 3% Consols, which she had bequeathed to the Corporation in trust, and the interest of which was to be devoted annually to the purchase of clothing for the poor of St. Michael's parish.]

Friday the 9th day of January 1834

At this Council application was made . . . for the Consent of this Corporation to the intended London and Southampton Rail Road being carried along over the Marsh to the Ditch on the North side of the Road

Resolved that this Council do consent thereto but dissent to its going further

[In the margin of this entry there is the following:

"We protest against the subjoined resolution because we consider it the first great step towards transferring the Trade and a chief part of the Business of Southampton to Chapel and the Banks of the River Itchen—to the great injury of existing Interests in the town and the almost certain destruction of the dues on . . . the New Pier lately created and tending to a breach of faith towards those who have lent their money thereon. (Signed) J. R. Keele. S. Lintott."]

¶ Though the protest was cast in somewhat exaggerated terms and its authors were directing their gaze to the Itchen rather than to the area where the railway terminus and afterwards the docks would be built, they had correctly foreseen that the trade of the old commercial centre at the bottom of the High Street, as well as the New Pier, would suffer through the new development.

Monday the 20th day of January 1834

[The examination of the accounts for 1833 showed a balance of £770.15.6 due to the Corporation.]

At this Council a Letter was read from the Commissioners for improving this port stating their apprehensions of injury to the Pier revenue if the intended line of rail road be carried into effect [and] that an act will be obtained for constructing Docks for the Benefit of Private Individuals, and therefore applying to this Corporation for the first Refusal of the Mudlands Eastward of the Platform in order to secure the Interest of those who have lent their Money on the . . . New Pier.

Resolved that the Corporation will give the Commissioners of the Pier the first Refusal.

At this Council Mr. Edward Harrison one of the Solicitors for the Bill intended to be brought into the ensuing Parliament for building a Bridge over the River Itchen at or near the present Ferry attended to obtain the Assent of this Corporation that a Road to such Bridge should be made across the Marsh and this Council taking the same into their consideration and fearing some Injury to the Navigation of the River Itchen to Chapel and Northam are of opinion that they cannot consent thereto but must be considered as Neuter in the Business.

¶ This last entry refers to what was in effect the first form of the Floating Bridge project—the formation of a company to build a bridge across the Itchen near the old ferry. It was fiercely opposed by the Northam Bridge Company, since their tolls would be threatened by the shorter and more convenient route to and from Southampton that would be opened up to more people than the ferry had been able to accommodate; and was also attacked or regarded with suspicion by those who feared that it would interfere with the trade of the Itchen and/or that the Company would charge heavy tolls on the road or roads which they would build across the Marsh. After being hotly debated at a stormy public meeting on 31 January, the plan nevertheless began to gain support and in the altered form of a floating bridge (at the Admiralty's suggestion) eventually carried the day. An act was secured in 1834 and the bridge was opened on 23 November 1836.

Saturday the 29th day of March 1834

This Council taking into consideration the Bill now before Parliament for a Floating Bridge at Itchen Ferry are of opinion that the several Clauses respecting the taking Tolls nearer Southampton than the Bridge or making any Fences across the Marsh or preventing Cattle in the Marsh crossing the Road and taking Gravel from the Waste Lands or Shore without

Recompense are highly improper and injurious to the Inhabitants of this Town and . . . should be struck out. . . .

Resolved that the members of Parliament for this Town . . . and also the southern part of Hampshire be written to requesting their aid in getting such clauses struck out and the Act altered accordingly and that the Solicitors of the Bill be informed that unless such alterations are made the Corporation must oppose the Bill.

¶ The bill was in fact withdrawn because of the strong opposition and a somewhat less objectionable one introduced next year with success.

Friday the 20th day of June 1834

Resolved that Mr. Mayor Mr. Atherley and Mr. Keele be a Committee to examine into the Records Charters Books and Papers of this Corporation to see what will be proper to supply the Record Commissioners with in answer to their Inquiries and that they be authorised to have the Assistance of Mr. Allchin an Examiner of ancient Records as well as the Town Clerk.

¶ The enquiries referred to here are also alluded to in a letter from the Town Clerk printed in the Report of the Commission on the Public Records, 1837, app. 2, p. 483:

"   Southampton, 20th August 1834
Sir,

I beg to acknowledge the receipt of three letters from you, making inquiries respecting the ancient records and manuscripts of this Corporation, for the use of His Majesty's Commissioners on the Public Records . . . and to acquaint you that the letters have been often laid before the Mayor and Common Council, but I could obtain no instructions as to answering your letters, nor were any steps taken till within the last two or three months. I can only account for it by knowing they were unwilling to decline giving any information in their power, but were not willing to incur any expense about it, as there was reason to expect that all the present corporators might be turned out of office by the legislature; and upon so uncertain a tenure they did not like to incur debts which might never be paid out of any corporate funds. As soon as it appeared that this would not take place during the session lately closed, they employed Mr. Allchin, a reader of ancient records, and a committee of corporators was appointed to examine their records and papers, and prepare a return to the Commissioners' queries, which has now been completed; and I transmit the same, by desire of the Mayor and Corporation of Southampton. . . ."

Although the Corporation was slow in attending to this matter, it was in fact more co-operative than most others, and their return shows that no records of importance have subsequently been lost.

Friday the 29th day of August 1834

At this Council the Town Clerk produced a letter he had received . . . by Command of His Majesty's Commissioners on the Public Records

Returning their thanks for the very full and interesting Return made to their Circular Questions and stating that Instructions have been given to the King's Printers to forward such of the Publications of the Board as are not out of Print to Southampton for the use of the Corporation.

[At this Council the following were proposed as serving burgesses:

Edward Home Hulton of Bevis Mount;
John Sammon Down, Doctor of Medecine;
Samuel Silver Taylor, brewer;
George Hunt, brewer;
John William Bovill, timber merchant;
Richard Eldridge the Younger, timber merchant.]

¶ Fifty-three volumes of the publications referred to above were received on 17 October.

Monday the 29th day of September 1834

[W. J. Le Feuvre was sworn Mayor.
James Bovill was sworn Sheriff on 7 October, and Dr. Down and E. H. Hulton, who had just been made burgesses, were sworn members of the Council and then Senior and Junior Bailiffs respectively, on 14 October.]

¶ It seems likely that the Corporation, faced by imminent extinction, was finding it difficult to persuade members to undertake office.

Friday the 31st day of October 1834

At this Council a Letter was received from Mrs. Anna Lintott the Widow of Mr. William Lintott late an Alderman of this Town stating her great Distress and applying to be permitted to participate in the Fund of Mr. Alderman Taunton for the Relief of distressed Aldermen and their Widows and . . . it appearing that Mrs. Lintott is a proper Object for Relief from the said Charity

Resolved that a Common Council be holden . . . on Friday the 7th day of November next to consider further her application. . . .

At this Council the Minutes of three Meetings of a Committee of Gentlemen, acting with a View to the Preservation of the Rights of the Inhabitants in the Public Lands of East and West Magdalens Hoglands Houndwell and Porters Meadow . . . and Copies of Letters to and from some of the Proprietors of these Common Lands were received and read by which it appeared the Committee were desirous the Sense of the Town should be taken on the Best Course for establishing and preserving the Public Rights in those Fields—and the same having been taken into Consideration It is

Resolved that search be made among the Corporation Records to see if anything further can be found respecting the Common Fields and that an Opinion of the Recorder be taken on the Subject. . . .

¶ See the entry for 18 February 1831 and note. Further search in the records failed to settle the renewed dispute and despite the Recorder's opinion (below) it continued to flare up intermittently until the project for the reclamation of the Marsh offered a solution.

Friday the 7th day of November

[Mrs. Lintott's application was considered and, Mrs. Durell and Mr. Rowcliffe being still alive, it was decided to divide the residuary interest of Taunton's Charity money equally between the three of them in future.]

Friday the 30th day of January 1835

[The examination of the accounts for 1834 showed a balance of £343.14.2 due to the Corporation.]

Friday the 20th day of February 1835

At this Council the opinion of Mr. Bingham upon the Case laid before him . . . respecting the Common Fields was . . . read whereby it appears that Mr. Bingham advises no Proceedings being taken unless the Proprietors attempt to build thereon and that in any case the Corporation have no power to act in such cases [and] that It appears to him that the Commoners have a Right of turning their Cattle into those Fields . . . but that the Owners of the Fields have a right to till them as they please

Resolved that the Town Clerk do send to the Committee . . . who addressed the Corporation respecting the Common Fields a Copy of the Questions laid before Mr. Bingham and his Opinion thereon. . . .

Friday the 8th day of May 1835

This day the Corporation consisting of Twelve Common Council Men and Eight Burgesses with the Town Clerk and Coroners . . . in Company with all the Clergymen of the Town and Neighbourhood . . . and very many of his Parishioners attended the Funeral of the Reverend Thomas Mears at All Saints Church. . . He was very generally respected and beloved by the Inhabitants of the Town at large. . . .

Friday the 18th day of September 1835

This day being the Friday before the Feast of Saint Matthew is the Day appointed by the Charters of this Town for the Election of Mayor and other Officers for the Year ensuing But it appearing to the Mayor Bailiffs and Burgesses assembled that an Act of Parliament was passed on the ninth day of September Instant intituled "An Act to provide for the Regulation of Municipal Corporations in England and Wales" [wherein] It is enacted that in every Borough where by Charter any Election of the Mayor Aldermen and Common Council Men is appointed to be holden between the day of the passing of that Act and the first day of May next no such Election shall be holden but every person holding Office in any Borough on the day of passing that Act shall continue to hold such office until the time provided in that Act for going out of Office—The Mayor Bailiffs and Burgesses present proceeded to the Town Hall and elected only the Inferior Officers of this Corporation the Mayor Sheriff Bailiffs and other Officers of the Government Body . . . remaining in Office according to the said Act. . . .

Friday the 9th day of October 1835

At this Council Lieut.-Col. Henderson and Mr. Barney [a solicitor] attended on behalf of the Rail Road and applied for six acres of the Marsh at about the South West Corner thereof for a Station . . . and the further Consideration of the same is deferred to the next Council. . . .

Friday the 16th day of October 1835

At this Council Lieut.-Col. Henderson and Mr. Barney with Mr. Giles the Surveyor attended and renewed their Application . . . to make a Station or Terminus of the Rail Road at the South Western End of the Marsh. . . .

Resolved that this Corporation . . . are willing to execute a Conveyance of the Land applied for . . . for the sum of one Guinea. . . .

Friday the 27th day of November 1835

Ordered that George Atherley Esquire be paid off his two bonds for fifty Pounds each . . . with the Interest due thereon

That Mr. Ridding be paid off his four Bonds for Three hundred and fifty Pounds . . . with the Interest due thereon

Resolved that the Royal Pier Bond for one hundred Pounds be sold for that Amount and the Interest due thereon

[And in another hand than Ridding's] Resolved unanimously that a Piece of Plate of the Value of Fifty guineas be presented to Mr. Ridding, as a mark of respect from the Corporation for the valuable services he has rendered the Corporation as Town Clerk during the last twenty five years. . . .

Friday the 18th day of December 1835

Ordered that Philip Cartaret Fall Esquire be paid off his two Bonds . . . for one hundred pounds each with the interest due thereon . . .

At this Council the following Letter was received from the Town Clerk and It is ordered that the same be entered in the Journal—

Mr. Mayor and Gentlemen of the Common Council,
I cannot but express my Feelings of Gratitude and sincere Thanks for the Honour done to me by your Resolution of the last Council and by your Vote of a Piece of Plate to me . . . I am extreamly [sic]

glad that my public services for so many years past should have met with the approbation of so respectable a Body . . . and I feel highly gratified by the Expression of your opinion contained in such Resolution.

I trust, Gentlemen, you will not consider me as undervaluing such a handsome Resolution and offer of a munificent Present when I decline accepting it. The Resolution coming so unexpectedly quite took me by surprise, and I hardly know what I said or how I thanked you for it, but I know it immediately struck me as objectionable [sc., in a legal sense] and that it was improper for me to receive the present. By the late Act of Parliament Corporate Funds are appropriated to particular services for which formerly they were not liable nor indeed applicable. Hitherto Corporations have had a power over their Funds, which arose from Corporate Property alone, and were not mixed up with any Burthen or Tax upon the Community. Now any Deficiency in the Funds of the Corporation is to be made up by a Borough Rate upon all the Inhabitants. Therefore the cost of this present . . . would eventually be defrayed and borne by the Persons paying the Taxes of the Town and you will in my humble Opinion, by your Vote of Kindness to me, be rendering yourselves liable to a charge of misappropriating the Corporate Funds. It would be a Dereliction of my Duty if I did not thus freely give you my Opinion on this, as I have hitherto done on other Subjects under your Consideration, which you have kindly received, though sometimes differing from yours; and I should be more than doubly blameable, if when it concerned myself I did not most clearly and fully point out to you the Irregularity of your Proceeding herein. To show you how desirous I am of a Testimonial of my Conduct for so long a Period as a Quarter of a Century, I beg leave humbly to suggest that it would highly gratify me to receive a Certificate under the Hands of the Members of the Common Council and under the Corporate Seal of my having served them faithfully and to their Satisfaction. I must request you Mr. Mayor and Gentlemen to consider this Letter not as in any way slighting your handsome Gift but as wishing you not to give occasion for anyone to say that you have misapplied the Public Monies. For however Corporators may be blamed by unreasonable and thoughtless people, I have great satisfaction in testifying that there is no Ground for such Imputation against any of the Corporation of Southampton. . . .

[In accordance with Ridding's suggestion a very warmly worded resolution expressing gratitude for his services and testifying to his industry and abilities was passed unanimously and entered in the Journal. A copy inscribed on vellum, with the corporate seal affixed, was afterwards presented to him.]

Monday the 21st day of December 1835

[Numerous bills were ordered for payment.]

Thursday the 24th day of December 1835

[More bills were ordered for payment, and the accounts for 1835 were examined, showing a balance of £287.10.8 in the hands of Messrs Atherley & Fall, the Corporation's bankers. (This, it should be repeated, did not take account of debts due on mortgages, bonds, etc. See the extract from the minutes of the new Council's Finance Committee for 8 July 1836.) A unanimous vote of thanks to the Mayor was passed for "the great urbanity, kindness and hospitality and diligence" with which he had discharged the duties of his office for the unprecedented period of one and a quarter years.]

II

The Council Minutes 1835–47

A List of the Names of the Persons elected Councillors . . . pursuant to the Act to provide for the Regulation of Municipal Corporations in England and Wales.

WARD OF ALL SAINTS—12 COUNCILLORS

Peter Breton of the Polygon Esquire	164 votes
George Atherley of Upper Moira Place . . . Banker	132
William Hook Steere of No. 26 Above Bar . . . Chemist	131
Samuel Silver Taylor of No. 13 Hanover Buildings . . . Esquire	129
Thomas Griffiths of New Place House . . . Esquire	128
Charles Tinling of Carlton Crescent . . . Rear-Admiral	128
Edward Toomer of High Street . . . Merchant	127
William Samways Oke of Portland Terrace . . . Doctor of Medecine	123
Charles Ducane of Carlton Crescent . . . Esquire	120
George Bennett of Above Bar . . . Grocer	120
Samuel Benness of the Tything of Portswood . . . Esquire	119
William Oke of Grosvenor Place . . . Merchant	118

WARD OF HOLY RHOOD—3 COUNCILLORS

Richard Eldridge of Orchard Lane in the Parish of Saint Mary . . . Merchant	[Page torn]
John Lamprey of Kingsbridge House in the parish of All Saints Esquire	50
William James Le Feuvre of Cumberland Place in the parish of All Saints Merchant	47

WARD OF SAINT LAWRENCE—3 COUNCILLORS

Martin Maddison of Castle Square in the parish of All Saints Banker	59
Henry Buchan of High Street in the parish of Saint Lawrence House Decorator	54
George Hunt of High Street in the parish of All Saints Brewer	52

WARD OF SAINT MICHAEL—3 COUNCILLORS

James Hawkins Thring of High Street in the parish of Holy Rhood Merchant	60

Edward Langdon Oke of High Street in the parish of Holy Rhood Merchant	59 votes
Joseph Lomer of High Street in the parish of Holy Rhood Merchant	56

WARD OF SAINT MARY—9 COUNCILLORS

Thomas Bradby of Love Lane . . . Gentleman	270
John Rubie of Bellevue Place . . . Shipbuilder	265
Joseph Hill Junior of Union Terrace . . . Surveyor	256
James Whitchurch of Bittern . . . Solicitor	198
Daniel Brooks of Three Field Lane . . . Surveyor	193
Charles Fox of Love Lane . . . Gentleman	188
Robert Young of Love Lane . . . Merchant	180
Edward Coles of Cross House Merchant	175
Joseph Lankester of Bernard Street Ironmonger	170

¶ The Ward of All Saints included the parish (except for the ancient ward of All Saints Infra), the tything of Portswood, the Common, which was extra-parochial, and the part of Millbrook parish within the town boundaries; St. Lawrence comprised the parish and the old ward of All Saints Infra; St. Michael the parishes of St. Michael and St. John; and Holy Rhood and St. Mary's corresponded to the parishes of those names. The numbers of votes cast show that from the first the rapidly growing (and Radical) ward of St. Mary's was under-represented in proportion to population.

Although the elections had not been contested so completely and bitterly on party lines as were those which followed, they had resulted in a large Conservative majority of 22 against 7 Liberals and Radicals, with one declared non-partisan, Brooks, who subsequently ranged himself with the Liberals and in due course became the first Liberal mayor. Only Holy Rhood and St. Michael's voted solidly Conservative; two Liberals, Atherley and William Oke, got in for All Saints, no doubt on grounds of personal esteem; and one, Buchan, for St. Lawrence's; while the representation of St. Mary's was divided. The sprinkling of retired officers in the old Council was reproduced in the new by the election of Captains Breton, Griffiths and Ducane for the "gentlemen's ward" of All Saints and of Bradby, a retired naval lieutenant, for St. Mary's. The last-named, who was presumably one of those many officers without means or influence who were unable to reach captain's rank, became a local Radical leader.

Thursday the 31st day of December 1835

[At this meeting all 30 members were present; the late Mayor, Le Feuvre, was elected to the chair; and after discussion it was decided that the Press should be allowed to be present henceforward, and, by a narrow majority, that the ten aldermen to be elected should not be chosen from among the councillors. The ten were Captain Rainier, John Jolliffe, John Ling of Marland Place (merchant), C. H. Hammond the ex-Recorder, Captain Ward, George Brown of Mount Place Esquire, Thomas Sloane Moody

Esquire, Joseph Lobb (mercer), Job Ede of Laura Place Esquire and Peter Dickson of York Buildings Esquire (who had held the position of Master of the Ceremonies for many years); the five last-named going out of office in 1838. Hammond declined the honour on grounds of age, however, and at the next Council Richard Eldridge was substituted.]

Friday the 1st day of January 1836

[After Alderman Rainier had been elected temporary chairman, Captain Peter Breton was chosen Mayor, George Hunt Sheriff, and S. S. Taylor and E. L. Oke Senior and Junior Bailiffs respectively. Ridding was appointed Town Clerk, his announcement of his intention to retire being overridden. He took care nevertheless to lay before the Council a letter declaring his determination to avail himself of that clause of the recent Municipal Corporations Act which allowed those who had been town clerks under the old dispensation to claim compensation for loss of office or diminution of income due to the change, pointing out that his situation would be "materially altered" (by which he meant that his duties would become heavier and his remuneration less, and that he would probably lose, as in fact he did, subsidiary offices which he had held by virtue—in practice—of being Town Clerk). A Watch Committee including members of both parties was also elected.]

Wednesday the 13th day of January 1836

Resolved that the Treasurer be paid a Salary of Fifty Guineas a year.

At this Council James Dott Hulton Esquire of Bevis Mount . . . was appointed Treasurer.

JUSTICES OF THE PEACE

It appearing that by the Act for regulating Municipal Corporations this Borough is to have a Grant of a Commission of the Peace and a Letter having been written to the Mayor from Mr. Phillipps the undersecretary of State . . . stating that any recommendation from this Council of persons qualified to be entrusted . . . with the Commission of the Peace of the Borough will have its due weight with the advisers of the Crown

Resolved that this Council do recommend the following Gentlemen . . . [George Atherley, Hulton, Eldridge, Lieutenant Bradby, William Oke, Captain Ward, Fall, Lomer and Captains Griffiths and Breton.]

¶ This list included representatives of both parties, though the majority were Conservatives, and was accepted by the Home Office.

Thursday the 28th day of January 1836

Resolved that the Watch Committee shall be allowed such sum as they shall find necessary for wages and allowances to the Police Constables not exceeding One thousand two hundred and fifty pounds for one year.

[A committee was appointed to consider terms of the renewal of leases.]

¶ The Watch Committee had decided to establish a new police force on the London model. They subsequently appointed a Southampton man, Inspector Enwright of A Division of the Metropolitan Police, as Superintendent (though he continued more often to be called Inspector) at 30s. a week. There were also two sergeants, one (Terry, one of the former constables, who eventually proved rather unsatisfactory) at 25s. and the other at 20s., and 22 constables at 16s., less 2s. for clothing. The watch house and lock-up at Bargate were rebuilt as a station-house, and another established in St. Mary's. The quality of the previous force may be gauged from the fact that when Superintendent Enwright made his preliminary tour of inspection he could not find all the existing watchmen until he began to look in the public-houses, whereupon he discovered five drinking in the "Rose and Crown".

Friday the 19th day of February 1836

At this Council an application was made by Mr. Smith and Mr. James Sharp two of the Solicitors to the Promoters of the Wet Docks and works proposed to be made on the Mud Lands according to the plan now exhibited by them for the assent of this Council to the proposed undertaking prior to the application for an act to effect the same and the same having been considered . . .

It is Resolved that this Council are of opinion that the formation of Docks at Southampton at the Terminus of the Rail Road from London will with proper management be productive of great advantages to the Town and Neighbourhood, and highly beneficial to the Commerce of the Nation, but they dissent to the application, because the proposed plan embraces a much larger quantity of the valuable mud lands than they think can possibly be required for the purpose, and because sufficient data have not yet been afforded.

¶ The successful progress of the railway company had revived the plan for the building of docks. A meeting of merchants and inhabitants on 15 October, with Mayor Le Feuvre in the chair, had elected a provisional committee to take the steps necessary for the formation of a joint-stock company, of which Captain Ward was to be Superintendent, and for an application to Parliament for leave to bring in a bill.

Friday the 18th day of March 1836

At this Council a Deputation from the Provisional Committee of the Dock Company attended and stated the views of the Company and their Bill now before Parliament and the Deputation having withdrawn

It was proposed that this Council do for the present continue their dissent to the application of the Southampton Docks Company—upon which the following Resolution was moved as an amendment

That this Council, convinced of the great and beneficial effect of the *works proposed . . . by the Committee of the Southampton Docks Company, are willing to assent generally to the measures if the terms can be agreed upon satisfactorily to this Council*—which amendment being put to the vote was decided in the affirmative.

Resolved that a Committee be appointed to confer with the Deputation from the Dock Company as to the compensation to be made by them for the land required for the purpose of their Docks. . . .

The Committee having retired and conferred with the Dock Committee [*sic*] returned and reported that the following terms had been submitted to them by the Dock Committee. . . .

"That as a Compensation to the Corporation for the Mudland to be taken for the purposes of the Dock Company it is proposed by the Provisional Committee that the Corporation shall be entitled to participate in the proceeds of the Undertaking in the shape of a Rent Charge equivalent to a Dividend on One Hundred Shares regarded as paid up Capital without liability to calls or claims . . .

"The Corporation shall be entitled to ten votes in respect of their interest in the undertaking of all Meetings of the General Shareholders—

"The Corporation to have the option of receiving Five thousand pounds as a gross sum on the Company taking possession of the Land in lieu of the proposed Rent Charge until the Dividend distributable among the general Shareholders shall amount to Ten per cent when the Corporation shall be entitled to a Rent Charge equivalent to a Dividend on Twenty shares . . ."

It was afterwards resolved that the above terms be accepted.

[Subjoined]

We protest against the resolutions of this day's council because, in our opinion, the lands and privileges of the Town entrusted to the Town Council have been hastily and unadvisedly given away because the value of the Land far exceeds the consideration offered, and because we will not be participators in a scheme which will benefit the Company without giving to the burgesses of the Town those advantages which they have a right to expect from their valuable property.

[Signed] Joseph Hill Junior
John Rubie
Thomas Bradby
James Whitchurch.

PROTEST

First because I believe no greater misfortune could befall the Port of Southampton or be more injurious to the Trade and Prosperity of the Town than to suffer the principal Docks and Warehouses . . . to get into the Hands of a Trading Company, whose interest it is, and ever will be, to make the most of their capital—whereas if the same are constructed and kept in the hands of Commissioners acting on behalf of the Town, they can have no other interest than to keep the Dock Rates and Harbour Dues as low as possible.

Secondly Because if the Mudlands are sold to a private Company the Corporation yield up the only improvable lands in their possession, and the Town . . . can never reap the full benefit they would otherwise have from an increasing Borough Fund arising from their Pier, Dock and Harbour Dues, etc., if the lands are kept in their own possession, but will have to make good any deficiency by an increase of Poor Rates and other municipal charges.

Thirdly Because we have not sufficiently enquired into the extent of our own resources, and I fully believe it will be found we have ample power and should find means to accomplish the work ourselves, and thus save the Town from the evils of a monopoly for the benefit of a Trading Company and the Trade of the Town from the burthen of an everlasting tax without a prospect of redemption or very little of reduction.

Fourthly because we have not been allowed sufficient time to consider all the bearings of this most important question—that the measure has been hurried on by many interested persons—that the inhabitants of the Town have only had one side of the question laid before them—in short, sufficient information has not yet been obtained to arrive at a wise decision on this important matter.

[Signed] Charles Tinling

¶ The Dock Company had also applied to the Pier and Harbour Board for its consent to their bringing a bill into the House of Commons. The discussions which took place on the Board involved most of the same persons and followed the same course as those of the Borough Council. The Board at first resolved that while it did not disapprove of a docks project it must reject the present application because too much land was asked for and not enough information given, but at a later meeting gave its assent. At both the Council and the Board meetings Admiral Tinling hotly rejected any suggestion that "gentlemen" were not interested in public works and would never consent to improvements. All he wanted, he reiterated, was to be sure that those in charge of such improvements should be known to be responsible men who could carry through what they undertook, and he pointed to the example of the Corporation of Liverpool in keeping their docks under their own control. Others joined him in expressing hostility to the idea of Londoners coming in, under cover of the Dock Company's need for capital, to kill the trade of the old quays and control the town. The Company's London solicitor and Captain Ward explained that, as with the railway company, it was absolutely necessary to bring in London capitalists because there really was not sufficient capital or enterprise in Southampton, and that a relatively large area of the mudlands had been asked for in order to have room for later expansion and to prevent the possibility of a rival company coming in. They also pointed out that the finances and borrowing powers of the Pier and Harbour Commissioners were much too limited to enable them to construct docks; and prophesied (though wrongly, as the future proved) that the trade of the present quays and pier, and with it the Board's revenue, would be increased by the general development of the port which the docks would bring about. They agreed, however, to reduce the land asked for by so much as would leave room for a tramway from the Town Quay to the site of the proposed railway terminus.

Wednesday the 6th day of April 1836

At this Council the Minutes of the Proceedings of the Committee appointed . . . to peruse and settle the special Clauses in the intended Dock Company's Bill were read, stating their Objections and Observations to some parts not only of those Clauses, but of certain other Clauses in the printed Bill; and the special Clauses as since amended and altered and a Print of the Bill as now altered in compliance with such Objections and Observations and a Letter from the London Solicitors expressing the Readiness of the Provisional Committee of the intended Docks to comply with the suggestions of the Committee of this Council were laid before the Meeting, and the same are to be further perused and settled by the said Committee. . . .

It was also proposed that the Council . . . lay the particular Circumstances of the Case before the . . . Treasury for . . . Directions as to the Course to be adopted . . . before the Committee of the House of Commons to whom the Southampton Docks Company's Bill will be referred. [This was negatived, but another protest by Whitchurch, Hill and Rubie was thereupon entered in the Minutes.]

Thursday the 5th day of May 1836

It was proposed that the Corporate Seal be affixed to the Bill now before Parliament for constructing Docks at Southampton as altered, upon which an amendment was moved:

That we feel it our duty not to assent to the Borough Seal being affixed to the Dock Bill without further information, which amendment . . . was negatived.

The original Question . . . was then put and carried.

[There follows a protest entered in the Minutes by Lankester, Bradby, Brooks, Jolliffe, Tinling, Whitchurch, Hill, Young and Rubie against the resolution, "because no member of the Town Council has assured the Council that the letter of the bill carries into effect the alterations agreed to, and because the Dock Committee have not abandoned their claim to purchase the whole of the mud lands at the very inadequate price of £5000".]

Friday the 27th day of May 1836

BOROUGH RATE

The Report of the Committee appointed to consider the propriety of levying a Watch Rate separately from a Borough Rate was read in which

Report the Committee stated their opinion that a separate Watch Rate should not be levied and that they had made an Estimate of the Amount in addition to the Borough Fund sufficient for payment of the Expenses to be incurred . . . to the first day of September next and found that it would be necessary to raise the Sum of Five hundred pounds and the same being taken into consideration It was resolved that [this] Sum . . . be raised by a Borough Rate upon the several parishes and Tything in this Town and County in the proportions following . . .

All Saints	£241
Holy Rhood	60
St. John's	10
St. Lawrence's	20
St. Mary's	121
St. Michael's	30
Portswood	18 . . .

COURT OF QUARTER SESSIONS

His Majesty having been graciously pleased to grant that a separate Court of Quarter Sessions shall be henceforward holden in and for the Town of Southampton . . . upon condition that the Council will put the Town Gaols into a fit and proper state for the confinement of Prisoners and the due maintenance of Prison discipline, or if the existing Gaols will not admit of it that they will build a new Gaol, or will contract with the Magistrates of the County . . . for the reception of the Borough Prisoners in the County Gaol and House of Correction at Winchester

Resolved that this Council do accept such Grant of Quarter Sessions upon this condition . . . and that they will provide for their prisoners accordingly.

TOWN GAOL

Resolved that such of the Borough Justices as are of the Council be a Committee to make enquiry respecting the Gaols and the best mode of providing for the prisoners. . . .

[Ridding was appointed Clerk of the Peace, and the report of a committee which had been appointed to consider his claim for compensation for the loss of the office of Clerk to the Justices, recommending a payment of £100 a year, was read and adopted.]

¶ A table of the amounts raised by borough rates in the next twelve years will be found in Appendix B.

Thursday the 16th day of June 1836

FINANCE COMMITTEE

Resolved that a Committee of Finance shall be appointed to whom shall be referred all matters connected with the income and expenditure of the

Borough and that they be also requested to make an Inventory of the Corporation property. . . .

SOUTHAMPTON DOCKS

At this Council an Application from the Southampton Dock Company for the purchase of the Mudlands according to the Resolution of the 18th day of March last having been read and taken into consideration. . . .

It was proposed [by the opposition to the transaction] that this Council are not prepared to say whether they will accept Money or Shares till the whole proceedings of the Common Council with the Dock Company shall be laid before the Lords of the Treasury and the opinion and sanction of their Lordships as to the quantity and price to be paid for the same shall be made known

Which being put to the vote was negatived.

After which it was proposed

That the agreement entered into with the provisional Committee of the Dock Company on the 18th day of March last be now confirmed

Upon which an amendment was moved

That so much only of the said Mud Lands be received by the Dock Company as may be necessary for the construction of Docks and Warehouses and Roads connected therewith

Which on being put to the vote was negatived.

The original proposition was then put and carried in the affirmative.

It was then proposed that the Borough Council having deliberately considered the offer made by the Dock Company for the purchase of the Mudlands do decide on accepting their offer in Shares instead of Money

Upon which an amendment was moved

That Money be received instead of Shares

Which on being put to the vote was negatived.

The original proposition was then put and carried in the affirmative.

It was then proposed that a memorial be forthwith presented to the Lords of the Treasury requesting their Lordships' approval of a Grant of the Mudland to the Dock Company in consideration of the shares as proposed

Whereupon an amendment was moved

That the Corporation having by their vote this day determined that it is expedient that the Council should take shares in payment for their valuable Lands . . . the Lords of the Treasury be memorialized by the Council to take the whole matter . . . into their serious consideration. . . .

Which on being put to the vote was negatived.

The original proposition was then put and carried.

It was then Resolved that a Committee be appointed to prepare a memorial to the Lords of the Treasury to confirm the Sale made to the Dock Company. . . .

[There follows, in Whitchurch's handwriting]

"We protest against the resolutions of this day's Council relating to the proposed gift or sale to the Southampton Dock Company, which if carried into effect would alienate for ever an extensive valuable and most improveable freehold estate belonging to the Burgesses of Southampton.

We record our determined opposition to this proposed sacrifice of property

Because it is a hasty and improvident bargain—

Because the estates of the Town are held *in trust* by the Mayor Aldermen and Councillors and were confided to them to be managed improved and *retained* for the benefit of the *present* and *future* Inhabitants of Southampton—

Because no irrevocable sale of any part of these estates should take place without the consent of a majority of the Burgesses of the Town which consent should be obtained at public meetings after free fair and open discussion of the advantages and disadvantages of any such proposed sale—

Because the present incumbrance and increasing expenses of the Corporation require the greatest economy and best management to support them—

Because the lands and property given away at this meeting would with good management have produced a large revenue to this Town and rendered unnecessary that Borough Rate which must now be laid as a burden on the toil, industry and enterprise of the productive classes in Southampton—

Because we know nothing and the Burgesses know nothing of the chief promoters of this Dock scheme—

. . .

Because a great portion of the land will if taken by the Company lie useless, unimproved and unprofitable, whereas if retained by the Corporation and let out on leases under proper restrictions its improvement would be rapid and constantly progressing—

Because the land and Baths [the now declining Royal Gloucester Baths, which lay within the area sold] have been bartered away for shares in a company managed by strangers in London the value of which shares as an investment is most doubtful—

And because a majority in the Council including many members who are directors shareholders or otherwise interested in the Company have voted away the property of the town without calling in the aid of any Engineer or Surveyor to assist their judgments or bear out their proceedings

(Signed)   James Whitchurch Town Councr. Ward St. Mary
    Joseph Hill Junior „ „ „ „
    D. Brooks   „ „ „ „
    John Jolliffe Alderman
    Joseph Lankester „ „ „ „
    Robert Young   „ „ „ „
    John Rubie   „ „ „ „
    Thomas Bradby „ „ „ „
    Ch. S. Tinling   „ „ of the Ward of All
                       Saints.

¶ This was the stormiest meeting which the new Council had yet known. The Docks Bill had now passed through Parliament, despite a petition against it from Whitchurch, Hill, Bradby and Rubie, who also sent a memorial to the Treasury complaining that the Council had violated the Municipal Corporations Act by treating with the Dock Company for the sale of the Mudlands without having previously obtained the Treasury's sanction. In his reply, however, the Secretary to the Treasury declined to accept this contention. When the Company now came to the Council for confirmation of the sale, the opposition, who in view of the variety of their motives must be regarded as co-belligerents rather than allies, fought a dogged rearguard action from amendment to amendment and finally to a protest that was virtually a manifesto. The division over the question was not originally a party one, but as Tinling fell somewhat into the background and the lead was taken by the little phalanx of councillors from St. Mary's, which was establishing itself as a definitely Radical ward, it assumed rather more of a party complexion. The protest, in particular, contained in embryo what became the Radical argument that the Council was financially improvident and was therefore laying needlessly heavy taxation on the town.

Only five members of the Council (Ward, Le Feuvre, E. L. Oke, Ede and Buchan) were directors or shareholders in the Company. At the next meeting the protesting minority brought forward a motion that these should not vote when its affairs were under discussion, but this was defeated.

Wednesday the 6th day of July 1836

At this Council . . . a Letter received by the Mayor from Mr. Baring the Secretary to the Treasury . . . was read, requiring particulars of the Corporation property, receipts and expenditure.

Resolved that the Finance Committee be desired to examine into the Debts and Credits and Estate and Effects of the Corporation and the probable receipt and Expenditure in order that the Mayor may be enabled to answer the four enquiries contained in the Letter from Mr. Baring. . . .

CONTRACT FOR PRISONERS IN HANTS HOUSE OF CORRECTION

The Mayor reported to this Council that he had applied to the Visiting Magistrates of the Hants County Gaol to permit the Prisoners from hence to be removed there for punishment and that they had consented to report favourably for their being received for one year, and that he had attended at the Hants County Sessions at Winchester on Tuesday . . . last when the Justices in Sessions agreed to take the Prisoners at the Expense the County may be put to respecting them. . . .

Resolved that this Council do approve of the Prisoners convicted and sentenced to more than fourteen days imprisonment being removed to Winchester.

¶ This agreement with the county justices was renewed from time to time.

[EXTRACT FROM THE FINANCE COMMITTEE
MINUTE BOOK, FRIDAY 8 JULY 1836

Meeting to examine into the debts, credits, estate and effects of the Corporation, as requested by the Council of 6th July, to enable the Mayor to answer the enquiry from the Treasury of July 2nd re:

(1) Amount of debts or liabilities
    Due on bond at 4%   £1800
    „ „ mortgages of the Corporation's one-fifth of the
    port dues to certain persons as trustees for a fund for
    decayed aldermen under Taunton's will   £3229
    Due on mortgage of the Audit House and Market to
    certain persons as trustees for Fifield's, Freeman's
    and Sadleir's Charities   £1750
    The interest of these sums is paid to the Charities as stated
    in the account of annual expenditure.

    Floating balances for which the Corporation is liable for
    several Charities as stated on 1 Jan. last:

Steptoe's Charity	£1774.5. 7	
Sir T. White's Charity	597.5. 5	
Charity fund: various small sums	71.9.11	
Apprentices' Fund	13.1. 0	£2456.1.11

                                       £9235.1.11

(2) Amount of Corporation's Property or other Assets.
    Consists chiefly of houses in Southampton let for terms of 40
    years renewable every 14 years on a fine of $1\frac{1}{4}$ years' rent
    The fines which have been received in the last 14 years amount
    to £10,001.10.4 or, on average, £717.7.0 p.a.
    Difficult to put an exact value on the property as renewals cannot
    be depended on—
    Supposing these renewals worth 20 years' purchase the
    property is worth   £14,280[1]

[1] There appear to be one or two errors of calculation in this part of the statement.

Quit rents on the foregoing leases £341.18.0
Capon money   do.   34.13.0

               £376.11.0
      at 20 years' purchase is worth   £7341

                                    £21,811

Land adjoining Free School let at £25 p.a.   £500
Annuity of £90 p.a. granted by the Commissioners of
   the Port being for the purchase of houses, store-
   houses and wharves adjoining the shore, formerly
   Corporation property, and of Mudland near the
   Town Quay secured on the Port Dues valued at
   25 years' purchase   £2300
Timber on Common: supposed value   £2000
One-fifth of Port Dues, in lieu of Petty Customs,
   anchorage and groundage, calculated on an average
   of 3 years £365.10.4, which at 18 years' purchase
   equals   £6579.6.0
2 bonds of the Port Commissioners for 100 each at 5% £200
Audit House and Market shops, valued at   £3000
Balance of cash in Treasurer's hands   £287.10.8

                        £36,667.13.8

The Corporation also possess the following property belonging to
   Charities not available for Corporation purposes—
     Fee farm rent on Woolston estate of   £38.2.6
     In 3% Consols
        Miss Bird's Charity   £1260
        Taunton's Fund   £256.1.3
        Spink's Charity   £270.3.2
     Estates under Alderman Steptoe's Will
        At Aspernam [?] near Romsey:
        Rent   £40.2.0
        At Yeovilton near Lymington:
        Rent   £40.2.0

               £80.4.0

(3) Estimated Annual Expenditure.
   Alderman Taunton's Aldermen's Fund   £129.3. 2
   Fifield's, Sadleir's and Freeman's Charities   66.1.10
   Charity monies which the Corporation are annually
   liable to pay   292.1.11

Payments of fee farm rents and in the nature of salaries, pensions and allowances, repairs, insurance of Corporation property and other permanent outgoings	£956.18. 0
Interest on Bond Debt	72
Expenses of police	1300
Payments made out of County rates previous to Municipal Reform Act: Repairs of Guildhall	20
Repairs of Gaols	70
Cost of Prosecution of Felons, including removal to Hants Assizes	190
Keep of prisoners in gaols and Estimate of removal for punishment in Hants County Gaol	300
Gaolers' salaries	145
Clerk of Peace's bill	50
Coroner's ,, for inquests	45
Chaplain to gaols	50
Surgeon ,, ,, and casual paupers	25
Taxes assessed on gaolers' apartments	6.10. 0
Inspectors of Weights and Measures	40
Impressing waggons for soldiers	1
Printing and advertising	20
Incidents	5
	£3783.14.11

(4) Estimated annual income.

Fines received on renewal of leases on an average of 14 years (but they vary a good deal, which means great variation in the amount of the borough rate)	£700
Annual rents, quit rents and capons	376.11. 0
Rent of Free School Play Ground	25
Interest on port bonds	10
Rents of Market shops	120
Annuity from Port Dues	92
One-fifth of Harbour Dues	365
Charity Funds charged as paid in the expenditure Woolston Rent of Mrs. Chamberlayne	38. 2. 6
Dividends on £1260 3% Consols (Bird's)	37.16. 0
,, ,, £256.1.3 Consols (Taunton's)	7.13. 6
,, ,, £270.3.2 Consols (Spink's)	8. 2. 2
Steptoe's Rents	80. 4. 0
	£1860. 9.2]

¶ In reply to the Council's memorial asking the Treasury to confirm the sale of a part of the Mudlands to the Dock Company (see 16 June above) a Mr. Cubitt had been sent down to investigate the matter on the spot. After interviewing all the parties concerned, he had reported that in his opinion the area to be sold, about 216 acres, was not excessive and the price offered was "ample and liberal". He recommended, however, that in view of the statement of the Corporation's finances with which the Treasury had been furnished and which showed both a considerable debt and a large annual deficiency that would have to be met by a borough rate, a lump sum of £5000 should be taken rather than shares. He also advised that in the agreement with the Company it should be definitely stipulated that the latter should leave sufficient space clear for a road or tramway from the Town Quays to the railway terminus. The Treasury had therefore sanctioned the transaction, provided that these recommendations were accepted, which the Dock Company had already professed its willingness to do and which the Council at this meeting now did, despite one more unsuccessful amendment from the opposition minority that it was inexpedient to proceed further.

Wednesday the 7th day of September 1836

LIGHTING CERTAIN PARTS OF THE BOROUGH

Resolved that such of the Magistrates as are Members of the Council be a Committee to consider the propriety of lighting such parts of the Borough as are not within the limits of the paving and lighting acts. . . .

¶ A majority of the inhabitants of "the upper part of the town" in All Saints Ward Above Bar, where most of the gentry resided and much of which had come into existence since the paving and lighting acts were passed, had recently made an application for its inclusion in these acts, without which they would continue to be dependent on their own private enterprise for illumination.

Wednesday the 19th day of October 1836

LIGHTING CERTAIN PARTS OF THE BOROUGH

The Committee appointed at the last Council . . . presented their Report, stating that, having had laid before them the particulars of the parts of the Borough most advisable to be placed within the provisions of the Acts . . . and also a statement showing the expenses of lighting the parts already within their limits, and having considered the 87th section of the Municipal Act and the proviso therein limiting the Rate to be raised for the purpose of defraying the expenses of lighting any part of the Borough ordered to be within the provisions of the local Acts to the average expense in the £ of the lighting the other parts of the Borough; it appeared to them that, inasmuch as the lighting of the great majority of the present Lamps is contracted for at a very low rate and the expense of lighting any other part of the Town would very much exceed the average expense of lighting the parts within the limits of the local Acts, it would be impossible for the Council to carry into effect the matters referred to them under the provisions of the 87th section of the Municipal Corporation Act; and the same having been read

Resolved that this Council do approve of the same.

HIGHWAY RATE

At this Council a Certificate under the Hands and Seals of three of His Majesty's Justices of the Peace for this Town and County was delivered in, . of the charges of putting the Highways Bridges and Causeways belonging to this Borough . . . into Repair and keeping them so for the year ensuing. . . .

It is ordered that the sum of One hundred pounds be raised . . . on the several undermentioned parishes within this Borough . . . by the following proportions, viz

Holy Rhood	£23
St. Lawrence's	6.10.0
St. Michael's	15
All Saints	39
St. John's	3. 5.0
St. Mary's	13. 5.0
	£100. 0.0

IMPROVEMENT OF THE TOWN

Resolved that a Committee be appointed to consider whether any and what specific improvements can be effected which may tend to increase the value of the Town property, to relieve the Borough Rate, and generally to improve the appearance and traffic of Southampton. . . .

¶ This was the beginning of the Council's first but abortive attempt to achieve "improvements".

Tuesday the 1st day of November 1836

[In the municipal elections (for one-third of the seats on the Council), which were now contested with strong party feeling, the Liberals or Radicals gained four seats. In All Saints Ward James Weld of Archers Lodge and Joseph Newman "Esquire" of 15 Bedford Terrace won election, though Weld as a Roman Catholic could not take the usual oath and had to avail himself of the alternative formula provided; and in St. Mary's a crushing Radical majority re-elected Joseph Lankester and replaced two Conservatives by George Laishley of English Street, grocer, and J. T. Tucker of Hanover Buildings, auctioneer. In the other three wards Conservatives were elected or re-elected with little or no opposition.]

Wednesday the 9th day of November 1836

[Captain Charles Ducane was elected Mayor, S. S. Taylor Sheriff and E. L. Oke and W. H. Steere Bailiffs. The Watch, Lease, Finance, Improvements and other more temporary committees were elected with little change in personnel.]

Monday the 21st day of November 1836

CHARITABLE TRUSTEES

It appearing to this Council that the powers of this Corporation in managing the Charities ceased on the first day of August last by virtue of the Municipal Corporation Act sectn. 71, and that it is therefore necessary that Trustees should be appointed,

Resolved that a petition be presented to the High Court of Chancery praying that Trustees may be appointed accordingly. . . .

[A motion to memorialize the Home Secretary for the increase of the representation of St. Mary's Ward from 9 to 12 was defeated.]

Tuesday the 13th day of December 1836

Resolved that the following Gentlemen be recommended by this Council to the Master in Chancery to whom the petition stands referred to appoint Trustees for the Charity Estates and property as fit and proper persons to be appointed . . .—

[Dottin and Hoy, the M.P.'s for the borough; the Reverends T. L. Shapcott (Vicar of St. Michael's), William Wilson (Vicar of Holy Rhood), J. E. Shadwell (Rector of All Saints), Edward Horne (Rector of St. Lawrence's and St. John's), J. W. Cary (curate of St. Mary's), Thomas Adkins (Minister of the Above Bar Independent Congregation); Admiral Tinling, Captains Ward, Ducane, Breton and Bradby; S. S. Taylor, W. J. Le Feuvre, Martin Maddison, Richard Eldridge, Stephen Judd, John Bullar (schoolmaster) and George Hunt (brewer).]

¶ The significant omission of the Rector of St. Mary's from the above list was due to the fact that he afforded one of the most scandalous examples of nepotism, pluralism and absenteeism in this period. In 1797 Brownlow North, Bishop of Winchester, had put his son Francis into the Rectorship, which he held until 1850, in plurality with the Mastership of St. Cross Hospital at Winchester from 1802. (The affairs of the Hospital in these years, incidentally, afterwards afforded Anthony Trollope material for his novel *The Warden.*) North's appearances in his parish were extremely rare, but, especially after he became Earl of Guilford in 1827, he drew heavily on its revenues to enable him to live the aristocratic life to which he was accustomed. His conscientious curate Mr. Cary was therefore the effective parish priest.

The Rev. Thomas Adkins, equally distinguished in appearance (he was nicknamed "the Beauty of Holiness" and said to be the best-dressed man in Southampton) and for his eloquence and learning, was unquestionably the leading nonconformist minister in the town. John Bullar, one of the principal members of his congregation, conducted a private academy in Prospect Place which deservedly enjoyed a high reputation from the early years of the century until his retirement in 1839. He was universally esteemed, even by those who differed from him on ecclesiastical and political questions, for his benevolence and scholarship.

The Master in Chancery chose Dottin, Hoy, the Revs. Wilson, Shadwell, Horne, Cary and Adkins, together with Tinling, Breton and Bullar, from the above list; and added J. R. Keele, Vice-Admiral Giffard of Carlton Crescent, James Weld, James Anderson of Carlton Crescent and Charles Maul, surgeon; thus giving rather more representation to nonconformists and Liberals.

Thursday the 1st day of January 1837

[After a somewhat lukewarm discussion a committee was appointed to consider whether a site could be found for the establishment of a cattle market. In due course this committee suggested a piece of the shore at the bottom of Simnel Street, but this proposal was voted down and the question slept for a time.]

Friday the 10th day of March 1837

BURIAL OF THE DEAD

At this Council the propriety of providing additional accommodation for the Burial of the Dead in this Borough having been considered,

Resolved that it should be referred to a Committee to consider what steps should be taken. . . .

Thursday the 4th day of May 1837

CHARITIES

Resolved that the following [6] Gentlemen be a Committee to meet the Committee appointed by the Trustees of the late Corporation Charities, for ascertaining the sums due and to be paid by this Corporation to such Trustees and for the delivery to them of all deeds books and papers now in the custody of the Town Clerk relating thereto. . . .

BURIAL OF THE DEAD

At this Council the Committee appointed to consider what means should be taken with a view of providing additional accommodation for the burial of the dead in this Borough reported that they had been attended by the several clergymen of the Town, and had considered the possibility of forming parochial Burial Grounds, but from the difficulty of procuring land in the smaller parishes they thought a Burial Ground for the Town generally would be the best.

That they had applied to the Right Hon. and Revd. Lord Guilford the Rector of Saint Mary's parish for a piece of the Glebe land on the East side of East Magdalens field for the purpose and after consulting the Lord Bishop of this Diocese on the subject a Deputation from the Committee had waited on Lord Guilford, who expressed his readiness to comply with the wish of the Committee but felt he could not in justice to his Successors alienate any of the Glebe land of St. Mary's without a proper consideration being paid for it and recommended [a field] near Charlotte Place on the eastern side of Love Lane as a spot better calculated for the proposed purpose and less expensive . . . but his Lordship was still open to any offer from the Council . . . on the subject. . . .

[The Committee had subsequently approached two lay landowners, both of whom asked prices which they considered too high.]

They therefore were of opinion that a statement of their proceedings should be sent to the clergymen of the different parishes recommending them to take immediate steps to bring the subject before a vestry meeting of each parish . . .

Resolved that the Report of the Committee be approved. . . .

Thursday the 22nd day of June 1837

CHARITIES

At this Council the Report of the Committee appointed . . . to meet a Committee of the Trustees of the Charities late vested in the Corporation for ascertaining the sums due and to be paid by this Corporation to such Trustees was read and the suggestions therein being approved of, it is Resolved that a Deed of Receipt and Release for the several monies paid and transferred to [the] Trustees . . . as proposed by the Committee be required of the said Trustees . . .

Resolved that the Treasurer of the Borough do pay to the Trustees . . . the sum of Three thousand three hundred and eighteen pounds, one shilling and one penny for the Capital Sums due upon the undermentioned Charities for which . . . the above Deed of Release is to be given and also the further Sum of one Hundred and forty pounds six shillings and ninepence the arrears of annual payments of those Charities due . . . to the 24th instant . . .

And it is Resolved and Ordered that the Treasurer of the Borough do sell so many of the Exchequer Bonds purchased by him with Five thousand pounds pursuant to the Order of the 12th day of January last as will be necessary to raise a sufficient sum for that purpose.

Resolved that the Committee appointed to meet the Charity Trustees . . . be authorized . . . to affix the Corporate Seal to a power of attorney enabling a Transfer to be made of the sum of £256.1.3 standing in the names of the late Mayor Bailiffs and Burgesses of Southampton in the three per cent consolidated Bank Annuities, part of the Taunton's Charity Trust monies, and also the Sum of £270.3.2 similar Stock standing in the same Names the Gift of Sarah Spinks for charitable purposes, unto Peter Breton of Southampton Esquire, The Reverend John Emilius Shadwell Clerk Rector of All Saints, Southampton, The Reverend Edward Horne Clerk Rector of Saint Lawrence cum Saint John, Southampton, and the Reverend James Walter Cary Clerk Curate of Saint Mary's Southampton four of the Trustees named by the said Trustees of the Charities for the purpose of such investment upon the trusts of the said Charities as soon as the said power can be obtained from the Bank of England.

IMPROVEMENT COMMITTEE

At this Council a memorial from several of the owners and occupiers of property in the ward of Saint Michael was received calling the attention of the Council to the disadvantages they laboured under for want of good roads and approaches to that ancient ward and expressing their unanimous opinion that a Street from the High Street to the Church of Saint Michael and a Street from Saint Michael's Square to the Long Rooms and a direct road from the Long Rooms to the Sarum Road at or near Four Posts would be of essential benefit not only to that ward but to the Town at large and requesting that the Council would by either of the means pointed out or by such other mode as might seem more feasible remove the injurious barriers which now impede their traffic and extend to them the assistance which has been given to other parts of the Town and the same having been read . . .

It was Resolved that the Report of the Improvement Committee [see 19 October 1836] be now . . . considered

And the same having been . . . considered . . .

It was proposed that so much of the Report as recommends the making of a Road from West Quay to Four Posts, an approach from the High Street through Saint Michael's Square to the West Quay and the widening of Bridge Street be adopted, and that an act for carrying into effect such improvements and such other improvements as the Council may here-after decide on be applied for by the Corporation in the next Session of Parliament

Upon which an amendment was moved as follows

That the Committee at the next or any subsequent meeting do lay before the Council a specific plan for the proposed improvement and a fair estimate of the Expense to be incurred by the Town for that purpose— which on being put to the vote was negatived.

The Original Proposition was then put and carried in the affirmative. . . .

Thursday the 3rd day of August 1837

[A committee was set up to consider the claim which Ridding had submitted to the Council for compensation for the loss of the office of

Clerk to the Trustees of the Charities, in which the new trustees had not continued him. He was awarded £20 a year, and also obtained £100 a year for his loss of the Clerkship to the Justices.]

COMMON GAOL

At this Council a Report from the Justices of the Peace of this Town ... was read stating that they had taken into their consideration the future management of the Common Gaol subsequent on the decease of William Spearing the late Keeper, and recommending that the Common Gaol and House of Correction should no longer be continued as distinct prisons, but that the same should be united and placed under the control and management of the Keeper of the House of Correction. That the Common Gaol should in future be appropriated for the use of female prisoners alone. . . .

IMPROVEMENT COMMITTEE

This Council having taken into their further consideration the report of the Improvement Committee and what further improvements should be included in the proposed act of Parliament to be applied for in the next Session

It was moved that the proposed Act do contain powers for inclosing the Marsh and letting of the same for building purposes

On which the following was moved as an amendment

That the contemplated Improvement Act be no further proceeded with

Which on being put to the vote was carried in the affirmative. . . .

¶ The Improvement Act project, which had received such tepid and ephemeral support on the Council, was on the whole a Radical measure. Taken up again in due course by the Paving Commissioners, it met with much criticism and opposition from the majority of the Council.

Friday the 22nd day of September 1837

[A highway rate of £100 was ordered to be levied for the ensuing year.]

Monday the 23rd day of October 1837

BOROUGH GAOLS

At this Council a Letter was read from the Secretary of State's Office to the Town Clerk, enquiring what had been done respecting the Gaols and the contracting for the reception of Prisoners in the Hants County Gaol

And it is ordered that the Town Clerk do inform the Secretary of State that the Council immediately on receiving the Grant of a separate Court of Quarter Sessions entered into a Contract with the Justices of the County of Hants for the reception of the Borough Prisoners in their County Gaol, and that with that aid the Borough Gaols appear sufficient for the purposes

of the Borough and that they have now made a further Order for an alteration in the present Gaols which will enable the Gaoler better to classify the
prisoners, and that they trust under a continuance of the Contract there
will be no occasion to build any Gaol here at present.

Wednesday the 1st day of November 1837

[In the municipal elections the Conservatives gained two seats, in All
Saints Ward where Weld (who was leaving the town) retired, and in
St. Lawrence's where Buchan was defeated.]

Thursday the 9th day of November 1837

[Joseph Lobb was elected Mayor (the St. Mary's Radicals unsuccessfully nominating Bradby against him), Captain Griffiths Sheriff, and
W. H. Steere and J. H. Thring Bailiffs. John Hunt the Younger was
appointed Treasurer, at a salary of £50 a year, *vice* J. D. Hulton who had
resigned.]

This Town having been visited with a dreadful fire on the night of the
7th instant which entirely consumed the spacious Storehouse and premises
of Messrs. King Witt and Company Lead Merchants at the end of the
High Street, and by which a great number of lives were lost, and this
Council feeling deeply for the sufferers and anxious to afford all the
Assistance in their power to the relief of the many persons who have
sustained injury by this Calamity, declined to proceed in the other matters
to be transacted and the meeting therefore adjourned.

¶ It is this fire which is commemorated on the two tablets at the sides of
the west door of Holy Rhood Church, which give the names of twenty-two
persons who lost their lives through it.

Friday the 24th day of November 1837

[A Highway Committee was appointed and requested to report to the
Council "what Streets or Highways have heretofore been repaired out of
the Highway Rate and what . . . not heretofore repaired out of the Highway
Rate ought to be so repaired; and whether any of the said Streets or High-
ways can or ought to be brought under the operation of the Pavement
Act . . .'.]

Friday the 19th day of January 1838

[A deed was signed transferring the funds of Taunton's and Sarah
Spink's Charities to the new charity trustees. A committee was set up to
consider the Town Clerk's salary.]

RESERVOIR, ETC., ON THE COMMON

At this Council application was made by the Commissioners of Waterworks for leave to appropriate about two acres of Land on the Southampton

Common for the purpose of making a reservoir and also such other portions as may be requisite in the construction of their works for supplying the Town with Water as specified in the plan laid before this Council . . . and the same and the plan having been considered . . .

Resolved that the Commissioners of Waterworks be permitted to appropriate two acres of land on the Common for a Reservoir and also such other portions . . . as shall be necessary for the construction of their works. . . .

¶ With the growth of the town the three reservoirs which the Waterworks Board had by now built on the Common (the third having been constructed in 1831) had become inadequate, as had also the powers of rating, borrowing and so forth granted to it by the acts of 1747, 1803 and 1810. Experimental borings undertaken on the Common by Clark, a London engineer, however, had led him to report that if these were developed an ample supply of water could be obtained. The Board had therefore secured a further act in 1836, enlarging its powers, and entered into a contract for the sinking of an artesian well, not with Clark who had submitted a plan for this purpose, but with one of its own members, Collyer, for whom four of his fellow-Commissioners came forward as sureties. It was for this project, rather than another reservoir, that the Board was now approaching the Corporation for a grant of ground. Collyer proved unsuccessful in his attempt, however, and his sureties (who were now rev⟨. . .⟩e been partners with him *sub rosa*) took over from him and p⟨. . .⟩mber of years without much success. Since the four were R⟨. . .⟩was a Radical majority on the Waterworks Board at the ⟨. . .⟩ matter became wrapped in an atmosphere of party bitt⟨. . .⟩onious accusations and counter-accusations. In 185⟨. . .⟩ed with Clark to continue the work, and it was not ⟨. . .⟩rtesian well was abandoned.

Thursday the 1⟨. . .⟩ ⟨Fe⟩bruary 1838

[The Finance Committee ca⟨. . .⟩cil's attention to the "vague and unsatisfactory manner" ir⟨. . .⟩cifications and estimates were drawn up.]

⟨HIGHW⟩AYS

The Highway Committee reported . . . that they had considered the several Streets and Highways heretofore repaired out of the Highway Rate, and what Streets not heretofore repaired out of the Highway Rate ought to be so repaired; and whether any of the said Streets could or ought to be brought under the operation of the Paving Acts:—And that the following streets and places have always been repaired as the Public Highways and paid for out of that Rate: viz.

Part of East Street . . .

Chapel Road from where the Waterhouse formerly stood to Lower
    East Street

Orchard Lane from East Street to the Platform

From the Platform to Cross House and from thence to the top of Marsh Lane adjoining East Street

Orchard Lane, Hanover Buildings and Paradise Row and the Sea Beach partially.

That the following Streets and Highways have not hitherto been repaired out of the Rate, but the Committee were of opinion that from the disgraceful state in which most of them are suffered to remain they are become a serious nuisance not only to the immediate neighbourhood but to the Town generally and ought therefore forthwith to be repaired—viz.

The interior streets and thoroughfares of Kingsland Place and the Street or Road called Eastern Place

King Street, Queen Street, Three Field Lane and Duke of York Street and Square

Charlotte Place and Northam Street, and

The Road west side of the Marsh from the End of Marsh Lane to the Glo'ster Baths.

That it was also the opinion of the Committee that the following Streets and Rows of Buildings should be brought under the Controul of the Paving and Lighting Acts, viz.

Bell Street, Cross Street, Mount Street, Union Street and College Street (being the intermediate Streets between Bernard Street and East Street)

Bernard Street and Orchard Lane . . .

Resolved that the Report of the Highway Committee . . . be approved.

Friday the 30th day of March 1838

At this Council a Memorial from a large number of the merchants and tradesmen of the Town was presented urging the Council to take immediate steps for the establishment of a Cattle Market.

[In view of the small attendance at this meeting it was resolved to postpone consideration of this memorial.]

Friday the 6th day of April 1838

SOUTHAMPTON DOCKS AMENDED BILL

The Town Clerk laid before this Council the Print of the Bill now before Parliament "for extending the time for making a Dock or Docks at Southampton" in order to its being considered whether there was any objection on the part of this Corporation to the extension of the time . . . from seven years to ten years from the passing of the Southampton Dock Act and whether any alteration in the intended Bill appears to be necessary, and the same having been considered, It was proposed [by James Whitchurch] that this Council hereby expresses its regret that the Southampton Dock Company should be persisting in their endeavours to hold a far greater portion of the Town Lands than can possibly be required for the construction of their Docks and by their present application to Parliament encumber their own undertaking and seriously injure the Town; and that this Council taking into consideration the representations made by the Company, before the Land was originally granted, that the works would be immediately proceeded with; taking also into consideration that no works have yet been commenced on the large tract of Land of which the Company have obtained possession . . .; taking also into consideration that the Company have not yet applied for the consent of the Council to their present proposed Bill . . . and being of opinion that if the Bill were merely to extend the time . . . the valuable reversionary interest of the Town would be postponed without any pecuniary consideration or prospective advantage to the inhabitants of the Borough—declares its strong objection to the proposed Bill . . .

Upon which it was moved as an amendment

That this Council . . . do hereby give their assent to the said Bill being passed into a law to extend the period for the completion of the said Dock or Docks and works . . . to three years beyond the seven years granted by the original Act

Which being put to the vote was carried in the affirmative. . . .

¶ The commercial panic of 1837 and the slow progress of the building of the London & Southampton Railway had reacted unfavourably upon the docks project. The Company's consequent resort to Parliament for an extension of its time-limit had naturally revived local criticism and opposition, though Admiral Tinling had now changed his attitude and spoke and voted with the majority in this debate.

Thursday the 3rd day of May 1838

CHARITIES

The Town Clerk laid before this Council a Statement of the Interest and annual payments on the several Charity Monies remaining in the hands of this Corporation now due to the Trustees of the Charities and the same having been considered

It is Ordered that [these sums] amounting to One Hundred and Seventy eight pounds eighteen shillings and one penny be paid by the Treasurer. . . .

Friday the 22nd day of June 1838

REPAIRS OF THE BRIDEWELL, ETC.

A Committee appointed the 1st February last to examine the work done at the Gaol and Bridewell . . . reported to this Council that it appeared to them after a minute examination of the Gaols that the whole of the works contemplated . . . had been satisfactorily executed . . . and that by these alterations a most essential improvement had been effected both as regards the classification of prisoners and the maintenance of a proper state of discipline within the prison . . .

[The Committee appointed to consider the establishment of a cattle market reported that it was desirable and could be effected without an act of parliament or any considerable expense, but as the Council was unable to agree upon a site it was resolved that the question should be submitted to a public meeting.]

Thursday the 16th day of August 1838

At this Council Mr. Thomas Ridding resigned his Office of Town Clerk . . .

Resolved unanimously that the thanks of this Corporation be given to Mr. Ridding for his zealous efficient and faithful Services as Town Clerk during the lengthy period of more than twenty eight years. . . .

At this Council Charles Ewens Deacon of . . . Southampton Attorney at Law was appointed Town Clerk. . . .

[It was resolved that the Town Clerk's salary should henceforth be £200 a year, an amendment moved by three of the St. Mary's Radicals that "taking into account the perquisites and emoluments likely to be derived by the Town Clerk" it should be £150 being defeated.]

Tuesday the 9th day of October 1838

[A highway rate of £80 was levied for the ensuing year and an invitation from the Chairman of the Directors of the Dock Company to the Mayor and Council to attend the laying of the foundation-stone of the first dock on the ensuing 12 October was accepted.]

Thursday the 1st day of November 1838

[The municipal elections, which were conducted more quietly this year, made no change in the relation of parties on the Council. For St. Mary's the retiring councillors were re-elected, while Conservatives were successful in all the other wards. Two notable newcomers to the Council were Joseph Rankin Stebbing, optician, who was afterwards to be a leading figure in the commercial and municipal life of the town, and Abraham Abraham, jeweller and silversmith. It was most unusual at that time for a Jew to be a member of a town council, and for one to hold office, as Abraham shortly afterwards did, was still illegal.]

Friday the 9th day of November 1838

[Joseph Bernard was elected Mayor, W. H. Steere Sheriff, and George Bennett and R. W. Guy Bailiffs. Of the retiring aldermen, Lobb, Moody, Dickson and Brown were re-elected, and Joseph Lomer replaced Job Ede.]

CATTLE MARKET

At this Council the Town Clerk reported the Proceedings of the Public Meeting held in pursuance of the Resolution of the Council. . . .

¶At this rather thinly attended public meeting a gravel field adjoining Houndwell had been chosen by a narrow majority as the site of the proposed market and a committee elected to carry this decision into effect.

Tuesday the 18th day of December 1838

DUTIES ON COALS

At this Council the Mayor laid upon the table the Resolutions passed at Public Meetings held at Winchester Romsey and Basingstoke relative to the Notice of the intention of the Commissioners of Pavement to apply for an Act of Parliament to enable them to levy Duties on Coals coming into the Port of Southampton or entering Southampton Water past Calshott Castle which having been read by the Town Clerk

It was moved that the Mayor be requested to acknowledge the receipt of the resolutions . . . expressive of the determination of those Towns to oppose in Parliament the Imposition of a Tax for the Improvement of Southampton on all coals etc. coming into the Port of Southampton or entering Southampton Water . . . and to express the full concurrence of this Council in the unjustness and oppressive nature of such a tax . . . not only as it would affect the Interests of those Towns and the County of Hants generally but also as it would affect the Interests and Welfare of the Inhabitants of the Town and Neighbourhood of Southampton and to assure those Towns of the Determination of this Council to resist the Imposition of such a Tax . . . whenever the subject may be brought under its consideration and whether the said tax extends to the County generally or be limited to the Town and Neighbourhood of Southampton only

Upon which it was moved as an amendment

That as the proposed Bill for improving the Town of Southampton originates with the Commissioners of Pavement and as the Commissioners are in communication with the several Towns on the subject of the resolutions which have been read this Council is of opinion that they should merely acknowledge the receipt of the Resolutions and express their Satisfaction that the Commissioners have so promptly attended to them

Which being put to the vote was negatived.

The Original Motion was then put to the Vote and carried in the affirmative.

¶The political alignment described in the Introduction was now taking shape, based on the dichotomy in the government of the town—the Conservatives controlling the Council and giving their greatest attention and support to undertakings such as the railway and the docks which would promote trade, and the Radicals sometimes shaping the policy of the Paving (or Improvement) and Waterworks Commissioners and proposing measures which would benefit the inhabitants in general, such as new streets and an increased water supply, while at the same time rather inconsistently proclaiming the need to lighten the burden of the rates. The Paving Commissioners were now intending to apply for an act which would amend the existing paving and lighting acts and enable them to effect improvements and raise tolls or duties for such purposes. In response to the outcry which their proposed tax had provoked they had now amended their plan to taxing only coal landed at Southampton itself, which concession was the substance of the "correspondence with the several towns" referred to in the amendment moved by Whitchurch and his Radical supporters on the Council; but this did not have the effect of lessening the opposition very much.

POLICE

At this Council the Town Clerk laid upon the table
> A Return of the number of Convictions that have taken place since the Establishment of the new Police in . . . Southampton and the Cost of that Establishment from the 7th March 1836
> also a Return for the three Years preceding the 1st January 1835.

It was then moved [by the opposition] that a Committee be appointed to enquire into the efficiency of the Police Establishment with a View to the reduction of its Expenditure and in order to relieve the Burgesses as far as possible from the present Borough Rate
Upon which it was moved as an amendment
That this Council highly approves of the appointment of an efficient Police Force and considers that the present Force is not more numerous than is necessary for the proper protection of the persons and property of the Burgesses of this Town and this Council takes this present Opportunity of publickly expressing their approval of the Conduct of the Inspector and of the Force generally on all occasions
Which being put to the vote was carried in the affirmative. . . .

SOUTHAMPTON COMMON

At this Council an Application from [the] Secretary to the "Southampton Common Improvement Committee" was read.
It was then moved that this Council Meeting be adjourned
Which being put to the vote was carried in the affirmative.

¶Disputes between the six-months owners of the common lands and the commoners had continued from time to time, and several attempts to arrive at an agreement had broken down. At a recent public meeting to discuss the question Whitchurch, who was himself one of the owners, had voiced the suggestion that the common lands might be "improved" and turned to better account by their fringes being appropriated or leased for building purposes and handsome houses, squares and ornamental walks erected. The idea was taken up by others, applied to the Common, and the

Committee referred to above formed. In view of the origin of the suggestion, however, it inevitably and immediately became entangled in local politics and accusations of interested motives were bandied about.

Tuesday the 1st day of January 1839

SOUTHAMPTON IMPROVEMENTS

At this Council a Memorial from certain Rate Payers of the parishes of Saint Michael and Saint John in favour of the Improvements proposed by the Commissioners of Pavement was read.

SOUTHAMPTON COMMON

At this Council [the previous week's] application on behalf of the "Southampton Common Improvement Committee" requesting to be furnished with a copy of the Plan of the Southampton Common and also a copy of the Grant or Deed whereby the Corporation hold the Common and requesting permission for the Committee to hold their future meetings at the Audit House was taken into consideration. It was moved that the ... Committee be furnished with a copy of the Plan of the ... Common and the Grant ... at the Expense of the Parties applying for the same, and that the Committee be allowed to hold their meetings at the Audit House at such reasonable times as may not interfere with the Meetings of [public bodies].

Upon which it was moved as an Amendment

That this Council having considered the Application ... is of opinion that it is not expedient to grant such request....

The Amendment having been put to the vote was carried in the affirmative.

CATTLE MARKET

At this Council a letter from Mr. Alfred Oakley offering a Site for a Cattle and Hay Market was read ... and ...

It was resolved that the same be referred to the Cattle Market Committee appointed at a Public Meeting of the Rate Payers on the 25th day of October 1838....

[A motion to buy two stoves to warm the Audit House was opposed by an amendment that "the Town Council are not justified in taxing the ratepayers with the stoves, which are a luxury and should be paid for by private subscription", but this amendment was defeated.]

¶ The memorial from nearly sixty ratepayers of St. Michael's Ward referred to above claimed that the ward contributed to local taxation nearly 50% more than its neighbours in proportion to population, but had been kept in the background for the past thirty years and had no proper approach to it. The memorialists therefore expressed the strongest approval of the plans for a new street from the High Street into St. Michael's Square and a road from the Long Rooms to Four Posts which were among the Paving Commissioners' intentions.

Tuesday the 8th day of January 1839

COMMISSIONERS OF PAVEMENT

At this Council an application from the Commissioners of Pavement requesting to be informed whether the Council . . . assented to or dissented from or remained neuter in respect of their intended application to Parliament in the ensuing Session for an Act to alter amend and enlarge the Provisions of the several Acts for Paving Lighting Watching and Improving the Town of Southampton and the liberties thereof and for widening and forming certain Streets Roads Lanes and other Public Thoroughfares and Places therein and for establishing a Cemetery within the said Town . . . were laid before the Council and taken into consideration

It was moved That it is the opinion of this Council that the Town Clerk be instructed to signify to the Commissioners . . . that this Council will be neuter respecting the intended application to Parliament . . .

Upon which it was moved as an amendment

That this Council do dissent from the Bill proposed to be obtained by the Commissioners . . .

Which being put to the vote was carried in the affirmative . . .

COUNCIL MEETINGS

At this Council It was Resolved

That the Mayor be requested to provide sufficient chairs for the accommodation of such of the Burgesses as choose to attend the Council Meetings and also to provide a Table for the Reporters. . . .

¶ The successful motion that the Council should oppose the proposed bill was moved by Admiral Tinling, who presented a memorial signed by 500 persons attacking the project. The Commissioners at their next meeting, during which twenty-one of their own number who opposed the bill left the room in protest, made considerable alterations in it, striking out some roads from the list of those which it was proposed to form or widen and inserting a clause providing for the election by the parish vestries of all but the *ex officio* commissioners. In spite of this a public meeting on 22 January passed resolutions denouncing even the amended project and expressing a determination to oppose it; and when it was submitted to the vestry meetings all but St. Michael's condemned it. In face of this the Commissioners resolved on 13 February to drop the plan.

Monday the 25th day of March 1839

ITCHEN BRIDGE AMENDMENT ACT

At this Meeting a print of the Bill now before Parliament "for enlarging the powers of the Acts for establishing a Floating Bridge over the River Itchen . . ." was submitted and taken into consideration . . . and . . . It was then moved that this Council considering that the Bill . . . would be highly prejudicial to the interests of the Inhabitants of the Town . . . do earnestly request the Members for the Town and County to oppose the said Amended Bill to the utmost of their power. . . .

Which . . . was . . . put to the vote and carried in the affirmative.

¶ The bill provided for compulsory powers of purchase, which the Mayor asserted were to enable the Itchen Bridge Company to buy Northam Bridge and thus create a worse monopoly than it had been established to break down. It also provided for an increase of tolls to a level considered exorbitant.

Tuesday the 16th day of April 1839

At this Meeting the Print of the [Itchen Bridge] Bill now before Parliament . . . with the alterations proposed thereto by the Promoter of the Bill and approved by the Itchen Bridge Company and also the correspondence with the Members for the Town . . . and the Southern Division of the County and also with . . . the Solicitor to the Promoter of the Bill were taken into consideration and Mr. Sharp the Clerk to the Itchen Bridge Company having been heard on the subject of the Bill with the proposed Alterations

It was Resolved unanimously that such Alterations appear to meet the views of this Council so far as they affect the interests of the Public and that this Council will not oppose the passing of the said Bill if the proposed alterations with such others (if any) as the public interest may require are fully carried into effect.

¶ As Mr. Sharp explained, the bill had not been promoted by the Company itself but by Mr. Hugh Mackintosh, a partner in the London firm of contractors who had built the Bridge. The struggling and near-bankrupt Company had fallen so heavily into debt to him that he had ended up as the owner of the Bridge property. The bill, however, had now been modified by striking out the clause giving power of purchase, cutting down the increase of tolls to one-third above the present level, and deleting another clause which bore hard on the local fishermen.

Thursday the 2nd day of May 1839

ABOVE BAR AND CHAPEL FAIRS

At this Council a Petition from certain Members of the religious Society of Friends and others of the same Persuasion resident in Southampton and its neighbourhood praying the Council to take such steps as shall prevent the evils that at present arise from the fairs . . . was received and read.

Friday the 10th day of May 1839

CATTLE MARKET

[The question of a site for this was still unsettled. The Secretary of the committee of inhabitants set up (see 1 November 1838) to promote its establishment had notified the Council that a position in either the East or West Magdalens was desired, but at this meeting it was voted that lands on which the ratepayers had rights of pasturage for six months in the year could not be appropriated for this purpose.]

Friday the 28th day of June 1839

[An application was received from the London & Southampton Railway Company (which shortly afterwards became the London & South-Western) for some additional strips of the Marsh to enable it to make approaches to its Terminus Station. The Council readily agreed to surrender its interest in all but one of the strips for a nominal consideration. A town meeting, however, influenced by fear that the Company would use the land for building, refused to agree, and the Company was compelled to invoke the powers of compulsory purchase with which its act had endowed it. The jury empanelled according to the procedure which such acts laid down awarded £1000 compensation to be divided equally between the Corporation and the ratepayers.]

Thursday the 1st day of August 1839

[A letter from Mr. Alfred Oakley offering part of his garden in Love Lane for a cattle market was considered, and the offer was accepted subject to further details being obtained from him.]

Tuesday the 24th day of September 1839

[The Town Clerk reported that Mr. Oakley had supplied further particulars of his offer, explaining that he would gravel the whole site and provide coops and other appendages at his own expense, and proposing to charge 3d. per head for beasts, 2d. for cows, 1d. for calves and 6d. per coop for sheep and pigs. It was resolved that the Council would sanction the establishment of a cattle market in the place and on the terms proposed, at Mr. Oakley's risk and responsibility.]

¶ The market, adjoining the Cricket Ground and the Railway Terminus, was opened on 24 October following, and was held on alternative Tuesdays to Salisbury Cattle Market.

POLICE AT HIGHFIELD AND PORTSWOOD

At this Council a Memorial was received . . . from certain inhabitants of Highfield and Portswood praying [it] to extend the Protection of the Police Establishment to their respective Districts.

And the same having been considered it is moved that the Watch Committee be instructed to add not less than three nor more than five Police Constables to the existing Police Force of the Borough to be employed . . . for the general protection of the property of the inhabitants of the Town and neighbourhood especially Portswood and Highfield.

[This motion was carried over an amendment that not more than two constables should be added.

A highway rate of £100 was levied for the ensuing year.]

Friday the 1st day of November 1839

[The municipal elections followed the same pattern as those of the previous year, the Radicals being successful in St. Mary's Ward and the Conservatives in all the others, so that there was no change in the balance of parties in the Council.]

Saturday the 9th day of November 1839

[Captain Breton, whom the Conservative *Hampshire Advertiser* described as "both a gentleman and a man of business", was elected Mayor for the second time; John Hole was chosen Sheriff and J. R. Stebbing and Edward Mayes Bailiffs. The Watch, Lease, Highway and Finance Committees were elected; and the Treasurer was instructed to pay the Trustees of the Charities £153.2.11 due to them.]

Thursday the 23rd day of January 1840

FELONS LANDING AT SOUTHAMPTON FROM GUERNSEY AND JERSEY

At this Council it was resolved that a Committee be appointed to inquire into the practicability of preventing the Captain or Master of any Vessel trading between this Port and the Islands of Guernsey and Jersey from landing or causing to be landed any Person or Persons convicted of Felony in those Islands (for the purpose of expiating his or their Offences) on the shores of Southampton.

DANGEROUS STATE OF THE CANAL IN HOUNDWELL

At this Council the Presentment of the Grand Jury at the General Quarter Sessions of the Peace held at the Guildhall . . . on Monday the 30th day of December 1839 complaining of the state of the canal running through the Houndwell common field and that it was a nuisance and detrimental to the health of Her Majesty's liege subjects and recommending its removal, was received and read.

Thursday the 6th day of February 1840

BURIAL OF THE DEAD

The Mayor having called the attention of the Council to the state of the Burial ground in the parish of St. Mary . . . and the Minutes of the Proceedings of the Committee appointed on the 10th day of March 1837 to consider what means should be taken with a view of providing additional accommodation for the Burial of the Dead having been read and considered

It was moved by Mr. Whitchurch and seconded by Captain Ward and Resolved that this Council again records its opinion that a Public Cemetery should be immediately constructed in or near the Town and requests the Committee already appointed to consider immediately which will be the best site for the same and what steps should be taken by the Council to provide a Burial ground which shall not increase the present expense of Funerals of the Poorer Classes.

CANAL AND TOWN POND

A committee which had been appointed to consider the state of the old canal recommended a public subscription being raised to defray the cost of filling it in

¶ The identity of the mover and seconder of the motion in favour of a town cemetery reflects the non-party spirit in which the Council, at least, was approaching this question.

Thursday the 5th day of March 1840

FELONS LANDING AT SOUTHAMPTON FROM GUERNSEY AND JERSEY

At this Council the Committee appointed on the 23rd day of January last reported that Mr. Abraham Jones Le Cras attended the Meeting of your Committee and rendered them much valuable Information. He stated that he had resided ten years in the Island of Jersey and was during that time the Editor of two weekly Journals published in that Island . . . and that he lately published a work on the Laws and Customs of that Island. He informed your Committee that his Occupation and Attendances in the Courts of Justice had afforded him great opportunities of becoming conversant with the affairs and laws of Jersey and Guernsey, that as there were no criminal laws in those Islands the Punishment of crime was left entirely to the direction of the court, both as to its nature and duration, and that convicts instead of receiving such exemplary punishments as are calculated to restrain vice and encourage virtue are transported to Southampton Portsmouth Weymouth and Plymouth and there let loose against the peace and security of the Inhabitants of those places, to commit Plunder Rapine and Murder for their subsistence—that he had kept a list of persons banished from Jersey for Housebreaking Highway Robbery and other Offences during his Residence there and that they amounted to nearly a thousand . . . and that the greater part of them were landed on the shores of Southampton—that of late years it has been the practice to imprison Natives convicted of Offences in the Islands but oftentimes if the Native Convicts are poor and likely to become chargeable [i.e. to poor relief] they are banished from the Island as well as the English Irish and Scotch who may have resided there. The sentence is banishment for a term of years which . . . is carried into execution not by transmitting the convicts to the Hulks at Portsmouth but by landing them at Southampton and letting them loose among the community. Mr. Le Cras also stated to your Committee that he had recognised in Southampton several persons who had been convicted of Felony in the Island of Jersey and who were transported to this Place, to expiate their crimes. . . .

Your Committee were of opinion therefore that these monstrous abuses were calculated to have a demoralising effect upon the population of this Town, to render both person and property insecure, to require a larger Police force than would otherwise be necessary, to increase the amount paid under the head of casual relief, and thus to augment the already heavy annual expenditure of this Borough and recommended this Council to memorialize the Secretary of State and petition both Houses of Parliament to cause measures to be taken to remedy these serious grievances . . .

It was Resolved that the same be adopted. . . .

Thursday the 7th day of May 1840

THE LATE RECORDER

At this Council it was resolved unanimously that . . . having received intelligence of the Resignation by Mr. Bingham of the Office of Recorder . . . in consequence of his Appointment as a Metropolitan Police Magistrate, while they congratulate him on the opening of a wider field for the exercise of his eminent judicial talents, [they] cannot but express their extreme regret at the loss of his valuable services to the town at large. . . .

Tuesday the 16th day of June 1840

[Mr. A. E. Cockburn was appointed Recorder.]

At this Council the Town Clerk laid on the table a communication . . . informing the Council that His Royal Highness the Duke of Sussex and other distinguished persons intended to honor Southampton with their company on the 20th instant, it being the day fixed for the Public Celebration of the Opening of the Railway and requesting the Council to adopt such Measures upon the Occasion as they may deem most proper.

The same having been considered

It was resolved that an Address be presented to His Royal Highness . . .

on his arrival at Southampton on . . . the 20th instant and that the Mayor and Council do attend at the Railway Terminus for the purpose of presenting such Address. . . .

Monday the 13th day of July 1840

At this Council the Town Clerk laid on the table a letter . . . from Richard Blanchard Esquire Clerk to the Commissioners of the Port and Harbour enclosing a List of Articles upon which the Commissioners propose to reduce the Dues payable under the Pier Act and requesting the consent of this Corporation to such Reduction and the same having been read and considered

It was moved . . . that the consent of the Corporation be given . . .

Upon which it was moved as an amendment by Mr. Tucker and seconded by Mr. Laishley [two of the St. Mary's councillors]

That the scale of dues now presented be referred back to the Commissioners of the Pier requesting them to supply the Corporation with a schedule of the present Dues in order to ascertain the amount of the proposed Reduction

Which being put to the vote was negatived

The original motion was then put . . . and carried in the affirmative. . . .

Thursday the 6th day of August 1840

COUNCILLORS FINED

. . . Only Eleven Members of the Council attending within a quarter of an hour after the time fixed for this Meeting . . . a motion was made that the eighth bye law be read and the same having been read and a greater number than one third of the Council having shortly after attended

It is Resolved that all Members of the Council who were not present when the eighth bye law was read be fined the sum of five shillings each pursuant thereto, unless sufficient cause to the contrary be shown at the next Meeting. . . .

FELONS LANDING AT SOUTHAMPTON FROM JERSEY AND GUERNSEY

At this Council the Town Clerk read a Letter . . . from the Honorable Fox Maule, written by direction of the Marquis of Normanby, informing the Council that his Lordship had communicated with the Governor and Bailiff of Guernsey on the subject of the complaint set forth in the Petition of the Council, and that his Lordship thought the authorities in Guernsey could not be blamed for sending away Paupers and Vagrants not being Natives. But with respect to the practice of banishing Culprits to England from Guernsey his Lordship disapproved of the same, and would not fail to consider any case which might accrue of that Description which may be brought under his notice, and take such steps as may appear to be necessary.

¶ Lord Normanby was the Home Secretary and Fox Maule (afterwards Lord Panmure and then Earl of Dalhousie) the under-secretary of state in the Home Office.

Monday the 26th day of October 1840

[It was resolved to levy a highway rate of £100 for the ensuing year.]

Monday the 2nd day of November 1840

[In the municipal elections the Conservatives were again successful in all wards except St. Mary's, so that the relation of parties on the Council remained unchanged.]

Monday the 9th day of November 1840

[Joseph Lobb was elected Mayor, J. R. Stebbing Sheriff (Charles Davies having been unsuccessfully nominated by Tucker and Joseph Lankester against him) and A. Abraham and Robert Miller Bailiffs. As a Jew, Abraham could not make the usual declaration "on the true faith of a Christian" and was therefore exposed to the risk of being proceeded against in the Court of Queen's Bench if, as the new Mayor said, "anyone had the bad taste to do so". The Watch, Lease, Highway and Finance Committees were also duly elected.]

TOWN IMPROVEMENTS

At this Council the late Mayor submitted (in pursuance of a Resolution passed at a Meeting of the Rate Payers . . . on the 6th Instant) the Report of a Committee appointed at a Public Meeting of the Rate Payers held on the 30th day of September last to enquire into the necessity of certain proposed New Roads and other Improvements within the Borough.

¶ Since the Paving Commissioners had decided in February of the previous year to drop their projected Improvements Bill, the question had slept for some time. Then on 30 September 1840 the ratepayers' meeting referred to above had elected a committee to consider the desirability of widening some streets, making some new ones and filling in the old canal. This committee had reported in turn to the further meeting on 6 November in favour of widening Bridge Street, West Street and the upper end of East Street, making certain new streets and filling the canal. The meeting had then recommended the report to the Council's consideration.

Thursday the 4th day of February 1841

COMMUTATION OF THE PORT AND HARBOUR DUES

At this Council Application was received from the Commissioners of the Port and Harbour informing the Council that the Peninsular and Oriental Steam Navigation Company were about to use this Port if an arrangement could be effected between them and the Commissioners for a commutation of the Dues, by payment of One Hundred Pounds for each Vessel for one Year from the time that each such Vessel should first make entry at the Custom House, and requesting the consent of this Corporation to the proposed arrangement. . . .

It was . . . resolved that the sanction of the Corporation be given. . . .

PACKET STATION

At this Council the Mayor reported that he had received an official communication from the Treasury Chambers informing him that the Lords Commissioners of Her Majesty's Treasury having under their Consideration the Report of the Committee appointed to examine and Report on the different Harbours and their Merits as Stations for the Embarkation of the West India Mails, and also the several Papers and memorials on the same subject, were of opinion that the selection of the Committee should be adopted, and that the Port of Dartmouth should be selected. . . .

¶ Great hopes had been entertained that the projected docks, of which the first was now in course of construction, would lead to the choice of South-ampton as a packet station for the West India mails if they were removed from Falmouth. In June 1839 a committee elected by a public meeting had drawn up a memorial to the Treasury on the subject; and when the newly-formed "P. & O." Company, which had obtained the contract for these mails, selected Southampton as the port of departure for its steamers these hopes were greatly strengthened. There was corresponding disappointment when the committee appointed by the Admiralty, to which the Government had referred the matter, recommended Dartmouth and their recommenda-tion appeared to be endorsed. The "P. & O.", however, continued to make Southampton the home station for its steamers, which merely called at Dartmouth for the mails; while in due course a committee of the House of Commons declined to ratify the choice of the latter port. The matter was thus re-opened and in 1843 Southampton was chosen after all to replace Falmouth.

Monday the 22nd day of February 1841

JEWS' DISABILITIES BILL

This Council approving of a Bill now before Parliament for enabling Persons professing the Jewish Religion to subscribe the Declaration of the 1st and 2nd Victoria on their election to Municipal Offices

It is resolved that the following petition be adopted by the Council and forwarded to both Houses of Parliament . . .

". . . Your Petitioners have observed with much satisfaction that a Bill is now before Your Honorable House entitled 'A Bill to enable Persons professing the Jewish Religion to subscribe the form of declaration con-tained in the Act of the first and second Years of her present Majesty for the Relief of Quakers Moravians and Separatists elected to Municipal

Offices' And Your Petitioners respectfully and earnestly pray that Your Honorable house will pass the said Bill and take such steps as may be required to afford the same indulgence to the Hebrew People of this Country as has been afforded to all other religious Sects

"And Your Petitioners will ever pray, etc. . . . ."

¶ Mr. Abraham's civic prominence and the respect felt for him were no doubt partly responsible for the Council's support of this measure.

Thursday the 6th day of May 1841

[£666 was received from the sale of timber from the Common, and appropriated to the reduction of Corporation bonds.]

Thursday the 5th day of August 1841

[The Finance Committee reported that no borough rate need be levied for the ensuing quarter.]

Friday the 22nd day of October 1841

INCLOSING THE MARSH

At this Council It was . . . Resolved that considering the great public works [i.e. the railway and the docks] which are in progress in the neighbourhood of the Marsh and the great value the same is become for building purposes It is expedient that an Act of Parliament be obtained inclosing the same and improving the approaches thereto, and also that powers be obtained for regulating the Flys within the Borough [and]

That a Committee be appointed for considering the best mode of carrying the same into execution and that in the mean time the Town Clerk do give the necessary notices for the next Session of Parliament.

¶ Flys, which had made their appearance in the 1820's as a means of transport in and near the town, had now become so numerous that there were complaints of their standing so thickly together as to block certain streets. and of the "improper and noisy conduct" of their drivers. Their fares also required regulation.

Monday the 1st day of November 1841

[In the municipal elections the Conservatives won two of the three St. Mary's seats contested, besides retaining their hold on all the other wards. This may have been in part a local reflection of the Conservative reaction in the country as a whole which had given Sir Robert Peel's ministry a majority at the general election of this year. It may also have owed something to the association of the local Conservatives with the railway, docks and other enterprises which were increasing the trade of Southampton.]

I

Tuesday the 9th day of November 1841

[Peter Dickson was elected Mayor, A. Abraham Sheriff, and Henry Fricker and Thomas Collard Bailiffs. Of the five retiring aldermen, Richard Eldridge, John King, W. J. Le Feuvre and Captain Ward were re-elected, while Colonel Henderson replaced John Jolliffe. Edward Toomer was also elected an alderman in place of George Brown who was no longer qualified.]

CEMETERY

It was . . . Resolved that the Town Clerk be directed to give Notice of an Application to Parliament at the next Session for a Bill to establish a Cemetery or Burial Ground at the North East corner of the Southampton Common and comprising about Twenty acres of the said Common [and] . . .

That a Committee be formed . . . to take such preliminary steps as may be considered necessary in furtherance of the above Resolution.

INCLOSING THE MARSH

At this Council the Town Clerk submitted a Draft of the intended Application to Parliament for power to inclose the Marsh and for improving the Approaches thereto and also for regulating the Flys within the Borough, and which have been approved of by the Marsh Inclosure Committee.

CANAL IN HOUNDWELL

At this Council a Letter was received and read from Mr. Thomas Sharland respecting the dangerous state of the canal in Houndwell.

And . . . It was . . . Resolved that the subject of filling up the Barge River in Houndwell, with the letter this day received respecting the dangerous state of the same, be referred to the Marsh Inclosure Committee.

¶ The project of a town cemetery had been dropped for several years after 1837, when (see the entry for 4 May of that year) it had been found impossible to buy land cheaply for the purpose since owners could command good prices for it as building sites owing to the expansion of the town and the construction of the railway.

Tuesday the 7th day of December 1841

CEMETERY

At this Council the Committee appointed . . . to take preliminary Measures . . . for obtaining an Act in the next Session of Parliament to establish a Cemetery . . . on the Southampton Common reported that at a Meeting held on the sixth day of December last Mr. Doswell attended and submitted a Plan showing the locality of the proposed cemetery . . . which met the approval of your Committee, and they . . . recommended the same to the Council for adoption. . . .

The Committee further reported that the Reverend Charles Parsons, curate of the Parish of Saint Mary, attended and having stated . . . that he should be in a situation to furnish . . . Information in the course of a few Days as to the Number of Deaths and fees paid in Burials in the Church Yard of Saint Mary's, and your Committee being desirous of a conference with the Clergy of the Town to discuss the merits of the Question . . . directed the Town Clerk to invite the following Clergy to attend Your Committee on Saturday then next . . . viz.

The Revd. Dr. Wilson

The Revd. J. E. Shadwell

The Revd. T. L. Shapcott

The Revd. C. Horne and

The Revd. C. Parsons

And Your Committee accordingly adjourned until that Day whereon [the above clergymen] attended and afforded Your Committee much general Information upon the subject of the proposed cemetery. . . .

Your Committee proceeded to make out an estimate of the probable Expense of erecting the Cemetery and the incidental Expenses thereto, and also the annual Expense of the same. [The probable expense of building was estimated at £4400 and the annual expenses at £100 for a chaplain and £100 for a clerk and sexton.]

It appeared to your Committee necessary to have powers in the Act to raise £7000 upon Mortgage.

Your Committee further . . . recommended that powers should be also obtained in the said Act to enable the Council to contract with the Guardians of the Poor for the Burial of the Paupers at the Cemetery which would have the effect of affording immediate relief to the present overcrowded church Yard of Saint Mary's Parish.

Your Committee are happy to inform the Council that the major part of the Clergy who attended . . . approved generally of the proposed Cemetery, and all admitted the necessity of some measure being adopted for remedying the existing Evils.

Your Committee further recommended that the leading Principle which should be adopted, should be the application as far as possible of the funds to be derived from the Interment of the Rich to reduce the charges attending the Burial of the Poor.

Your Committee likewise recommended that the Council do memorialize the . . . Treasury, for consent to the appropriation of the portion of the Common for the purpose proposed, and that the Town Clerk be directed to prepare and lay before the Council the Draft of the intended Bill to be submitted to Parliament . . . during the next Session.

The Report of the Cemetery Committee having been read and considered,

It is . . . Resolved that the Report . . . be adopted and that the Committee be authorized to sit again and to take such further steps as may be necessary. . . .

INCLOSING THE MARSH

At this Council the Committee appointed . . . to consider the best mode of inclosing the Marsh and improving the approaches thereto . . . reported that Mr. Doswell submitted to Your Committee Plans showing the Marsh Lands proposed to be enclosed, containing in the whole 16 acres three roods and 32 perches or thereabouts, together with the property situate in Bridge Street . . . and Marsh Lane and the Road opposite Ogle Place in the parish of Saint Mary and also part of Porters Meadow proposed to be taken under the powers of the Act for widening and improving the approaches to the Marsh.

The Committee having taken the same into their consideration recommended to the Council that the following Streets Roads and Ways . . . communicating with the said open fields commons or Marsh Lands called the Marsh should be accordingly widened and improved vizt.

Bridge Street . . . Marsh Lane, as far as the Marsh . . . The Road opposite to Ogle Place between Saint Mary's Church Yard Road and Marsh Lane . . . The Road adjoining to and on the South side of Porters Meadow. . . .

Your Committee likewise recommended that general Powers be applied for so far as the rules of Parliament will admit, to form widen and improve all or any other of the Streets Roads and Approaches to the said Marsh as well as . . . within the said Town . . . which might hereafter be deemed expedient or necessary, and also for the proper Drainage etc. of the Land proposed to be enclosed, and for repairing and keeping in repair the present Roads, and any hereafter to be made.

Your Committee also further recommended that any Streets Roads or Ways when formed improved or widened should be placed under the control and power of the Commissioners of Pavement, and also that compulsory powers be obtained for purchasing the interests of the Owners and Lessees of the Properties that will be required for the purposes of this Act, and also that powers be obtained for purchasing the interests of the Owners in Fee and Lessees of a sufficient part of the Lammas and other Lands.

Your Committee having also considered the subject of regulating the Flys and other Public Vehicles plying for hire within the Borough recommended that they should be placed under the authority of the Council and that the Fares should be fixed and rules made for their management and that such Bye-Laws should be made as hereafter may appear advisable and that powers be accordingly obtained in the said Act for that purpose.

Your Committee further recommended that the Town Clerk be directed to prepare the necessary Schedules of Properties required for the purposes of this Act, and to prepare and give the proper Notices to the Parties as required by the Standing Orders of Parliament, and to prepare and lay before the Council the Draft of the intended Bill to be submitted to Parliament in order to carry into effect these important objects, and . . . to inform the Earl of Guilford . . . that a part of the Deanery would be required in carrying into effect the proposed Plan.

The Report . . . having been . . . considered

It is . . . Resolved that it be . . . adopted.

Thursday the 3rd day of February 1842

CANAL IN HOUNDWELL

At this Council the following recommendation was received from the Jury upon the Inquest on view of the Body of Mary Tubbs held on the 23rd day of December last, who on the evening previous was drowned while crossing Houndwell, by slipping into the Canal

"The Jury beg to recommend to the Town Council that in the proposed application to Parliament for enclosing the Marsh, powers should be obtained to fill up the canal in Houndwell and thereby prevent the recurrence of similar frightful accidents, and effect a great Improvement in that part of the Town".

And the same having been read and considered

It is Resolved that the recommendation of the Jury be referred to the consideration of the Marsh Inclosure Committee.

[The Council also resolved to subscribe £5 towards the expenses of draining the Canal.]

Friday the 18th day of February 1842

CEMETERY

At this Council the Town Clerk submitted the following Proceedings of the Vestry Meetings of the several Parishes in this Borough, relative to the proposed Application about to be made by the Council for an Act to establish a Public Cemetery on the Common

All Saints Vestry

[Resolution] "That the Churchyard in Saint Mary's parish has long been entirely inadequate to supply the wants of the Town, and from its overcrowded state is likely to prove injurious to the health of the Neighbourhood, it is highly expedient that an additional Burying Place should be provided for the Town, this Meeting approves of Application being made by the Council . . . for an Act to appropriate a portion of the Common accordingly".

Saint Mary's Vestry

[Resolution] "That the consideration of the Question of the Cemetery be adjourned for one Month, and that a Draft of the intended Bill be then laid before the Vestry, that the clauses may be thoroughly examined, and either rejected or adopted as shall then be determined".

Saint Lawrence Vestry

[This resolution was identical in wording with that of All Saints, though better punctuated.]

Holy Rhood Vestry

The Town Clerk reported that he had received a communication from the Churchwardens of the Parish of Holy Rhood informing him that at a Vestry Meeting held yesterday . . . to consider the propositions contained in his letter, sent by direction of the Council. . . .

It was Resolved to give their dissent to those propositions.

Saint Michael's Vestry

[Resolution] "That a Cemetery is indispensable to the health and morals of the Town, and that this Meeting pledges itself to entertain that Question with a view to its establishment, with as little delay as possible, and with due regard to the feelings, the convenience and the circumstances of the Poor, but with a fixed determination of preventing the Town Council . . . from embarking in the speculation, which is contrary to the spirit and intention of the Municipal Act, may be disastrous in its results, and may hereafter be urged as a Precedent for embarking in speculations still more extensive and hazardous".

The foregoing proceedings having been considered

It was proposed . . . and seconded . . . that the proposed Cemetery Bill be postponed for one Year

Upon which it was moved as an amendment . . . that as the Vestries of this Town have expressed their unanimous Opinion as to the necessity of a New Burial Ground, it is expedient to proceed with the Intended Cemetery Bill without delay

Which being put to the vote was carried in the affirmative.

It was then moved that the Mayor be authorized to affix the Corporate Seal to the Petition to the House of Commons on the subject of the Cemetery

Upon which it was moved as an amendment . . .

That under the circumstances that the vote for proceeding with the Bill for the Cemetery has been carried by a majority of one only, in a Council consisting of seventeen members, this Council do not feel themselves justified in incurring any further expense in obtaining the proposed act of Parliament

Which being put to the vote was negatived.

The Original Motion was then put to the vote and carried in the affirmative.

INCLOSING THE MARSH

[The Town Clerk also submitted resolutions passed by the vestry meetings of the several parishes defining their attitudes to the Council's projected application to Parliament for leave to bring in a bill for enclosing the Marsh. The attitudes and even the resolutions of most of the meetings resembled those adopted with regard to the cemetery proposals, but in this case only St. Lawrence's supported the Council; though it is clear that in All Saints an attempt had been made to carry the same set of approving resolutions, but had been stopped by the defeat of the first of them.

St. Lawrence's Vestry resolved

"1. That the Marsh in its present state is of very little advantage to the commoners, and there is no doubt that by its appropriation to building purposes a very considerable income might be derived, which would be applicable for the benefit of all Parties interested therein. This Meeting approves of Application being made by the Council . . . to Parliament for an Act to enable them to appropriate the Marsh accordingly.

"2. That it would be desirable that the money to be raised under the Authority of such Act should after defraying the Expenses of Obtaining the same and putting it into execution, be applied as follows: vizt., In the first place, in widening and improving the approaches to the Marsh, vizt., the Road on the southern side of the Porters Meadow, Marsh Lane, the Road opposite Ogle Place, part of the Itchen Bridge Road and Bridge Street, and such other Roads and Streets in the Town as are not sufficiently commodious to the Public: in the next place in draining and filling up the canal in Houndwell: and in the next place, in acquiring on reasonable terms, for the benefit of the commoners, the interests of the Owners of the Soil in the Porters Meadow, East Marlands, West Marlands, Houndwell and Hoglands.

"3. That when the interests of the Owners of the Soil in the aforesaid common fields shall have been acquired, it will be desirable that such Fields shall be open to the commoners during the whole Year, as is now the case with the Common and the Marsh. . . ."

In All Saints the first of the above resolutions was moved but negatived.

St. Mary's resolved that "this Meeting be adjourned for One Month, that then the Corporation be requested to lay before the Meeting a Draft of the intended Bill, with Plans and Estimates, and the probable cost of the intended Improvements".

Holy Rhood, as it had done regarding the Cemetery, sent a brief intimation that it dissented from the Council's proposals, though in both cases the brevity seems to have been due to the fact that the vestry meeting had been held only on the evening before that of the Council.

St. Michael's resolved that "the Parishioners do most cordially agree that Improvements such as widening the Streets . . . are wholly necessary, and likewise that the Marsh in its present state is of no advantage to the Rate Payers, but regret that under the present Bill they are entirely excluded from any participations of the benefits arising therefrom, thereby feeling themselves justified, however anxious for Improvements, in giving their unqualified dissent to this Application".

In face of these resolutions the Council decided to postpone for the current session of Parliament the proposed bill for the enclosure of the Marsh.]

¶ The chief objections to the proposal of a cemetery on the Common were: that the Council, which was already being accused of extravagance, would be very ill-advised to borrow a relatively large sum on mortgage; that the commoners' rights would be infringed; and (especially in St. Mary's Ward) that the people of the poorer districts would have to walk two or three miles in each direction when attending funerals.

The opposition to the enclosure of the Marsh was at least partly regional, though there was again an element of suspicion of an apparently speculative venture. It came chiefly, however, from interests centred in Holy Rhood and St. Michael's wards which were increasingly and very naturally alarmed by the way in which the railway, the now imminent docks, and the development of wharves, warehouses and workshops on the banks of the Itchen were drawing the town's centre of gravity away eastward from the bottom of the High Street, the old Town Quay and the Royal Pier. To them the enclosure seemed a further strengthening of the "Itchen interest". Since many of these objectors whose commercial roots were in the old "bottom of the town" were Conservatives, while Whitchurch and other St. Mary's men belonged to the "Itchen interest", the division on this question cut across parties.

Wednesday the 16th day of March 1842

[Further communications were received from the vestries of St. Mary's and Holy Rhood, expressing opposition to the cemetery project. The Council thereupon reversed the decision taken at its previous meeting and resolved to postpone its intended bill.]

GREAT ROYAL AGRICULTURAL SOCIETY

At this Council a communication was received . . . on the subject of an Application to be made from the Town Council to have the Great Royal Agricultural Society Meeting held in this Town in the Year 1844.

And . . . it was . . . Resolved that a Committee be appointed to communicate with the Chairman or Secretary of the . . . Society on the subject.

Thursday the 5th day of May 1842

At this Council the Mayor submitted a letter which he had received . . . enclosing a copy of a resolution of the Council of the Royal Agricultural Society requesting certain Information prior to any Town being selected for the country meetings

And the same having been read and considered

It is Resolved that the consideration of the said letter and Resolution be referred to the Committee appointed at the last Council.

Thursday the 1st day of November 1842

[In the municipal elections the Radicals recaptured the two St. Mary's seats which had been lost in the previous year, thus recovering the whole representation of that ward; while the Conservatives continued to hold all the others. James Whitchurch, who now retired, was replaced by Richard Andrews, the leading coachmaker in the town (an industry which had developed into prominence during the "Spa" period of Southampton's history, but was now declining). Besides Andrews, who was afterwards an outstanding Liberal leader and mayor, another newcomer to the Council was the Radical Dr. Francis Cooper.]

Wednesday the 9th day of November 1842

[Edward Mayes was elected Mayor, A. Abraham being unsuccessfully nominated against him by Joseph Lankester and Dr. Cooper. Henry Fricker became Sheriff and W. R. Mabson and Richard Coles Bailiffs.]

VOTE OF THANKS TO THE LATE MAYOR

At this Council it was moved . . . that this Council offer their sincere thanks to Peter Dickson Esquire late Mayor for the able and efficient manner in which that Gentleman has discharged the Duties of the Office. . . .

Upon which it was moved as an amendment by Mr. Joseph Lankester and seconded by Mr. Francis Cooper that this Council are not justified in recording their votes in favour of the Original Proposition

1st because the Mayor . . . during his Mayoralty, has exhibited towards those who differed from him in Municipal and Political Subjects an acrimoniousness of feeling, coupled with a peevishness and petulance of manner wholly unbecoming the high station he has occupied.

2nd That during this Mayoralty, beyond any former Precedent, the paid officers of this Council, with the permission and sanction of the Mayor, have exhibited themselves before the Public as violent political partizans to the great disgust and annoyance of the Inhabitant Rate Payers, who have thus witnessed their property squandered for other than Municipal purposes.

3rd That in refusing the aid of the Police Force to prevent the disturbance of a Public Meeting convened to discuss an Important Public Question in a legal and Constitutional manner, of which intended disturbance his Worship was previously informed, was [sic] a tyrannical usurpation of power calculated to bring the Office of Chief Magistrate into disrepute and contempt.

4th That in refusing to call a Public Meeting as requested by upwards of 200 Rate Payers . . ., to take into consideration their alarming condition and that of the Town in general, for want of a supply of good and wholesome Water, the Mayor adopted an unprecedented course—one clearly showing his dread of public opinion and indicating that his Motives and Conduct would not bear this Investigation.

Lastly that this Council with deep regret record that whilst during this Mayoralty the Expenditure of the Council was greatly increased, they fail to perceive that the Town has derived the least benefit, there having been a total absence of all plans for Public Improvement or for the amelioration of the social moral and physical condition of the Inhabitants, and that for those several reasons this Council deplore that they cannot now accede to a proposal which for the last seven years has been carried without a dissentient voice

Which being put to the vote was negatived

The Original Motion was then . . . carried in the affirmative. . . .

¶ In this meeting political and personal animosities in the Council reached their highest point. Dickson, who remained in the chair throughout since his successor Mayes was not present, refused for a long time to put the amendment, and at a later stage threw into the fire a copy of the Radical *Hampshire Independent*, which he declared had been calumniating him for months, "amidst the tumultuous applause" of his supporters. There can be little doubt that his urbanity in public office fell short of that which he displayed as the town's Master of the Ceremonies. At the same time it should be remembered that as holder of this latter office he must have had more cause than almost anyone else to resent the changes in Southampton, which were destroying the value and meaning of the post; and that even though his fellow-Conservatives by their support of the railway and docks had had much to do with these changes he may have associated them rather with "new men" and Radicals such as the Lankesters. Nevertheless the fact that he was the only one of the next batch of five aldermen to go out of office who was not re-elected may mean that even his own party felt at bottom that he was a doubtful asset to them.

The year of his mayoralty, besides being one of rising expenditure (see the table of the borough rate in Appendix B) had been marked by particularly fierce political and personal bitterness, arising chiefly from three issues: the annulment of the Southampton parliamentary election of 1841, the wrecking of an anti-Corn-Law meeting, and a water shortage.

After the Conservative victory in 1841 the Liberals had petitioned against the return of the new members of parliament, Lord Bruce (afterwards Earl of Elgin) and C. C. Martyn, on the ground that their agents had been guilty of corruption. Bribery, direct and indirect, had in fact been so rife throughout the country in this election that the House of Commons it produced was nicknamed "the Bribery Parliament", and petitions were brought forward in many places besides Southampton. It is clear that both political parties in the town had been in the habit of using corrupt practices during the elections of the past ten or twelve years, though the Liberals claimed that they had only been driven to do so in self-defence; but in this instance it was the Conservatives who as the victors were vulnerable and were exposed. The election was quashed, though sufficient was also shown up about the Liberal practices for their candidates not to be declared elected, and in a fresh contest a new pair of Conservatives, Mildmay and Hope, were successful. Among the small fry of the party who were proved to have acted as bribing agents in the original election were the town crier and one of the town sergeants.

While tempers were stretched to the limit on both sides over this petition, the Rev. T. Adkins, the minister of the Above Bar Independent congregation, who was a prominent member of the Anti-Corn-Law League and had been chairman of a recent national conference of nonconformist ministers who advocated the repeal of the Corn Laws, arranged a regional anti-Corn-Law conference in Southampton. Its first meeting, in the Long Rooms, was broken up by a tumultuous mob which it seems clear was organized and encouraged (on the spot in at least one case) by leading Conservatives. When a deputation headed by Adkins asked the Mayor to provide police protection for a second meeting, Dickson refused, taking the ground that if disorder was feared the meeting ought not to be held. It did in fact take place, behind locked doors guarded by a force of bludgeonmen which the repealers in their turn had organized.

Further exacerbation was provided by the fact that the four contractors who had undertaken to sink a well on the Common from which the town's water-supply could be obtained were now finding the task beyond them. A dispute had broken out between them and the Waterworks Commissioners, which in the prevailing atmosphere of party hostility had inevitably become a political question, and it was in connection with this that Dickson had taken what was indeed the very dubious step of refusing a requisition to call a public meeting.

The Radical leaders must have realized that they had little or no hope of carrying their amendment, but were no doubt aiming at placing it on permanent record in the Council Minute Book.

Wednesday the 16th day of November 1842

SOUTHAMPTON DOCKS

At this Council the Town Clerk submitted a notice which had been transmitted to him by . . . the Court of Directors of the Southampton Dock Company, of an intended application to Parliament in the ensuing Session, for an act to alter, explain, amend, extend and enlarge the powers and provisions of the Company's Acts . . .

And the same having been . . . considered

It was . . . Resolved that a Committee be appointed to consider and watch the Bill . . . and to Report to the Council thereon. . . .

¶ The Company was seeking power to borrow an additional £50,000 to enable it to complete its tidal dock, which had nevertheless been officially opened on 29 August.

Thursday the 2nd day of February 1843

CANAL IN HOUNDWELL

At this Council Mr. Doswell reported that the filling up of the canal in Houndwell was now proceeding. . . .

CEMETERY

This Council having taken into their consideration the Necessity of appointing a Committee to devise the best means to be adopted for selecting and obtaining a spot of land suitable for the purposes of a cemetery . . . and also to determine on the most preferable mode of raising the funds required . . .

It was . . . Resolved that a Committee be appointed. . . .

Wednesday the 15th day of February 1843

CEMETERY

At this Council the Committee appointed at the last Meeting . . . reported that Mr. Parker the Assistant Poor Law Commissioner now a Resident in Southampton attended and informed your Committee that Sir James Graham the Secretary of State for the Home Department had applied to the Poor Law Commissioners for Evidence as to the Accommodation throughout England for the Burial of the Dead; that the Commissioners had already afforded to Sir James Graham much information on the subject.

Mr. Parker further stated that having visited the Church Yard of Saint Mary, he had found the same to be densely filled, and the soil of that Nature (in consequence of the great accumulation of animal matter therein) as to be productive of Dangers to the Health of those living in the Neighbourhood, and that the difficulty of finding space for the Burial of the Dead was daily increasing. Mr. Parker suggested to the Committee that a representation should be made to Sir James Graham of the total want of accommodation for the Burial of the Dead, and of the great Increase of Buildings and Population in the Borough, in order that the Evils might be remedied in the general measure which he thought would be introduced by Sir James Graham during the present Session of Parliament.

The Committee further reported that The Mayor also informed [it] that he had seen the Reverend Charles Parsons, the Curate of the Parish of Saint Mary, who informed him that he considered the Church Yard to be now completely filled, and that he did not think that burials could be continued there during the ensuing summer. . . . The Town Clerk informed Your Committee that he had communicated with his parliamentary agents as to the possibility of proceeding with a Bill during the present Session [and that they had replied suggesting a procedure by which this might be accomplished if no time were lost].

The foregoing . . . having been carefully considered, and Your Committee being unanimously of Opinion that the present accommodation afforded in Southampton for the Burial of the Dead was totally insufficient . . . and the state of the Church Yard of Saint Mary . . . a most serious Evil, and the frequent exposure and Disturbance of Corpses recently interred a most painful necessity and not only productive of danger to the health of those living in the Neighbourhood but lacerating to the feelings of Surviving Friends and Relatives and distressing to the Inhabitants in General, and being also of Opinion that the present Session of Parliament ought not to be permitted to pass without obtaining a remedy of these most serious Evils either by the general measure contemplated by Sir James Graham or by an Act of Parliament to be obtained for the purpose . . . recommended the Council . . . to direct the Town Clerk to take the necessary steps. . . .

And . . . It was . . . Resolved unanimously that the Report . . . be adopted.

At this Council the Town Clerk submitted a Petition to the . . . House of Commons praying leave to introduce a Bill for the establishment of a cemetery on part of Southampton Common

And . . . It is Resolved unanimously that the same be . . . adopted. . . .

Monday the 27th day of March 1843

CEMETERY

At this Council the Cemetery Committee reported that at a meeting . . . the Town Clerk reported that the Petition to the House of Commons had been duly presented to the House and had been referred to the Committee on Petitions who had reported that the Standing Orders had not been complied with. The Town Clerk also reported that the Petition had since been referred to the Committee on Standing Orders.

The Town Clerk laid before your Committee a Statement to be submitted to the Select Committee on Standing Orders with a view of having such Standing Orders suspended, and your Committee having considered the same [it] was approved . . . and the Town Clerk was instructed to take the necessary steps. . . .

COPY OF STATEMENT

On the part of the Promoters of the Bill

The Town of Southampton comprises the Parishes of . . .

All Saints which with a Population of 6891 according to the last census has a Burial ground of very limited extent (being only one rood and twenty two perches) and some catacombs under the Church

Holy Rhood [which] with a Population of 1989 has no Burial Ground nor any catacombs

Saint Michael's [which] with a Population of 2151 has no Burial Ground nor any catacombs

Saint Lawrence's [which] with a Population of 814 has no Burial Ground but has some catacombs

Saint John's which with a Population of 704 has a Burial Ground of very limited extent (being only 16 perches) but no catacombs.

In the Churches of Holy Rhood and Saint Michael there are some vaults but they are all occupied.

Saint Mary's has a Church Yard of 2 Acres 2 Roods and 9 Perches. The Population of Saint Mary's was 14,535 but the Church Yard of that Parish has, in consequence of the limited accommodation for Burials elsewhere, in effect been the Burial ground for the whole Town, the Population of which according to the last census was 27,084.

The Population of the Town was 7609 according to the census of 1801. Its increase has been very rapid of late Years, and it is estimated that in the two Years which have elapsed since the last census . . . upwards of Two thousand has been added to its numbers.

The completion of the Railway and the approach towards completion of the Docks are daily bringing new residents into Southampton and there is every probability that for some Years to come the increase of its Inhabitants will proceed in a still more rapid ratio than it has hitherto done. As some Evidence in support of this Proposition it may be stated that the Foundations of upwards of Two Hundred new Houses were laid in the Parish of Saint Mary alone in the course of the last Year.

The cost of Interments in the Catacombs within the Town is such as to confine their use almost exclusively to the Wealthy, while the Vaults are generally if not wholly appropriated. There is some slight accommodation for the Burial of Dissenters in addition to what has been mentioned but it is in the nature of private Property. . . .

Saint Mary's Church Yard is now crammed full. The accumulated human remains which have been deposited in it have raised it in every part several feet above the Pavement of the Church and the surface of the Surrounding Lands, with which it was formerly on a level. Its walls now encircle a mass of soil principally consisting of animal matter, in various stages of decomposition, extending over an area of more than two acres and a half and probably averaging fifteen feet in depth, and in consequence of the danger which is apprehended to the health of the town from the Poisonous Malaria arising from it the officiating Clergyman of the

Parish has stated that he does not think it safe that Burials should take place there during the ensuing Summer. . . .

These facts . . . can be proved to the Committee by the Clergymen and by some of the most eminent Medical Gentlemen of the Town; abundant additional Evidence if required can be brought to prove that the Church Yard, which is situated near a densely populated part of the Town, is an offensive and even dangerous nuisance. . . .

The Burials in that Church Yard were ascertained in 1841, on the average of that and the preceding two Years, to amount to no less than Five Hundred and Ninety five, and the number of Deaths in the Town must now be considerably greater than in either of those Years, owing to the increase of the Population; the average of the Burials there in Vaults and Brick Graves during the same Years was under thirty, and thefore it may be fairly assumed that nearly the whole of the Dead buried in that Church Yard were buried there, and not elsewhere, from sheer compulsion.

The rich resort to other places; but the great bulk of the Inhabitants cannot do so, owing to the heavy Expense of distant Funerals, which is always increased by the extra fees for burying non-parishioners. If some substitute for Saint Mary's Church Yard be not provided . . . the Burial of the Poor must, it is apprehended, be effected at the Expense of the Rate Payers, or by Subscription, or must take place as in times of plague.

In the Year 1837 the Town Council took the subject into consideration. It was found that the formation of distinct parochial Burial Grounds was impracticable; and endeavours were made to obtain a piece of ground suitable for a cemetery for the Town at large. Negotiations for this purpose were entered into, but they all failed, chiefly from the high price required for the ground, which was valuable for Building purposes. . . . The Town Council at length resolved to apply to Parliament for . . . an act similar to that for which they are now Petitioners.

All the notices required . . . were accordingly given, previously to the last Session, and the House of Commons granted leave for the Bill to be brought in. Shortly afterwards one of the Honorable Members for Lymington introduced a general measure for the establishment of cemeteries in Populous places, which was considered to afford the Town a prospect of having a cemetery established under its provisions and the Town Council therefore resolved not to press their application to Parliament.

That Bill however did not pass, and though now again introduced . . ., no certainty appears that it will be adopted, and . . . the Town being now on the verge of an absolute destitution of the means of burying their Dead, the Town Council have felt it to be their imperative duty to renew their application to Parliament. . . .

The Council feel that they have no alternative but to make every exertion in their power to obtain the sanction of Parliament at the earliest possible moment to their proposed Bill. . . .

It may be observed that the piece of Common land which the Council had originally selected for the cemetery was objected to by some as being too remote from the Town; they have chosen another piece of the same common, well adapted for the purpose, lying three Quarters of a Mile nearer to the Town. . . . They are prepared to substantiate all the allegations in this Statement by indisputable Evidence; and they trust that the extreme urgency of the case, and the Public Nature of the Interests involved, will afford sufficient grounds for such a suspension of the Standing Orders as may enable the Bill to pass into a Law in the present Session.

The Committee further reported that at a subsequent Meeting . . . the Mayor reported that . . . he had accompanied [a] Deputation with the Town Clerk to London, and that they had been examined before the Select Committee on Standing Orders in support of the allegations contained in the Statement, and that the Select Committee . . . considering the case to be one of absolute necessity had consented to suspend the Standing Orders. . . .

The Town Clerk reported to your Committee that he had . . . given the usual notices and he was directed to continue the same in order that the Council might be in a situation to proceed with the Bill during the present Session, which in accordance with the rules of the House had been read the first time. . . .

The Report of the Cemetery Committee having been . . . considered It was . . . Resolved unanimously that it be . . . adopted.

¶ It will be noticed that in its statement for the benefit of the Standing Orders Committee the Council was somewhat disingenuous in ascribing its abandonment of its previous application for leave to bring in a bill to the introduction of a more general measure instead of to the strong local opposition voiced in the vestry meetings. No doubt it feared that its case might be weakened if it revealed that even at that time there had been so much opposition to its proposals. The member for Lymington referred to was W. A. Mackinnon, who had brought in a private member's bill but had been so strongly discouraged by Sir James Graham the Home Secretary with the argument that the matter should be left to subsequent government legislation that he had dropped it.

Thursday the 13th day of April 1843

CEMETERY

At this Council the Town Clerk submitted certain resolutions which he had received from the Churchwardens of the Parish of Saint Mary . . . passed at a Vestry Meeting . . . relative to the Establishment of a Cemetery. . . .

At this Council the Committee appointed . . . to devise the best means . . . for selecting and obtaining a spot of land suitable for . . . a Cemetery and . . .

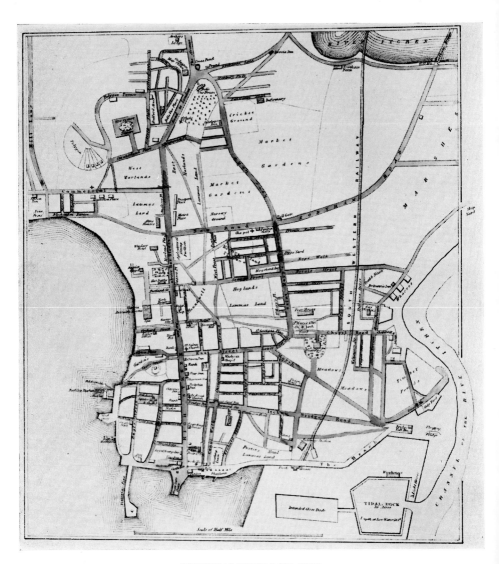

SOUTHAMPTON IN 1844
(Reproduced from *The Southampton Atlas* published by the Southampton Record Society, 1907.)

instructed to take such steps and give such Directions as they might deem necessary, with the view of obtaining an Act of Parliament for the Establishment of such Cemetery, and to consider the Print of the Bill for that purpose . . . submitted the following Report . . .

Your Committee . . . have taken a view of the site for the proposed Cemetery and also the site of the cemetery as proposed last year and . . . were unanimously of opinion that the site at the South West Corner of the Southampton Common is the most desirable and advantageous spot for the purpose. . . .

The Committee further reported that they conceived that the great saving of distance . . . was an important feature in the plan, relieving as it would do the humbler classes from much inconvenience and loss of time, as well as Expense, besides which the proposed site will have the advantage of an approach from Hill Lane thereby affording increased facilities for the conveyance of Corpses to the Cemetery by different routes. . . .

Your Committee were of opinion that a cemetery on the site in question might be so established as to be Ornamental to the Town as well as attractive to Visitors without interfering with the present Race Course, or destroying the beauty of the Common.

Your Committee at five protracted meetings have carefully and maturely considered the Draft of the Bill . . . and have made such alterations and addition thereto as seemed . . . most suitable and proper.

Your Committee, which consists of members of the Council who may be said to represent all the several religious sections in the Borough, after several days of anxious deliberations upon the details of the intended measure, are happy in being able to state that they have been with one or two exceptions . . . unanimous in their approval of the draft Bill which they now submit with confidence for the consideration and adoption of the Council. . . .

[The proposed bill was then considered clause by clause and certain clauses amended or struck out.]

Wednesday the 19th day of April 1843

[The consideration of the proposed Cemetery Bill clause by clause was resumed and completed.]

Thursday the 27th day of April 1843

CEMETERY

At this Council the Town Clerk submitted certain Proceedings passed at a Public Meeting of the Inhabitants . . . holden at the Guildhall on Tuesday the 25th. Instant relative to the intended Cemetery. . . .

¶ Although the Council, including the Radical members, were now unanimously in favour of the cemetery project, there was still opposition in the town and particularly in St. Mary's Ward, based as before on the remoteness of the site from the poorer districts and on doubts of the Council's wisdom in borrowing so relatively large a sum as would be needed. At the town meeting on 25 April the proposal was vehemently defended by Lankester and Cooper (who as a campaigner for the promotion of public health was particularly strong in its support) against attacks from some of their fellow-Radicals. Petitions, including one from the Board of Guardians, were sent to Parliament against the bill but met with no success.

Wednesday the 31st day of May 1843

[The Town Clerk reported that the Cemetery Bill had passed the House of Commons.]

Thursday the 6th day of July 1843

[The Town Clerk having reported that the Cemetery Bill had passed the House of Lords, a committee was appointed to carry it into effect.]

SOUTHAMPTON PORT

This Council having taken into their consideration the propriety of appointing a Committee to obtain Evidence and to take all such steps as may be considered necessary with the view of Southampton being rated a second class Port

It was . . . Resolved unanimously that a Committee . . . be appointed to prepare a Memorial to the . . . Treasury . . . and that for the furtherance of this object the Committee be empowered to confer and to act in conjunction with a committee of the Harbour Commissioners. . . .

SOUTH HANTS INFIRMARY

At this Council a communication was received from the Secretaries of the South Hants Infirmary requesting the attendance of the Corporation on the occasion of laying the Foundation Stone of . . . the Infirmary

And . . . It was . . . Resolved that the Mayor and Corporation do attend the Ceremony. . . .

Thursday the 3rd day of August 1843

[The Town Clerk reported several presentments by the Court Leet Jury of encroachments and nuisances, which were referred to the Lease Committee for enquiry and report.]

Wednesday the 16th day of August 1843

SOUTHAMPTON PORT

At this Council the Committee appointed . . . to prepare a Memorial to the . . . Treasury praying that Southampton may be placed on the footing of a second class Port . . . reported that the committee appointed by the Harbour Commissioners met your Committee . . . and that Mr. Firmin the receiver of the Harbour Dues attended and afforded the Committees much Information upon the subject . . . and the Committees . . . Resolved that the following Memorial . . . be presented to their Lordships. . . .

. . . The Memorial of the Mayor Aldermen and Burgesses of the Borough of Southampton
Sheweth

That since the opening of the London & South Western Railway in 1840 the Trade of the Port of Southampton has very greatly increased particularly in regard to Steam Vessels

That the number of arrivals weekly prior to the opening of the Railway did not exceed four whereas at the present time there is a daily Communication to and from Havre . . . as well as a daily communication to and from the Channel Islands and through them to and from the South of France, in addition to which the Government have selected the Port . . . for the dispatch and arrival of the Peninsular Oriental Mediterranean and West India Mails, which Steamers take their departure from and arrive at the Port regularly.

That such Steamers bring numerous Passengers with large Quantities of goods and merchandize, which are generally warehoused here and sent under bond to London.

That the late opening of the Southampton Docks will in the opinion of your memorialists greatly increase the number of Vessels frequenting the Port and that extensive Warehouses are in course of construction by the Dock Company . . .

That your memorialists humbly pray that Your Lordships will be pleased to take the circumstances into consideration and in consequence of the increased and increasing Importance of Southampton, it may be placed on the footing of a second class Port. . . .

And your memorialists will ever pray, etc. . . .

At this Council a communication . . . was received from Her Majesty's Treasury that the Board of Customs were then engaged in the revision of the Customs Establishment with the view to submit an Augmentation thereof but that the Classification of the outports was purely a matter of official Regulation and that the advancement of Southampton to the second class would in no way whatever confer any public facility or accommodation.

[It was reported that the Royal Agricultural Society had accepted the Council's invitation to hold their annual meeting at Southampton in 1844.]

TOWN IMPROVEMENTS

At this Council It was . . . Resolved that . . . it is highly expedient to take into consideration the propriety of appropriating a belt or proportion of the outskirts of the Southampton Common and the unoccupied part of the Southampton Marsh for the purpose of Buildings with the view as well to an Increase of the Income of the Borough as also to increased accommodation to the Public for recreation on other lands, over which common rights are exercised within the Borough . . . and

That a Committee be appointed to take into their consideration the subject of the foregoing Resolution. . . .

Thursday the 7th day of September 1843

RESERVOIR ON THE COMMON

At this Council an application was received from the Commissioners of the Southampton Water Works requesting the consent of the Council to the construction of an additional Reservoir on the Southampton Common. . . .

And the same having been . . . considered

It was moved . . . that this Council do give consent. . . .

Upon which it was moved as an Amendment . . . that a Committee be appointed to confer with the Commissioners . . . and report upon the application

Which being put to the vote was carried in the affirmative.

Thursday the 14th day of September 1843

RESERVOIR ON THE COMMON

At this Council the Committee appointed at the last Meeting . . . reported—

Your Committee, being anxious to obtain all possible Information on the important subject referred to them, have caused various Questions relative to the existing Works on the Common to be put to Mr. Doswell the Engineer . . . [and]

On a careful consideration of the Information which [they have] been able to collect, they [are] of opinion that a sufficient case [has] not been made out for proceeding immediately with the construction of the Reservoir, and they would recommend that another Season be allowed to pass before a decision shall be come to on the subject. . . .

It was . . . Resolved that the Report of the Committee be . . . adopted.

¶ The Commissioners had, however, recently constructed works at Northam from which a supply of water was obtained to augment that available from the unsatisfactory enterprise on the Common.

Monday the 30th day of October 1843

TOWN IMPROVEMENTS

At this Council the Committee appointed by the Borough Council to consider the propriety of appropriating a belt or portion of the Southampton Common and the unoccupied part of the Southampton Marsh for ... Building ... reported that having first taken into their consideration ... the enclosure of the Marsh they were of opinion that the Marsh in its present state comprising about Sixteen Acres was of very little advantage to the Commoners and that there was reason to believe that by its appropriation to Building Purposes a very considerable sum of money might be raised which would be applicable for the benefit of all Parties interested therein, and recommended that the Council should make an application to Parliament at the ensuing Session for an act to enable them to appropriate the Marsh and apply such sum accordingly.

Your Committee having proceeded to the consideration of the Question as to the application of the money to be derived from the enclosure of the Marsh were unanimous in their opinion that the money to be raised thereby be applied for the purposes of making ... the necessary Roads in and upon the said Marsh lands and of draining and filling up the canal in Houndwell and that powers should be obtained for purchasing for the benefit of the Commoners the Interests of the Owners of the Soil in the Porters Meadow East Marlands West Marlands Houndwell and Hoglands and making the same Common during the whole Year instead of Six Months as at present. . . .

Your Committee also recommended that any Roads when made should be placed under the control and power of the Commissioners of Pavement. . . .

In making the recommendation to the Council as to the appropriation of the money to be raised by the disposal of the Marsh lands which are now totally unproductive and unattractive either to the Inhabitants or Visitors Your Committee felt that ... they were acting in strict conformity with the Spirit and intentions of the Municipal Act by giving to the Commoners an equivalent for those rights of which they are already and will hereafter be deprived, and by rendering the other Common lands more useful to the Commoners, more suitable for recreation, and more ornamental and attractive. . . .

Your Committee having directed their best attention to the Question referred to them as to the propriety of appropriating a belt of the Common for Building purposes were of Opinion that it is expedient that a belt or portion of the outskirts ... should be appropriated for Building purposes with a view to the future preservation of the Pasturage of the Common, the drainage and embellishment of the same and a diminution of the Borough Rate by the receipt of a large annual amount in the shape of Ground rents.

Your Committee not being unanimous as to this last recommendation and feeling that much difference of opinion exists, as well in the Council as out of it, did not recommend that the proposed Bill should embrace the project for appropriating a belt of the Common for Building purposes without the approbation of the Rate Payers of the Town in Vestry assembled. . . .

It was moved by Captain Ward and seconded by Mr. Joseph Lankester that the Report of the Committee be . . . adopted so far as relates to the Marsh and that Instructions be given to the Town Clerk to take the necessary steps for procuring an Act of Parliament for the Enclosure of the remaining portion of the Marsh not at present occupied by the Railway Company or the Itchen Bridge Company

Upon which it was moved as an amendment . . .

That the proposed Bill . . . be abandoned

Which being put to the vote was . . . negatived.

The Original Motion was then . . . carried in the affirmative.

It was then . . . Resolved that the Committee be requested to continue their services and to consider the Details of the Bill and to report further . . . thereon.

[The remainder of the Committee's report, recommending the appropriation of a belt of the Common for building purposes, was not adopted.]

Wednesday the 1st day of November 1843

[The municipal elections made no change in the relation of parties on the Council.]

Thursday the 9th day of November 1843

[Colonel George Henderson was elected Mayor (perhaps with the imminence of further railway development in mind), Richard Coles Sheriff (the proposal of Daniel Brooks by Dr. Cooper and Richard Andrews being defeated), Joseph Ball Senior Bailiff (the proposal of J. W. Beavis by Andrews and I. Baker being defeated) and John Aslatt (unopposed) Junior Bailiff.]

TOWN IMPROVEMENTS. THE MARSH

At this Council certain Resolutions were received and read from the Churchwardens of Holy Rhood . . ., relative to the Enclosure of the Marsh, as having been passed at a Vestry Meeting held this day in that Parish. . . .

¶ There was considerable opposition to the enclosure of the Marsh, especially that part of it used as a cricket field, on the ground that the common lands were "the lungs of the town" and must be kept for recreation. The rising hostility throughout the country to enclosure in general seems to have been an element in this opposition, which was again strongest in St. Mary's.

Thursday the 16th day of November 1843

TOWN IMPROVEMENTS. THE MARSH

At this Council the Town Clerk submitted certain Resolutions . . . passed at Vestry Meetings held in the several Parishes of Saint Mary, Holy Rhood and Saint Lawrence . . ., relative to the intended Application to Parliament to improve the Marsh and for other purposes.

It was moved by Captain Breton and seconded by Mr. Francis Cooper that no further proceedings be taken for an act for the Enclosure of the Marsh in the ensuing Session of Parliament

Upon which it was moved by Mr. J. R. Stebbing and seconded by Mr. Joseph Lankester that . . . the Council now resolves to proceed . . . but that in deference to the opinions of the Rate Payers expressed in Vestry assembled the Town Clerk is hereby instructed to take the necessary steps to set apart for the recreation of the Inhabitants that portion of the Marsh . . . now called the Cricket Ground and that such land hereafter shall not be alienated from such purpose but with the consent of the Rate Payers in Vestry assembled

Which . . . was carried in the affirmative. . . .

PAVEMENT IMPROVEMENTS

At this Council the Town Clerk submitted a Notice which he had received from Mr. Henry Page, Clerk to the Commissioners of Pavement, of the intention of the Commissioners to apply in the Ensuing Session of Parliament for an act to alter and amend their present Act, and to effect other Improvements in the Town, and which was accompanied by a Schedule of the several Properties belonging to the Corporation proposed to be affected by the Improvement Act

And the same having been . . . considered

It was . . . Resolved that a Committee be appointed to consider the Application of the Commissioners . . . and to report . . . thereon. . . .

¶ The Pavement Commissioners, declaring that the town's growth rendered some new local enactments absolutely essential, had decided, at exactly the same time as the Borough Council resolved on the enclosure of the Marsh, to bring forward an improvements bill which was very like the one which they had been forced to drop in 1839, but without the tax on coal and of course the cemetery which was now otherwise provided for. They proposed to include all the town and what were now the suburbs of Portswood and Highfield within the jurisdiction of the Board, which was to be placed on a somewhat more democratic basis, in that besides the members of the Borough Council *ex officio* there were to be an increased number of elected commissioners chosen by the ratepayers. The sewerage and streets of the whole urban area would thus be brought under the Board's control, involving the purchase of all private sewers and pavements; and it was proposed to widen or build various roads (see 1 February 1844). For these purposes powers of compulsory purchase and of borrowing £25,000 would be included in the bill.

Thursday the 1st day of February 1844

TOWN IMPROVEMENTS. THE MARSH

At this Council a Deputation from a Meeting of the Inhabitants of the Parish of Saint Mary . . . attended on the subject of the Improvement of the Marsh and stated to the Council their objections to the same and read a Petition which they proposed to present to Parliament relative thereto.

At this Council the Committee appointed on the 16th . . . of August last on the subject of improving the Marsh . . . reported that . . . the Town Clerk [had] submitted the Draft of the proposed Bill and Your Committee [had] proceeded to examine and consider the several clauses and made such alterations and additions thereto as appeared . . . necessary, and [had] directed the Town Clerk to get the same printed and circulated for the use of the Town Council.

The Committee further reported that they had instructed the Town Clerk to prepare the necessary Petition to the House of Commons. . . .

It was Resolved that the Report of the Committee be received.

PAVEMENT IMPROVEMENTS

At this Council the Committee appointed at the last Meeting . . . to consider the Application of the Commissioners of Pavement reported that in taking into their consideration the subject referred to them . . . [they had been] of opinion that previous to any Determination being come to the following Information should be obtained from the Pavement Commissioners

What portion of the Original Plan has been since abandoned?

What Improvements it is proposed to carry into effect?

What amount it is proposed to borrow?

The Estimated Costs of the several Undertakings.

The Estimated Return for the outlay.

And they [had] directed the Town Clerk to obtain the foregoing Information from the Clerk to the . . . Commissioners and to submit the same to . . . the Committee.

The Committee further reported that at a subsequent Meeting . . . the Town Clerk had reported the reply of . . . the Clerk to the Commissioners . . . [which was to the effect that the principal alterations and improvements proposed were]

. . . To widen Bridge Street

To form a Street from St. Michael's Square through Blue Anchor Lane to West Place, and to construct a raised or Terrace Road from the Long Rooms along the shore to Four Posts.

To widen Hanover Buildings . . . and form a Road across Houndwell and Hoglands through York Street to Marsh Lane.

To widen Marsh Lane as far as the Marsh.

To form a Road from Paradise Row to the South West Corner of Kingsland Place, and from thence by the West Front and Portland Place to the Northam Road; and from thence through the East Magdalens by Brunswick Terrace and Place into the London Road.

To form a Road from Love Lane across the waste to Rockstone Place . . .

To widen Pound Tree Lane and form a Road thence across Houndwell, along South Front Kingsland Place to Saint Mary's Street.

To form a Road from the South Front by Saint Mary's Place to York Street . . .

To place all the Highways and Sewers under the management of the Commissioners.

To empower the Commissioners to regulate the Flys and Hackney Carriages.

To extend the limits of the Paving and Lighting Acts to all parts of the Town except Portswood and the Common.

[The Clerk to the Commissioners also explained that the maximum which they proposed to borrow was £25,000, including their present debt of £2000; that they proposed to levy a rate not exceeding sixpence in the pound for paving, to extend the properties rated to the paving rate, and to impose a rate not exceeding one shilling in the pound on the whole town, except Portswood and the Common, for lighting, sewerage, repairing, highways and improvements; that they intended to take as long a time as Parliament would sanction for the accomplishment of these improvements; and that no estimate of the expense of the several undertakings or of the return for the outlay had yet been made, though the Commissioners had passed a resolution that no improvement should be carried into effect unless a plan and estimate had first been obtained and the necessary funds provided. He concluded by stating that a plan of the proposed improvements had been prepared by Mr. Doswell and that he was prepared to attend the Committee with it and give any further explanation that might be required.]

The Town Clerk having read the notice from the Commissioners of Pavement, with the List of the Properties belonging to the Corporation, proposed to be Scheduled and taken by the contemplated Improvements And the Committee having considered the same together with the foregoing Correspondence And Your Committee, having no probable Estimates of the outlay required for effecting the several Improvements and Alterations, or the return to be derived from the outlay for the same, . . . recommended that in the absence of the requisite Information the Council should Dissent to the Proposed Undertaking; at the same time Your

Committee approved of several of the proposed Improvements. . . .

The Committee further reported that they called the attention of the Council to some of the most Important of the intended Improvements—

The widening of Butcher Row on the Northern side as far as Simnel Street

> Your Committee having inspected the Plans of Mr. Doswell of this proposed improvement, were of opinion that it would entail a very heavy expense to the town and that little or no return would be derived therefrom

To form a street from Saint Michael's Square through Blue Anchor Lane to West Place, and to construct a raised or Terrace Road from the Long Rooms along the shore to Four Posts.

> Your Committee were of opinion that this . . . would involve . . . a considerable outlay and was quite uncalled for in the present state of the Borough taxation. . . .

> With respect to the several proposed Roads across the Common Lands, Your Committee observed that these . . . would very materially interfere with the Plans of the Corporation under the proposed Act to improve the Marsh, and . . . recommended that no Roads should be made across the common lands by the Commissioners . . . without their consent, or that they should be made by the Corporation and afterwards vested in the said Commissioners.

To form a Road from Paradise Row to the South West Corner of Kingsland Place and from thence . . . to the Northam Road, and from thence . . . into the London Road.

> Your Committee submitted that . . . this Road would also very much interfere with the objects of the Corporation in laying out the Lammas Lands for the Public Benefit, and also that the proposed Road from Pound Tree Lane across Houndwell and along South Front . . . will afford all the accommodation which appeared desirable.

To form a Road from Love Lane across the waste to Rockstone Place.

> To this . . . Your Committee saw no objection.

To place all the Highways and Sewers under the management of the Commissioners

> Your Committee approved of this Plan, the sum at present applicable for the repairs of the Highways within the Borough being totally inadequate. . . .

To extend the limits of the present Pavement Acts.

> As to the propriety of this measure the Committee was not prepared at the present time to offer an opinion. . . .

Power to borrow money and to levy rates.

> Upon this subject in the absence of all Estimates and Evidence relative

thereto Your Committee were entirely unable to form any opinion. . . .

Under all the circumstances . . . Your Committee recommend, as before stated, that the Council should Dissent to the proposed Application . . . and that a Committee should be appointed to confer with the . . . Commissioners on the proposed Improvements and to watch the Bill in its progress through Parliament and to take all such other steps as may be necessary. . . .

The Report of the Committee having been . . . considered

It was Moved . . . that the Report be . . . adopted, so far as regards the Dissent of this Corporation to this intended act as now constituted.

Which . . . was carried in the affirmative.

[The Cemetery Committee reported that they had plans drawn up and had invited tenders for the drainage of the land and the erection of the walls, and had accepted a tender, on the basis of which a contract had been drawn up. Tenders for making the main roads and cross walks had also been invited, and it was desirable that plans should be forthwith obtained for erecting the Chapel and Lodge and tenders for these likewise invited. This report was adopted.]

¶ The exclusion of Portswood and the Common from the proposed improvements bill was in response to a memorial which the Pavement Board had now received from a large number of residents in Portswood, declaring that since theirs was (they claimed) a rural and not an urban district they did not wish it to be included and burdened with the resultant rates.

Thursday the 15th day of February 1844

[The Marsh Improvement Committee reported that the Town Clerk had submitted to them a draft of the proposed Marsh Improvement Bill and they had considered its clauses, most of which they approved while in some others they recommended amendments. They also recommended that £10,000 should be the sum which the Council should seek power to borrow for the purposes of the Marsh enclosure project, and that a clause should be inserted in the proposed bill to prevent the Pavement Commissioners from making roads across the common lands without the Corporation's consent. The Council then in turn considered the draft of the bill as amended by the Committee, altering to £15,000 the sum which power was to be sought to borrow; after which the Committee were authorized to proceed with the task of piloting the bill through Parliament]

Monday the 19th day of February 1844

BRANCH RAILWAY FROM BASINGSTOKE TO NEWBURY

This Council having taken into their consideration the propriety of presenting Petitions to both Houses of Parliament in favor of the proposed Basingstoke and Newbury Branch Railway Line

It was Resolved unanimously that the following Petition be presented . . .

"Your Petitioners have heard with gratification that a Bill has been introduced into Your Honorable House for making a Railway from the London and South Western Railway at Basingstoke to the Town of Newbury

"Your Petitioners cannot fail to regard this further facility of Inland Communication from Southampton as a matter of great Interest and advantage not only to the Districts which will thus be brought into close connection with a Port possessing every natural and artificial accommodation, but also to Your Petitioners and the Trading Interests of Southampton in respect of the new market which will thus be opened to their enterprise.

"Your Petitioners confidently believe that a considerable traffic both of Passengers and goods between Southampton and Newbury and the parts beyond it will immediately result from the construction of the said Railway, and that Newbury and its Neighbourhood will be largely supplied with Seaborne Coals and all imported produce from Southampton at much cheaper rates than the same articles are or can be now obtained there from other quarters. And Your Petitioners are also assured that the produce of the Districts with which this line will connect Southampton will be exported from Southampton more readily and expeditiously than it has been or can be from any other Port.

"The prospective advantages which must result should the said Railway be continued northwards from Newbury to Swindon are of a yet more important character and as Your Petitioners believe of great national concern

"Your Petitioners therefore humbly Pray Your Honorable House that the said Bill may pass into a Law"

Resolved unanimously that a similar Petition be presented to the House of Lords.

LAZARETTO

This Council having taken into their consideration the propriety of memorializing the . . . Treasury praying for the Establishment of a Lazaretto in or near Southampton Water

It was Resolved unanimously that the following memorial be presented . . .

". . . The Port of Southampton has become a Place of increasing and great importance in reference to Foreign and general Shipping Trade, and of late with the Levant, to which in addition to Sailing Vessels a Steam communication has been opened by the Peninsular and Oriental Steam Navigation Company.

"The great facilities which have been secured to Shippers, Merchants and Owners frequenting this Port, both in reduction of Dues and

Improvements of the Harbour, as well as by the opening of the Great Tidal Basin of the Southampton Docks, the established Railway Communication now likely to be much extended . . . all tend to attract Shipping to Southampton and make any interruption to its Trade a very serious injury.

"Your Lordships' Memorialists have found that Vessels leaving this Port are unable to return to it with cargoes from the Levant, but are compelled at great risk and Expense to proceed to Standgate Creek [on the Kentish shore of the Thames estuary] in consequence of there being no Lazaretto within the Port of Southampton or near to it, and that in consequence thereof this Trade, instead of being extended, as it would doubtless be, will shortly be wholly lost, to the great injury of Merchants and Shippers and serious Damage to the Inhabitants of Southampton.

"Your Lordships' Memorialists therefore most earnestly Pray that Your Right Honorable Board will . . . be pleased to order the Establishment of a Lazaretto within the Port of Southampton. . . ."

BRITISH ASSOCIATION FOR THE ADVANCEMENT OF SCIENCE

This Council having taken into consideration the propriety of inviting the British Association . . . to hold their Annual Meeting in this Town in the Year 1845

It was Resolved unanimously that the Town Clerk be directed to communicate with the Association and to invite them to hold their Annual Meeting next Year in this Town.

COMMUTATION OF THE PORT AND HARBOUR DUES

At this Council Application was made by the Commissioners of the Southampton Port and Harbour, requesting the consent of the Corporation to a general power to enable the Commissioners to make such reductions and alterations in the mode of collecting the Harbour Dues as they may deem advisable for three Years from the first day of January last

And the same having been . . . considered

It is Resolved that the consent of the Corporation be given. . . .

PAVEMENT IMPROVEMENTS

This Council having taken into their consideration the propriety of appointing a Committee to consider the clauses of the Pavement Improvement Bill, and to confer with the Commissioners of Pavement relative to those clauses which affect the Interests of the Town Council and . . . of the Town

It was . . . Resolved that a Committee be appointed. . . .

¶ Behind the idea that a branch of the London & South-Western Railway from Basingstoke to Newbury would promote a considerable traffic between this area and Southampton there was also the larger hope of opening up an alternative route to the north that would not go through London, by subsequently extending the Basingstoke–Newbury line to Swindon (as the petition envisaged) and linking it there with a chain of lines already built or building which would give a through route *via* Gloucester, Birmingham, Derby and York. Communication between Southampton and the west and Wales would likewise be improved. Owing to successful opposition by the South-Western's rival the Great Western, however, the line was not built.

A lazaretto was a building or ship set apart for quarantine purposes. In response to the Council's memorial, an old 74-gun ship of the line was stationed at the Motherbank (the roadstead between Spithead and Cowes) for this purpose.

Thursday the 16th day of March, 1844

TOWN IMPROVEMENTS. THE MARSH

At this Council the Town Clerk submitted certain proceedings of a Vestry Meeting held . . . in All Saints parish . . . relative to the Marsh Improvement Bill.

LONDON AND SOUTH-WESTERN RAILWAY

At this Council Mr. Joseph Lankester presented a memorial from certain Merchants and shipowners residing in Southampton, and others, complaining of various grievances suffered by them under the regulations of the London & South Western Railway Company and alleging that the revenues of the Port and the income of the Corporation were greatly injured thereby, and praying the Town Council to propose such alterations in the Bill now before the House for enlarging the powers of the . . . Company, for the protection of their own privileges and maintenance of their own revenue. . . .

And this Council having heard the statements of Mr. Chaplin the Chairman of the Railway Directors and . . . the Solicitor to the Company relative thereto and also the statement of . . . the Solicitor on behalf of the Memorialists

It was . . . Resolved that the Memorial . . . be referred to a Committee in order that they may enquire into and report . . . upon the allegations contained therein, and also upon such other matters connected therewith as may affect the Interests of the Borough [and]

That the Committee be empowered to hold such correspondence and conference with the Directors . . . as they may consider expedient.

¶ The All Saints vestry meeting had resolved to oppose even the amended Marsh scheme. The parish was also the only one which opposed the Pavement Commissioners' improvement bill, the argument used in both cases being that it paid, or claimed to pay, more than half the rates of the town without getting any corresponding benefits in return, and would pay still higher rates and get no more if the two bills passed.

Between the town and the Railway Company relations were now deteriorating. Complaints were being raised that it was abusing the monopoly which it possessed by charging excessive goods rates, especially for the transport of coal. In this Council meeting its Chairman sought to justify these charges, but some concessions were afterwards made, which nevertheless did not prevent the Council and the commercial interests of the town from supporting various projects for a competing line or lines to Southampton in the railway boom that was now beginning (see 30 October 1844 and 30 July and 24 September 1845).

Monday the 25th day of March 1844

TOWN IMPROVEMENTS. THE MARSH

At this Council the Town Clerk submitted certain Resolutions passed at the Saint Michael's Vestry in favor of the Application to Parliament to improve the Marsh. . . .

[The Council confirmed the Cemetery Committee's decision to accept Mr. W. H. Rogers's design with such alterations and improvements as might seem necessary to it or to the Bishop of Winchester.]

Monday the 29th day of April 1844

PAVEMENT IMPROVEMENTS

At this Council the Committee appointed . . . to consider the clauses in the Pavement Improvements Bill and to confer with the Commissioners of Pavement relative to those clauses . . . reported that they had carefully . . . considered the several clauses . . . and that they had made such alterations and additions to the Bill and observations thereon as appeared . . . necessary and they submitted to the Council such Bill for their consideration and approval.

The Committee also reported that they had held a conference with a Committee appointed by the Commissioners . . . when the views of Your Committee as to various clauses in the Bill were considered and the Committee have much satisfaction in stating that the Commissioners . . . readily entertained the same and at once made many alterations in accordance with the opinion of the Committee whilst other objections remained over for their further deliberation and Determination the result of which the Commissioners undertook to communicate . . . with as little delay as possible. . . .

The Committee further reported that . . . the Commissioners . . . had [now] undertaken to prepare some additional clauses . . . by which the objections to the Bill as it now stood . . . would be removed.

The Committee also further reported that the Commissioners . . . had expressed their readiness that no Roads should be made across the Lammas Lands without the previous consent of the Corporation. . . .

The Committee further reported that they were of opinion that the Town Clerk should be instructed under the Directions of the Committee to watch the Bill through both Houses of Parliament in order that the several alterations and additions made thereto . . . might be fully carried into effect and to take all such other steps as may be thought necessary. . . .

And the Council having taken into their consideration the several clauses contained in the Bill and having made many alterations and additions thereto and having considered the Report of the Committee

It was moved . . . that the Report . . . be received and adopted. . . .

Upon which it was moved as an amendment . . . that the Improvement Bill . . . be no further proceeded with as it will entail too great an expense on the Town as the Commissioners . . . will not pledge themselves to Sewer the Town first, before other alterations are made, but are desirous of Enlarging Streets and Purchasing Property as their early Improvement for which the Town is likely to be rated

Which being put to the vote was negatived

And upon the Original Motion being put . . . there was not a sufficient number present to constitute a Council.

¶ When the Improvement Bill reached the committee stage in the Commons the Commissioners endeavoured to meet the objection voiced in the above amendment by agreeing to postpone all improvements of streets until they had laid out in sewerage and drainage £10,000 of the £20,000 which the Bill would empower them to borrow.

Thursday the 2nd day of May 1844

PAVEMENT IMPROVEMENTS

At this Council it was Resolved unanimously that the Report of the Committee submitted at the last Meeting . . . be received and adopted . . . [and]

That the Committee . . . be reappointed, and that they be requested and authorized to take such proceedings with a view to the alterations and amendments of the Bill as stated in their Report to the Council, subject to such Limitations as were proposed at the last and adopted at this Council Meeting.

TURNPIKE ROADS

At this Council the Town Clerk reported that he had received a communication from Mr. Moody the Clerk to the Trustees of the Turnpike informing him that Lord Shaftesbury had insisted on the insertion in the Pending Southampton Improvement Bill of the usual clause restraining the Trustees of the Turnpike from repairing or taking Toll on the portion of Turnpike within the limits of the proposed Bill, and that he was about to communicate the subject to the Trustees and requesting him to communicate it to the Council as it would be desirable to make an united effort to induce his Lordship to alter his Determination.

And the same having been read and considered

It is Resolved unanimously That the consideration of the same be referred to the Pavement Bill Committee and that they be authorized to take all such Proceedings to prevent the operation of the Clause or to obtain a Modification thereof as they may consider necessary.

¶ The Lord Shaftesbury referred to was not the great humanitarian but his father, to whose earldom he did not succeed until 1851.

A Turnpike Trusts Amendment Bill of 1843 had restricted trusts from laying out money on any roads lying within the limits of any local improvement act. Lord Shaftesbury's insistence on the application of this to the proposed Southampton bill would mean that the Southampton–Winchester Trust would lose much of the control which it had previously possessed over several of the main thoroughfares of the town; namely, the road from Bargate to the point in the Avenue where All Saints parish ended, that from the toll-gate on the corner of the present Commercial and London Roads to Four Posts Bridge, and that from St. Mary's Church to the corner of Cumberland Street and St. Mary's Street. The resultant loss of revenue would, it claimed, be more than double the saving in costs of maintenance.

Thursday the 13th day of June 1844

ROYAL AGRICULTURAL SOCIETY

At this Council the Mayor reported that the Magistrates of the Borough were of opinion that it was necessary that an Additional Number of Police should be appointed on the occasion of the visit of the Royal Agricultural Society to this Town and that they were also of opinion that Fifty Men from the county Constabulary should be engaged for the purpose. . . .

And the same having been . . . considered

It is Resolved unanimously that the matter be referred to the Watch Committee, and that the Committee be authorized to advance such amount as they may deem necessary for the payment of any additional Police that may be required. . . .

REPAIRING DOCKS AT THIS PORT

At this Council a report of the Committee appointed by the Commissioners of the Port and Harbour was submitted, on the subject of the construction of repairing Docks at this Port.

And the same having been . . . considered and this Council feeling the necessity existing for the immediate construction of a repairing Dock for the accommodation of the Trade of this Port

It is Resolved unanimously That the subject be referred to the consideration of the Lease Committee. . . .

¶ The Harbour Commissioners then approached the Dock Company, which replied that it was proposing to build a graving dock. In the bill which it then prepared to introduce into Parliament in order to secure the necessary powers, however, it inserted clauses which provoked much alarm and opposition. One of these would have empowered it to rent or buy, and the Commissioners to lease or sell, the Pier and quays at some future date; which aroused fears that it was aiming to monopolize the whole trade of the port in the same way as the London and South-Western monopolized its railway communications. Another provided for the repeal of those clauses of the Pier Act of 1831 which obliged vessels, under penalty, to call at the Pier to land passengers and goods. In return the Company offered to guarantee the Commissioners a revenue equal to their average annual receipts for the three years before the opening of the docks, by making good if necessary the amount by which their actual revenue might fall short of this figure. The Borough Council nevertheless feared that it might suffer a loss of income by the further falling-off (see Appendix A) of its fifth of the (actual) port dues collected.

Thursday the 1st day of August 1844

TOWN IMPROVEMENTS. THE MARSH

At this Council the Marsh Improvement Committee reported that the Owners of the Lammas Lands had submitted certain Proposals for their Interests therein which the Committee having considered declined to accede to [and] that a Proviso had been inserted in the Act that the Corporation should not interfere with any part of the Lands and Premises of the Southampton Dock Company without their consent.

The Committee further reported . . . the result of the Compromise made with the several Opponents to the Bill . . . the Owners of the Lammas Lands having agreed to the Terms proposed by the Committee conditionally that One Hundred Pounds was paid on account of the Expenses of the Opposition, which they thought it advisable to accede to. . . .

The Report of the Committee having been . . . considered

It was moved . . . that it be received . . .

Which . . . was carried in the affirmative. . . .

CORPORATION EXPENDITURE

At this Council a letter was received . . . forwarding a copy of a resolution passed by the Guardians of the Poor . . . that it was their Opinion that the Expenditure of the Corporation appeared very extravagant. . . .

TURNPIKE ROADS

At this Council the Pavement Bill Committee reported that in accordance with the resolution passed . . . on the 2nd day of May last authorizing them to take all such proceedings to prevent the operation of the Turnpike Clause in the Pavement Improvement Bill or to obtain a Modification thereof as they considered necessary they had instructed the Town Clerk to confer with Mr. Moody the Clerk to the Trustees of the Turnpike thereon and also to prepare the necessary Petition to Parliament and to take all such steps as he considered necessary with the view of procuring the clause to be struck out of the Bill in the Committee of the House of Lords and that a Petition had been accordingly presented against the clause.

The Town Clerk reported that Mr. Cockburn was retained to oppose the Clause in Question on behalf of the Corporation, the Inhabitants, and the Trustees of the Turnpike Roads, and the Evidence of Mr. McAdam was given before the House of Lords Committee showing the injurious effects of the clause, but the Committee resolved that the clause should form part of the Bill. . . .

¶ The "Mr. McAdam" referred to was William, a grandson of the great road engineer John Loudon McAdam. He acted as permanent engineer to a number of turnpike trusts, one of which was the Southampton–Winchester.

Wednesday the 30th day of October 1844

ROYAL AGRICULTURAL SOCIETY

At this Council a communication was submitted from James Hudson Esquire Secretary to the Royal Agricultural Society addressed to the Mayor informing him that at a meeting of the Society held in Southampton it was Resolved that the best thanks of the Society should be given to himself and the Corporation for the readiness with which he had on every occasion met the wishes of the Society and the efficient and successful manner in which he had done all in his power to promote its objects during the preparation and continuance of their late gratifying meeting. . . .

BRITISH ASSOCIATION FOR THE ADVANCEMENT OF SCIENCE

At this Council the Town Clerk reported that in answer to the invitation presented to the British Association . . . to hold their annual meeting in this Town next year, he had received a communication from the Society [sic] informing him that they had appointed its meeting for 1845 to be held in Cambridge. . . .

GRAVING DOCKS

At this Council a communication was received from the Clerk to the Commissioners of the Port and Harbour forwarding a copy of the second report of the Committee appointed by the Commissioners upon the subject of constructing Graving Docks, and submitting for the Information of the Council that conferences having taken place between the Committee and a Deputation from the Dock Company the Dock Company had undertaken to construct the proposed Docks, but as an application to Parliament was necessary for that purpose they contemplated an amended Dock Act, wherein they proposed in addition to taking Powers for the construction of Graving Docks to insert a clause among others to exempt Vessels frequenting the Docks wholly or in part from the Tonnage Rates now payable to the Commissioners, and that as the Council of the Borough had a considerable

Interest in the Port Revenues the Commissioners thought it right to take their Opinion upon the subject previous to deciding what Course to adopt.

And this Council having taken the same into their consideration

It was . . . Resolved unanimously that having considered the communication of the Commissioners . . . and being impressed with the Statement of its Committee [it] feels called upon to object to the reduction of the Tonnage Rates as proposed by the Southampton Dock Company . . . in the proposed amended Dock Bill, more especially as this Council is convinced that a considerable outlay will be required from time to time on the part of the Commissioners to dredge the channel from the injurious effects presumed to be produced therein by the construction of recent works in and upon the River and the great Disturbance of Mud by the Dock Company and other Proprietors of Water side Property. This Council is however prepared to entertain and give its consent to any well digested Plan to be proposed by the Commissioners . . . for the reduction of Tonnage on Vessels generally or a commutation of Tonnage on Vessels to the Docks as soon as they are satisfied that their probable permanent income will admit of so doing, and that such a course will increase the general Shipping Trade of the Port, and which the Commissioners have power [to do] without any further Legislative Enactment.

This Council will in other respects give the most cordial support to the Southampton Dock Company in seeking a Bill for the construction of Graving Docks and that a Committee be appointed to watch the said Bill. . . .

SOUTHAMPTON AND DORSETSHIRE RAILWAY

This Council having taken into their consideration the propriety of appointing a Committee for watching the Southampton and Dorsetshire Railway Bill and also with the view of obtaining the proposed Terminus at the lower part of the Town and with Instructions to report to the Council the propriety of opposing any Plan for carrying the Terminus to a Distant Situation from Southampton

It was . . . Resolved unanimously that a Committee be appointed to watch the Southampton and Dorsetshire Railway Bill. . . .

[The Cemetery Committee reported that the contract for building the two chapels and entrance lodge of the Cemetery had been concluded.]

¶ By now the leading elements which hoped to break the South-Western's monopoly by attracting a rival line to Southampton were those (already referred to in the note to the entry for 18 February 1842) whose commercial interests were centred in the "bottom of the town", the old town quays and the Pier. If a new line could be induced to enter Southampton by the Western Shore and make its terminus near the quays and Pier, they hoped for a revival of the commerce of this area, now suffering from the eastward pull of the South-Western's terminus and the docks. The projected Southampton and Dorchester (as it was more generally called) was at first very ready to concur in this, provided that it could have a connection with the

South-Western terminus by a tramway along the waterfront. But the Pier and Harbour Commissioners were reluctant to sanction the use of locomotives along any such tramway, and their reluctance led the Committee of the Commons to which the S.D.R. bill was referred to reject the proposed Pier route and insist on a line from Blechynden through a tunnel approximating to the old canal tunnel, which would join the South-Western a short distance north of the Terminus. By this time the S.D.R. Company had been constrained to lease its as yet unbuilt line to the South-Western's rival the Great Western; and it now became a bargaining counter in a deal between these last two, by which the Great Western transferred the lease to the South-Western in return for the latter's agreement to abandon any such opposition to its proposed Reading–Basingstoke branch as the abortive Basingstoke–Newbury line would have constituted (see 19 February 1844). The Southampton & Dorchester line, which was built during 1845-7, was completely absorbed into the South-Western in 1848.

Friday the 1st day of November 1844

[The municipal elections reflected the decline of party bitterness from its peak in 1842, which was no doubt due to the fact that in the subsequent two years the main subjects of discussion were matters of general concern —especially the recent railway aspirations. (It will be noticed how relatively frequently resolutions were passed unanimously.) The elections were conducted very quietly, with hardly any seats contested, and the balance of parties in the Council once more remained the same as before.]

Saturday the 9th day of November 1844

[Captain Griffiths was elected Mayor, Daniel Brooks being unsuccessfully proposed by Andrews and Cooper; Joseph Ball was elected Sheriff and John Aslatt and William Rogers Bailiffs.]

HIGHWAYS

At this Council the Highway Committee reported that . . . in consequence of the Pavement Improvement Act possessing powers in future to repair the Antient Highways within the Borough and thereby repealing that part of the local Highway Act relating thereto, they had accordingly ordered the . . . Balance of £91.14.3 [then in their bankers' hands] to be transferred . . . to the Treasurer of the Pavement Improvement Commissioners towards the general repair of the Highways now placed under their superintendence by virtue of the above mentioned Act. . . .

¶ The Improvement Act, passed in the previous summer, had empowered the Commissioners to raise £20,000 by loan and therewith to make or widen most of the streets referred to under 1 February above. It stipulated, however, that they must first construct the necessary sewers, laying out not less than £10,000 in the purchase of private sewers and the building of others within three years, and provide adequate lighting and paving of the streets now placed under their sole control.

Friday the 20th day of December 1844

SOUTHAMPTON AND DORSETSHIRE RAILWAY

At this Council the Committee appointed . . . respecting the Southampton & Dorsetshire Railway Bill reported . . . that at a Meeting of the Committee the Town Clerk reported that a Requisition signed by certain Inhabitants of the Town had been presented to The . . . Mayor, requesting him to convene a Public Meeting . . . for the purpose of taking into consideration the propriety of supporting the proposed Southampton and Dorchester Railway and that a Public Meeting would accordingly be held on Friday then next for that purpose. The Committee . . . requested the Town Clerk to inform Messrs. Castleman [the wealthy Wimborne solicitors a partner in whom, Charles Castleman, was the chief original promoter of the line and secretary of the Company] that in the unanimous opinion of the Committee it was very desirable to bring the proposed line of Railway near to the Royal Pier and that such an arrangement would ensure the general and cordial approbation of the Inhabitants. . . .

The Committee also reported that at a subsequent meeting Mr. Castleman attended and submitted a Plan of the situation of the Terminus near the Royal Pier, and which was in accordance with the views of the Council and of Your Committee, and pledged himself not to adopt any other Terminus unless compelled to do so by Parliament. . . .

The Committee also further reported that at a subsequent Meeting the Town Clerk submitted the Proceedings of the Public Meeting of the Inhabitants held . . . on the 15th day of November last in favor of the Southampton and Dorsetshire line of Railway. . . .

(Copy of the Proceedings)

At a numerous and influential Meeting of the Inhabitants . . . held at the Guildhall . . . It was unanimously resolved that this Meeting is strongly impressed with the advantages of Railway Communication between this Port and the South Western Coast of England and the Ports in the Bristol Channel, and regards the Southampton and Dorsetshire Railway terminating at or near West Quay . . . as having peculiar claims on the Inhabitants and as entitled to their entire support . . . [and]

That this Meeting pledges itself to support the Southampton and Dorsetshire line . . . both in and out of Parliament, and not on local grounds alone, but with regard to those great Public Advantages to which Southampton owes its present and daily growing Importance as the central Point in the British Channel for the easy and rapid transmission of Mails Passengers and goods to and from the Metropolis and every part of the Kingdom. . . .

This Council having taken into their consideration the propriety of presenting a Memorial to the Board of Trade in favor of the Southampton and Dorsetshire Railway and a Draft of a Memorial having been submitted to the Council for that purpose . . .

It was . . . Resolved that the Memorial now read be adopted and forwarded to the Board of Trade. . . .

Thursday the 6th day of February 1845

[The Cemetery Committee reported that the contracts for erecting the walls and constructing the roads, walks and drainage of the Cemetery were completed; and that the erection of the chapels, lodge entrance and gateway was progressing satisfactorily. They recommended that the planting of the Cemetery should now be commenced.

The Committee appointed to watch the progress of the Southampton & Dorchester Railway Bill reported that both Mr. Castleman and the directors of the Company had repeated in writing the pledge which the former had previously given verbally that they would "use their utmost endeavours to obtain" parliamentary leave for their line to run to the quays and Pier. Subsequently, their report continued, the Company's agents had apprised them that the Board of Trade had suggested the agreement with the Great Western Railway Company referred to in the note under 30 October 1844 above, "with the view of reconciling differences as to territory and traffic". They had also learnt that the substitution of the tunnel line of entry into the town for the line to the Pier had been mooted and was in the air. A motion was then passed that the Council's support of the bill was conditional on its providing for the line's entrance to Southampton by way of the quays and Pier.

An application from the Poor Law Guardians for a grant of land on the Common on which to erect a new workhouse was referred to the Lease Committee.]

Friday the 7th day of March 1845

DOCK COMPANY

At this Council the Town Clerk submitted a Print of the Bill now before Parliament to alter and enlarge the powers and provisions of the Dock Company's Act and the Pier Act of 1831.

At this Council a Memorial was presented from certain Merchants Traders and Inhabitants of Southampton praying the Council to oppose both in and out of Parliament certain objectionable clauses of the said Bill.

And this Council having considered the same and it appearing that certain Negotiations were pending between the Directors of the Southampton Dock Company affecting the penal Clause contained in the Royal Pier Act

It was moved . . . That in the Opinion of this Council it is imperatively necessary that the rights of the Corporation should be preserved untouched as respects all Dues derivable from the Pier and Harbour and that as the proposed repeal of the Penal Clause, as far as the landing of Passengers and goods are concerned at the Pier, contained in the Royal Pier Act, would affect the Interests of the Corporation, the repeal of the said clause as contemplated by the amended Bill of the Dock Company be opposed by the Council in Parliament.

Which being put to the vote was negatived. . . .

It was moved . . . and Resolved That the Corporation as the Conservators and Guardians of the Public Interests do feel called on to oppose in Parliament that part of the amended Bill of the Dock Company which relates to the purchasing or leasing of the Public Quays and Wharfs of the Town and that the Council do resist all such attempts on the part of any Public Body or Company for the furtherance of any Measure which may directly or indirectly . . . affect the Interests of the Corporation involved in the same.

BRITISH ASSOCIATION FOR THE ADVANCEMENT OF SCIENCE

At this Council the Town Clerk submitted a communication received by him . . . on the subject of the British Association . . . holding their Annual Meeting in the Town next Year

And the same having been . . . considered

It was . . . Resolved unanimously that in the opinion of this Council it is highly desirable that the meeting . . . should take place in Southampton in the year 1846, and this Council do cheerfully offer to the Society [sic] the use of the Guildhall and Audit House, . . . and that the Mayor be requested to take such measures as he may deem necessary to secure this desirable object.

Thursday the 1st day of April 1845

SOUTHAMPTON MARSH

At this Council the Committee appointed on the 1st day of August last to take into consideration and report to the Council on the best mode for laying out the Marsh for building purposes . . . reported that . . . being of opinion that it was desirable to obtain Information from Surveyors and other practical Persons . . . they had caused a Paragraph to be inserted in the Local Papers inviting them to send in Plans gratuitously. Your Committee were not disappointed in their expectation [for] they received plans, the whole of which possessed great merit, from [7] surveyors. . . .

The Enquiries of the Committee had been directed to three principal objects, viz:—

1st. The general Plan for laying out the land.

2nd. The formation of Roads.

3rd. The Sewerage.

In considering the first of these topics your Committee were unanimously of opinion the following objects should be constantly kept in view, viz: the revenue to be derived from the allotment of the land for Building purposes, the Health of the Inhabitants in respect of the free circulation of air, the means of communication through these lands, between the Docks and the other parts of the Town, and, as far as might be, the Ornamental character of the Plan for laying out the Marsh. The combination of these desiderata was felt by your Committee to be the great object of their Deliberations, and . . . they found considerable difficulty in choosing one out of seven distinct Plans. . . .

The Committee further reported that being desirous of obtaining the opinion of those Gentlemen who had favored them with Plans, on several Points, and also of giving them an opportunity of making such Statements as they might wish to make in addition to such as they sent in with their Plans, [they had] requested them to attend the Committee which they did. . . .

The Committee . . . being desirous of testing the Opinions and information given to them by the Gentlemen who contributed the Plans were of opinion that it was desirable that the several subjects which had engaged the attention of your Committee should be submitted to some practical surveyor unconnected with either of these Gentlemen. . . . With this view therefore they submitted the plans . . . to Mr. Joseph Hill who made a report in writing and also attended your Committee and answered satisfactorily numerous Questions they put to him. The Committee reported that they had maturely weighed the opinion given by Mr. Hill and entirely accorded with him that the plan of Mr. Guillaume was to be preferred. . . . The Committee therefore reported that it was their opinion that Mr. Guillaume's plan for laying out the land should be adopted subject of course to such minor alterations as the Committee to whom the Council may entrust the carrying it out shall consider to be advantageous. . . .

And the report of the Committee having been . . . considered as also Mr. Hill's report together with the several plans for laying out the Marsh

It was . . . unanimously Resolved that Mr. Guillaume's Plan . . . be adopted, . . . subject to such minor alterations as may be considered necessary. . . .

DOCK COMPANY

At this Council the Committee appointed on the 7th day of March 1845 for the purpose of carrying into effect the resolution of the Council passed on that day with the view of opposing in Parliament that part of the amended Dock Company's Bill which related to the Dock Company purchasing or leasing the Public Quays and Wharfs of the Town or which affected the Interests of the Corporation reported that . . . a conference took place between the Directors of that Company and Your Committee on the 15th instant, that Col. Barlow the Chairman of the Directors then informed Your Committee that until the report of the proceedings of the last Borough Council appeared in the Public Papers the Directors were not aware that any power had been taken to enable the Commissioners of the Port and Harbour either to sell or lease the Public Quays of the Town to the Dock Company and that he at once said that such powers should be immediately struck out from the Bill. . . . The Committee having also stated to the Directors the objection which existed to the Dock Company obtaining power to take on lease the said Quays, the Directors intimated that such objection would be considered. . . .

The Committee further reported that at a meeting held by them on the 24th instant the Town Clerk submitted the Amendments proposed by the Dock Company to the objectionable clauses. . . .

The Committee being of the opinion that such Amendments were not satisfactory directed the Town Clerk to acquaint the Directors . . . thereof.

The Committee further reported that at a subsequent meeting . . . on the 29th instant the Town Clerk submitted further Amendments as proposed by the Dock Company which they laid before the Council. . . .

The Committee were of opinion that neither of the proposed Amendments were satisfactory and that no ground was shown why the Dock Company should obtain the powers they sought . . . and the Committee were satisfied that the monopoly which if those provisions were enacted would be given to the . . . Dock Company might in many instances be productive of serious injury not only to the Corporation but to the general Shipping and other Trade attracted to the Port of Southampton as well as to the general prosperity of the Port and Borough. . . .

The Committee submitted to the consideration of the Council a Petition to Parliament against the objectionable clauses of the Bill which they recommended for adoption.

The Report of the Committee having been . . . considered

It was . . . Resolved that a Committee be appointed for the purpose of opposing those clauses in the Docks Bill now before Parliament which would empower the Company to purchase [not only] the Public Quays and Wharfs but also the private Quays and Wharfs and the rest of the River Frontage of the Town . . . and that such Committee be requested to take all such steps by Petition and otherwise before Parliament for insuring the rejection of such clauses and also unless some arrangement be come to (satisfactory to the Commissioners of the Pier and to the Town Council) to oppose the clause by which it is sought to repeal some of the provisions of 1st & 2nd W. IV c. 1 requiring Captains of Steam Vessels to call at the Pier. . . .

Monday the 21st day of April 1845

SOUTHAMPTON AND DORSETSHIRE RAILWAY

At this Council the [Council's] Southampton & Dorsetshire Railway Committee submitted the Print of the Southampton & Dorchester Railway Bill.

And this Council having taken the report . . . into their consideration.

It was . . . unanimously Resolved that the Committee appointed by the Council on this subject . . . be empowered to watch the Bill in a Committee of the House of Commons, and to present a Petition to Parliament to be permitted to appear before such Committee by Counsel and Agents. . . .

It was . . . unanimously Resolved that the Committee be instructed to offer the most strenuous opposition to those parts of the . . . Bill which apply to a line into the Town at any other point than at or near the Gates of the Royal Pier. . . .

DOCK COMPANY

At this Council the Town Clerk reported the result of the Negotiations between the Committee appointed . . . to oppose the objectionable clauses in the amended Bill of the Southampton Dock Company [and the representatives of the Company], and that the Parliamentary Committee on the Bill had adjourned / . . for the purpose of affording all parties the opportunity of considering and agreeing to the several clauses proposed to be inserted in the Bill for carrying into effect the Negotiations between the Committee and the Company.

¶ The Dock Company had agreed to strike out of the bill the clause which repealed the penal clause of the Pier Act and also that empowering them to buy the quays, while still guaranteeing to make good to the Pier Commissioners any amount by which their annual revenue might fall below £1700 until their debt of £8000 was paid off. On 1 May the Town Clerk reported to the Council that the bill might now be considered unobjectionable.

Wednesday the 16th day of July 1845

APPLICATION FROM THE GUARDIANS OF THE POOR FOR A GRANT OF PART OF THE SOUTHAMPTON COMMON TO ERECT A NEW POOR HOUSE

[The Lease Committee, to which this application had been referred on 6 February, reported that they "were of opinion that it was not desirable to build a new Workhouse on the Common".]

Wednesday the 30th day of July 1845

MANCHESTER AND SOUTHAMPTON RAILWAY

At this Council James Walkingshaw Esquire of Old Park Isle of Wight attended and informed the Council that a Company was about to be established to construct a line of Railway to communicate from Southampton to Cheltenham and from thence by lines already constructed to Manchester and to be called "The Manchester and Southampton Railway" and having explained to the Council the advantages which were likely to arise to the Town and Port of Southampton by the construction of the same and the Plan of the intended Railway . . . having been submitted to this Council

It was . . . Resolved unanimously that a Direct Line of Railway Communication between Southampton and Manchester such as is proposed . . . is calculated essentially to promote the Interests of . . . Southampton, the neighbouring Towns and Districts, the rich agricultural counties through which it will pass and afford to the great Manufacturing Districts the most direct communication with the English Channel the Mediterranean and all parts of the East and West Indies.

That this Council will therefore to the utmost of its power support the general features of this Undertaking and that a Committee be appointed to take such measures as may be most calculated to promote the object and secure the particular Interests of Southampton connected therewith. . . .

SOUTHAMPTON AND DORSETSHIRE RAILWAY

At this Council the [Council's] Southampton and Dorsetshire Railway Committee . . . reported . . . a communication from Mr. Castleman respecting the selection of a site for the proposed Station near Blechynden Terrace and that having considered the same they were of opinion that the piece of Land near the Shore lying to the West side of and opposite to King John's Pond and near the Eastern end of Blechynden Terrace would form a convenient site . . . and the Town Clerk was requested to inform Mr. Castleman thereof.

[Later in the meeting a letter from Mr. Castleman was read from which it appeared that there was an objection to this proposed site.]

¶ The great railway boom of 1844-6 was now nearing its height, during which no fewer than forty-two lines connected with or affecting Southampton were projected, though hardly any of them ever came to anything. The Council, disappointed by the Southampton & Dorchester Company but as anxious as ever to break the South-Western's monopoly, grasped eagerly at the new prospect laid before them by Walkingshaw, a London solicitor born at Romsey; especially since the promoters of the Manchester & Southampton Railway also promised to make their terminus near the Pier.

The site eventually chosen for the Southampton & Dorchester's Blechynden station was a little nearer the tunnel than that of the present Central Station. When it was opened in 1847 it soon "made that neighbourhood as lively and full of business as it was dull and monotonous before", to quote the *Hampshire Advertiser* of 12 May of that year.

Wednesday the 24th day of September 1845

OXFORD AND SOUTHAMPTON RAILWAY

At this Council a Deputation attended on behalf of the Oxford Newbury Andover Manchester and Southampton Junction Railway Company . . . and the Chairman of the Company having explained to the Council the advantages which were likely to accrue to the Trade and Port of Southampton by the formation of such railway and a Plan of the line of the intended Railway having been submitted to this Council

It was . . . Resolved that the proposed . . . Railway is calculated essentially to benefit the Town and Port of Southampton as well as to be of great Public Advantage and that in the Opinion of this Council the proposed undertaking is deserving their utmost support [and]

That the Committee appointed by the Meeting of the Council held on the thirtieth . . . July last to secure the particular Interests of the Town . . . be requested to promote the same objects with respect to the proposed Railway. . . .

Saturday the 1st day of November 1845

[With the townspeople largely absorbed in reading railway prospectuses, buying railway shares, and trying to secure properties whose value might be enhanced by possible new railways, the two parties made an agreement not to contest the municipal elections. In practice this broke down, however, since a section of the Liberals rebelled against it. The few contests which took place nevertheless once more made no change in the balance of parties on the Council, the Radicals still holding St. Mary's Ward and the Conservatives all the others.]

Monday the 10th day of November 1845

[Joseph Lobb was elected Mayor for the third time (Captain Griffiths declining to be re-nominated), and announced that like his predecessor he was resolved to give the new railway undertakings his firm and energetic support. The retiring Mayor's claim in his valedictory address that he had tried to allay "warring passions" was applauded by both sides. John Aslatt was elected Sheriff and William Rogers and Henry Brett Bailiffs.

It was reported that Mr. Castleman had been invited to indicate the exact spot on which the S.D.R. Company wished to erect their Blechynden station.]

LITERARY AND SCIENTIFIC INSTITUTION

At this Council a communication was read from Mr. T. H. C. Moody informing the Council that the Literary and Scientific Institution of this Town would shortly be dissolved and offering on the part of their Members their Museum of Specimens and Curiosities Scientific Apparatus and Books, subject only to the retention of such articles as the original donors may now require to be returned to them, to the Council at a valuation under the provisions of the act recently passed empowering municipal Councils to make such purchases.

And . . . it was . . . Resolved that the consideration of Mr. Moody's letter be referred to a Committee. . . .

¶ The Literary and Philosophic Institution, as it had been called in earlier years, had been founded in 1828, but after a few years of success had been struggling since the middle 1830's to keep alive.

Thursday the 29th day of January 1846

MANCHESTER AND SOUTHAMPTON RAILWAY

[The Council, having had more detailed plans of the proposed line laid before it, instructed the Town Clerk to inform the Company that they approved of it, and even resolved to petition Parliament in its favour, but reserved the right to object in Parliament to any of the details of the proposed bill.]

WILTS SOMERSET AND SOUTHAMPTON JUNCTION RAILWAY

[The Town Clerk having reported that he had been notified of the intended construction of this railway, a motion was proposed "that in the Opinion of this Council it is of much Importance to the Trade and Commerce of . . . Southampton that a direct communication should be established by railway between the Bristol and English Channels" and promising support to the undertaking; but as the meeting was by no means unanimous it was decided to postpone the consideration of the matter.]

Thursday the 5th day of February 1846

WILTS SOMERSET AND SOUTHAMPTON JUNCTION RAILWAY

It was . . . Resolved . . . that Petitions be presented to both Houses of Parliament praying that a Bill for the construction of the above Railway be passed into a Law . . . and

That the assent of this Council be given to the application of the Wilts Somerset and Southampton Railway subject to their approval of the Details of the Bill. . . .

[A petition to the Commons in support of the bill was drawn up and approved, and a committee appointed to watch and report on its progress.]

Monday the 23rd day of March 1846

ROMSEY AND REDBRIDGE BRANCH RAILWAY

At this Council the Committee appointed on the 29th of January last reported that in accordance with the resolution passed by the Council on that day they had presented a Petition to the House of Commons on behalf of the Council in favour of the proposed Manchester and Southampton Railway Bill. . . .

Your Committee considered it their duty to draw the attention of the Council to a report . . . that attempts would be made in the Committees in Parliament to compel the Manchester and Southampton Railway Company to connect their Line with that of the South Western Company either at

Romsey or some other point. Your Committee had no reason to believe that the promoters of the Manchester and Southampton Line had any intention of parting from the pledge given to the Council last autumn, that theirs should be an independent Line terminating at or near the Royal Pier, but they were apprehensive that efforts would be made by the South Western Railway Company to enforce the Junction to which allusion had just been made. Your Committee were of opinion that such a Junction would ultimately secure to the latter Company the working of the pro-jected line and give them an absolute Monopoly of every Railway access to the Town which can be contemplated, and deprive the Inhabitants of some of the principal advantages expected from the Manchester and Southampton Line.

The Committee were also of opinion and recommended that clauses should be inserted in each Bill for the purpose of securing the rights of the Corporation to the Mud Lands outside of either Line of Railway and also a carriage and foot road on the south west side of the outermost Line from the Royal Pier to Milbrooke. . . .

And this Council having considered so much of such report as relates to a Bill now before Parliament promoted by the London and South Western Railway Company for constructing a branch Railway from Romsey to Redbridge

It was . . . Resolved that a Petition be presented to both Houses of Parliament against the proposed Romsey and Redbridge Branch Railway, promoted by the South Western Railway Company, setting forth the injurious consequences which must result to the Town . . . should such a Bill pass into Law, placing as it would the whole Railway Communication with this Town in the hands of one great company, thereby creating a monopoly that cannot fail to prove disastrous to the Trade and Commerce of the Town [and]

That the Committee be empowered to take such steps as they may deem advisable in opposing the Romsey and Redbridge Branch Railway and to appear by themselves, counsel and Solicitor before the Committee of both Houses of Parliament in support of the Petition.

[Five members, not all of one party, protested against spending Corpora-tion funds in petitioning against any junction between the Manchester and Southampton and the London and South-Western Railways.

The Cemetery Committee reported that the chapels and lodge were completed.]

¶ In the Council's negotiations with both the Southampton and Dorchester and the Manchester and Southampton Railway Companies a secondary but nevertheless important object was to ensure that their proposed lines should leave a clear belt of reclaimable mudland along the Western Shore, with access from the landward side, on which a promenade could subsequently be made. This was all the more desirable since the construction of the rail-way terminus and the docks had ruined the old walk from the Platform eastward along the Beach which had been the townsfolk's favourite and fashionable constitutional earlier in the century. It was also hoped to construct pleasure gardens on this belt of shore, and there was even talk of docks being built there—an early anticipation of the New Docks of the twentieth century.

Wednesday the 29th day of April 1846

GAOL AND BRIDEWELL

At this Council the Town Clerk submitted a report from the visiting Justices setting forth the inconvenience arising from the present Gaol and Bridewell in consequence of its being too contracted for the present increase in the number of Prisoners and that it was quite impossible to carry out therein the adequate classification and the rules and regulations recommended by the Secretary of State. The Town Clerk also submitted certain resolutions passed at an adjourned Quarterly Sessions of the Justices . . . expressive of their opinion that some steps should forthwith be taken for providing a better and more commodious building for the confinement and classification of the Prisoners committed to the Gaol and Bridewell. . . .

And this Council having considered the same as also the propriety of appointing a Committee to consider . . . the subject

It was . . . Resolved that a Committee be appointed. . . .

THE CEMETERY

At this Council the Cemetery Committee reported that, application having been made to them by the members of the Jewish Persuasion residing within the Borough for the appropriation of a small part of the Cemetery for the Interment of their Dead, and your Committee having entertained such application, and being of opinion that a portion of the Cemetery should be appropriated for their Interment, had accordingly set out a suitable portion of Land for such purpose which according to their religious rites would render it necessary to erect a small chapel or room for their services . . . for their exclusive use, and also to erect a separate gate for the entrance to communicate with the chapel and ground; and your Committee being of opinion that the Corporation should be at such expense, accordingly recommended that the Chapel and Entrance gate should be erected at the Expense of the Corporation. . . .

[The Council resolved to attend the consecration of the Cemetery by the Bishop of Winchester on 7 May.]

Thursday the 7th day of May 1846

[A committee was appointed to make the necessary arrangements for the meeting of the British Association.]

Monday the 13th day of July 1846

NEW ROAD OPPOSITE WEST FRONT

At this Council the Town Clerk reported that he had received a Notice from the Pavement Improvement Commissioners of their intention to take and purchase a strip of Land being part of the Houndwell Common Field opposite to West Front Kingsland Place for forming a New Road therefrom to Portland Place.

And the same having been . . . considered

It is Resolved that the consideration of the same be referred to the Lease Committee. . . .

Tuesday the 21st day of July 1846

VOTE OF THANKS TO THE LATE RECORDER

At this Council the Mayor reported that Alexander Edmund Cockburn Esquire had resigned the Office of Recorder . . . Whereupon It was . . . Resolved that the cordial thanks of the Council be given to [him] for the able and impartial manner in which he has discharged the Duties of his Office. . . .

MANCHESTER AND SOUTHAMPTON RAILWAY

. . . At this Council the Committee appointed to watch the progress of the Manchester and Southampton Railway Bill reported that since the meeting at which they submitted their former report they had in compliance with the powers then given them adopted such proceedings as in their Judgement appeared necessary for carrying into effect the several resolutions then passed by the Council and in furtherance thereof the following Petitions were accordingly presented to the House of Commons, vizt.

A Petition against the then proposed Romsey and Redbridge Branch Railway.

A Petition against the proposed Manchester and Southampton Railway Bill for the purpose only of obtaining the insertion of certain clauses therein and

A Petition against any alteration of the Commencement of the said Railway at Southampton. . . .

The Committee laid before the Council the following Details of their Proceedings viz.

First with respect to the Petition against the Romsey and Redbridge Branch Line. Upon the Petition, as well as the others, Mr. Davies appeared for and on behalf of the Corporation, and the Committee of the House of Commons ultimately rejected the former and declared the preamble of the Manchester and Southampton Railway Bill proved.

Second. The Petition presented for the purpose of Inserting a clause in the Manchester and Southampton Railway Bill for protecting the rights of the Corporation in the Mudlands within the Borough has been inserted . . . [*sic*].

Third. The Petition against any alteration of the Commencement of the Line. . . . This important point was secured in the Bill as now amended by the Committee [sc., of the Commons]

The Committee laid before the Council a Print of the Bill for their consideration and informed them that the following clauses had been inserted therein affecting the Local Interests of the Borough vizt. . . .

> Clause 51. Empowers the Company to make a Tramway on the Public Quays.
>
> Clause 52. Imposes a Penalty for passing along the Tramway at a greater speed than 4 miles an hour.
>
> Clause 53. Provides for the erection of a Station between the East end of Bletchynden [*sic*] Street and Portland Terrace. . . .
>
> Clause 59. Compels the Company to make maintain and use a Terminal Station at the North Western Side of the Quay. . . .

The Committee reported that they felt great pleasure in reporting upon the successful termination of the Bill up to the present time. . . .

¶ The bill had now passed the Commons (an event greeted by much rejoicing and bell-ringing in Southampton), but the opposition of the London & South-Western Company, which had already delayed its passage through the committee stage, continued in the House of Lords.

Thursday the 13th day of August 1846

NEW RECORDER

At this Council the Mayor submitted a letter received by him from Edward Smirke Esquire Barrister at Law informing him that he had been appointed to the Office of Recorder of the Borough. . . .

THE MARSH

At this Council the Marsh Improvement Committee reported that as the Marsh Sewer was completed, they were of opinion that it was now desirable that a portion of the Marsh should be placed in the market for building purposes . . . and as soon as the necessary Funds were provided, and a Surveyor appointed, [they] were prepared and would proceed further in laying out the several Lots of Land, upon such terms and conditions as may appear necessary.

It was . . . Resolved that the report of the Committee be . . . adopted and that they be authorized . . . to advertise for Tenders for borrowing such sums of Money as they consider necessary from time to time in carrying into effect the provisions of the Marsh Improvement Act. . . .

Monday the 31st day of August 1846

MANCHESTER AND SOUTHAMPTON RAILWAY

This Council having taken into their consideration the best course to be adopted in consequence of the Temporary Defeat of the Manchester and Southampton Railway Bill in a Committee of the House of Lords . . .

It was . . . Resolved unanimously that this Council continues to entertain the strongest approval of the intended Line from Cheltenham to Southampton and will persevere in supporting any renewed effort for carrying the same into effect being strongly of opinion that the Line is calculated to be of great Local and Public Advantage and essential to the accommodation of the Towns through which it is intended to pass and Particularly to the Prosperity of the Port of Southampton.

¶ The opposition of the L.S.W.R. Company to the Manchester & Southampton's proposed line from Cheltenham through Swindon and Marlborough to Southampton had been withdrawn after a compact had been made, by which the M.S.R. was to use the Southampton & Dorchester (now effectively South-Western) line from Redbridge to Blechynden Station and pay half the cost of its construction, and the South-Western to use the M.S.R. line from Andover to Redbridge and from Blechynden Station to the Quay Terminus, the station at Blechynden being common to both lines. But the M.S.R. Company had then encountered the still more formidable opposition of the Great Western, which had a powerful influence on the House of Lords committee before which the bill had then come.

Friday the 9th day of October 1846

MEETING OF THE BRITISH ASSOCIATION FOR THE ADVANCEMENT OF SCIENCE

At this Council the Mayor reported that a vote of thanks to this Corporation had been proposed and carried by the British Association . . . at their late meeting for the manner in which the Association had been received here and for the use of the Public Rooms in the Town. . . .

Monday the 2nd day of November 1846

[In the municipal elections a swing of the pendulum in favour of the Liberals began to be apparent. Besides holding St. Mary's Ward, they made three gains (one in All Saints and the St. Michael's and St. Lawrence's seats which fell vacant this year), while a non-partisan was elected to the vacated Holy Rhood seat. The Conservatives were suffering from the local effects of the nation-wide schism in the party caused by Sir Robert Peel's reversal of policy in the repeal of the Corn Laws, and showed apathy in many cases and dissension in others.]

Monday the 9th day of November 1846

[W. J. Le Feuvre was elected Mayor, Henry Brett Sheriff, and P. Goepel and William Rogers Bailiffs. The Liberals, however, tried out their increased strength by contesting each election doggedly. Against Le Feuvre, whom they disliked personally for his hot partisanship and equally hot temper, they nominated five successive persons in vain, beginning with the moderate Liberal Daniel Brooks. Rogers, against whom seven successive nominations were made, subsequently declined to serve as Junior Bailiff, since he had already been Senior Bailiff and presumably resented being relegated to the foot of the ladder of office. W. C. Spooner was then elected in his place.]

Friday the 4th day of December 1846

ROAD OPPOSITE TO WEST FRONT

At this Council the Lease Committee reported that the Town Clerk had submitted the notice received from the Pavement Improvement Commissioners of their intention to take and purchase a strip or piece of land being part of Houndwell Common Field adjoining the roadway of West Front Kingsland Place . . . belonging to this Corporation for the purpose of forming a New Road or way by the Pavement Improvement Act authorized to be formed along the West Front of Kingsland Place and Portland Place to Northam Road [see 1 February 1844 and 13 July 1846] and the Committee having . . . considered the same regretted to find that the Commissioners . . . should think it necessary to make the said road, but finding that properties had already been purchased for the purpose of forming such road they did not recommend the Council to put any obstruction in the formation thereof and they directed Mr. Doswell to make a valuation of the land. . . .

They further reported that at a subsequent meeting Mr. Doswell . . . estimated [the Corporation's interest in] the land at the sum of £16.15.0.

TRAMWAY ACROSS THE QUAY

At this Council the Town Clerk submitted a communication . . . that it was the intention of the Commissioners of the Port and Harbour to construct a Tramway from the Quay to the South Western Terminus; and the same having been . . . considered

It was . . . Resolved that . . . this Council do give their consent accordingly to the laying of such [tramway] under the superintendence of their Engineer Mr. Doswell. . . .

MARSH

At this Council the Marsh Improvement Committee reported that . . . they had appointed Mr. Guillaume as Surveyor to the Corporation in carrying into effect his Plan for Building upon the Marsh. . . .

[They also reported that he had estimated that £4000 would be required to carry out the proposed works, that they had directed the Town Clerk to advertise for tenders for the loan of £5000, and that Guillaume had also estimated the total value of the Marsh land which was now being reclaimed and converted at £2000 a year.]

Thursday the 4th day of February 1847

NEW GAS COMPANY

At this Council the Town Clerk submitted a Print of a proposed Bill for better supplying with Gas the Town . . . of Southampton and certain places adjacent thereto.

THE MARSH

At this Council the Marsh Improvement Committee reported that . . . they had accepted Mr. John Aslatt's Tender for advancing £5000 under the powers of the Marsh Improvement Act at 4½ per cent. . . .

The Committee further reported that the Town Clerk having submitted the Draft Notice of the Corporation declaring rights of common and other rights affecting the Marsh extinguished which he had prepared in accordance with the terms of the Marsh Improvement Act; and the same having been . . . approved the Committee recommended the Council to accept the same, and that the Town Clerk be directed to publish the same in the manner directed by the . . . Act. . . .

¶ John Aslatt was a well-to-do coachbuilder. The public rights on the Marsh were extinguished as from the ensuing 12 April, except for the four acres preserved as a cricket ground.

Friday the 30th day of April 1847

A Borough Council was this day held . . . (pursuant to Notice for that purpose fixed at the Town Hall and Audit House and also given to each Member of the Council) in consequence of a Requisition presented to the Mayor to take into consideration a Bill now before Parliament for the construction of the Manchester and Southampton Railway, with reference to the property of the Town Council proposed to be taken under the powers of the Bill; and also with reference to the Terminus of such Railway at Southampton, and to take such steps thereon by Petition to Parliament or otherwise, and on the proposed measure generally so far as the Interests of the Town may be affected thereby as may be deemed advisable

At this Council the Town Clerk submitted a Print of the Manchester and Southampton Railway Bill. . . .

It was . . . Resolved that in the opinion of this Council the Manchester and Southampton Railway Company should be bound either by adequate penal clauses to construct their Terminal Station at Southampton at the spot and as otherwise provided in their Bill which passed the House of

Commons in the last Session of Parliament and to run all their carriages with Passengers and Goods arriving at or departing from Southampton to and from such Terminal Station . . . or to surrender the Compulsory Power of Purchase of the Mud Land and other Corporation property within this Borough, [and]

That a Petition be presented to the House of Commons against the said Bill in its present shape . . . with a view to the insertion of clauses to effect the foregoing object. . . .

¶ By now the knowledge of the compact which the M.S.R. had made with the South-Western was causing disappointment, suspicion and alarm in Southampton. "As in the parallel case of the Southampton and Dorchester", wrote the *Hampshire Advertiser* on 22 May, "the town has been deceived and betrayed into the hands of the very company of which it strove to be independent". The House of Commons Select Committee on Standing Orders, however, refused to allow the M.S.R. bill to proceed because of errors which it contained, and after this second failure and with the decline of the railway boom that part of the project which concerned Hampshire and Southampton was not revived again. The Council and the town were thus left to achieve co-existence with the London & South-Western Company from whose monopoly they had sought in vain to escape.

Tuesday the 11th day of May 1847

SOUTHAMPTON AND DORCHESTER RAILWAY:
BLECHYNDEN TERRACE STATION

At this Council the Town Clerk reported that a Petition had been presented to the House of Commons on behalf of the Council . . . against one of the Southampton and Dorchester Company's Bills praying for the insertion of certain clauses therein compelling them to make all proper and necessary Roads Avenues and Approaches to the Station at Blechynden Terrace, and that when the Bill came before the Parliamentary Committee for their consideration the reception of such Petition was opposed by counsel retained by the Company, and the Committee decided that the Corporation had no Locus Standi before them.

Wednesday the 29th day of September 1847

THE MARSH

At this Council the Marsh Improvement Committee reported that . . . they had had under their consideration a design proposed by Mr. Guillaume for the Elevation of the Dwellings proposed by him for erection on the Central Lots of Land in the Bridge Road, and that they had approved thereof and recommended the same to the Council for adoption; and that the front Lots . . . should be immediately put into the market.

The Committee further reported that having taken into their consideration the amount of Improvement which each Person should expend on such of the Lots . . . as are proposed to be put into the market, they were of opinion that the Purchaser of every Lot of Land in question should be compelled to expend not less than . . . £350 upon every Lot . . . purchased.

The Committee also . . . reported they were of opinion . . . that the Purchaser of every one of such Lots as hereinafter mentioned should have the option of taking, after the sale of such Lot, the Back Lot to such front Lot, at two thirds of the rent of such front Lot, provided that the intention of such Purchaser was signified to the Town Clerk within 14 days after the day of Sale, but that each of such Back Lots should be subject to the same Terms and Conditions as the front Lots; and the purchaser shall expend on each of such Back Lots on Improvements not less than . . . £200. . . .

It was . . . Resolved unanimously that the reports of the Marsh Improvement Committee be . . . adopted.

¶ The sewerage and drainage of the eleven acres or so of the Marsh which had been taken over under the Marsh Improvement Act of 1844 had now been completed, though to the accompaniment of complaints of the slowness with which it was alleged that the Act was being put into effect; and on 2 November part of the land was put up for leasing by auction. The good prices obtained were taken as confirming the Marsh Improvement Committee's estimate that it would be comfortably possible to raise the money necessary to buy out the six-months owners of the common lands, who had agreed to dispose of their rights at £250 an acre. These lands could then be planted and ornamented as parks and pleasure grounds, thus making the town more attractive.

Monday the 1st day of November 1847

[In the municipal elections the swing of the pendulum in favour of the Liberals which had begun in the previous year was completed. Encouraged by a walk-over in the recent parliamentary election, while the disunity and apathy of the Conservatives continued, they gained the four All Saints seats and the one St. Lawrence's seat vacated, so that with the previously non-partisan Holy Rhood councillor gravitating to their side they mustered eighteen in number. All ten aldermen were Conservatives, but five retired this year and were replaced by five Liberals (since the latter had a bare majority in their election), so that the eventual Liberal majority was 23-17.]

Tuesday the 9th day of November 1847

[The Conservatives accepted in a graceful spirit the defeat which they had foreseen. The retiring Mayor, Le Feuvre, to his great credit, had invited the leaders of both parties to a dinner at which the keynote was the necessity of working together on the current questions which were of such great importance to the town. On nomination day, therefore, Daniel Brooks, who had so often been proposed in vain for office, was unanimously chosen Mayor. Joseph Lankester, the fighting Radical leader of

St. Mary's Ward, was elected Sheriff, and John Parsons and G. T. Short Bailiffs.

A committee about equally representative of both parties was set up, "to be called the Revision Committee, who shall enquire into the duties of all the paid Officers of this Corporation and the amount of their salaries and perquisites with a view to the reduction of the number and the amount of salary if deemed advisable thereby to lessen the Expenditure of the Borough".]

The Corporation's Fifth of the Port Dues

These were paid in two half-yearly instalments, for the six months ending 25 March and 29 September respectively. For the first fifteen years or so they bear some relation to the rise of the port's prosperity, but after that they cease to do so, since practically all this development was connected with the Itchen wharves and the docks, from whose charges the Corporation drew nothing. Indeed the decline in the closing years of this table mirrors the falling-off in the revenues of the Pier and Harbour Commissioners which caused the anxiety referred to more than once in the text.

For the six months ending		29 September 1815	£181. 2. 7
,,	,,	25 March 1816	128.17. 4½
,,	,,	29 September 1816	146. 4.11
,,	,,	25 March 1817	103. 2. 5
,,	,,	29 September 1817	127. 1.10½
,,	,,	25 March 1818	120. 3. 5
,,	,,	29 September 1818	128.14. 2
,,	,,	25 March 1819	132. 5. 1
,,	,,	29 September 1819	203. 6. 4
,,	,,	25 March 1820	Accounted for
,,	,,	29 September 1820	as a lump sum, 559.14.10
,,	,,	25 March 1821	27 April 1821.
,,	,,	29 September 1821	191. 1. 0
,,	,,	25 March 1822	187.10. 0
,,	,,	29 September 1822	187. 2. 0
,,	,,	25 March 1823	187. 0. 0
,,	,,	29 September 1823	169.12. 0
,,	,,	25 March 1824	179. 4. 6
,,	,,	29 September 1824	180. 0. 6
,,	,,	25 March 1825	169.19. 4
,,	,,	29 September 1825	172. 7. 4
,,	,,	25 March 1826	181.13. 9
,,	,,	29 September 1826	230.16. 6
,,	,,	25 March 1827	193.15. 5
,,	,,	29 September 1827	246. 1. 9
,,	,,	25 March 1828	197.19.11
,,	,,	29 September 1828	222.12. 1

For the six months ending			
For the six months ending	25 March 1829	255.14. 9
,,	,,	29 September 1829	267. 6. 3
,,	,,	25 March 1830	218. 6. 5
,,	,,	29 September 1830	265.14. 9
,,	,,	25 March 1831	210. 8. 8
,,	,,	29 September 1831	228. 4. 9½
,,	,,	25 March 1832	198. 7. 5
,,	,,	29 September 1832	187.18. 9
,,	,,	25 March 1833	188. 4. 6
,,	,,	29 September 1833	169.15. 6
,,	,,	25 March 1834	162.13. 4
,,	,,	29 September 1834	192.17.11
,,	,,	25 March 1835	167. 9. 8
,,	,,	29 September 1835	215.10. 2
,,	,,	25 March 1836	196. 0. 8
,,	,,	29 September 1836	228.19. 5
,,	,,	25 March 1837	162.15. 2
,,	,,	29 September 1837	197.11. 1
,,	,,	25 March 1838	182. 3. 9
,,	,,	29 September 1838	224.19. 9
,,	,,	25 March 1839	196.13. 0¼
,,	,,	29 September 1839	243. 4. 6¾
,,	,,	25 March 1840	188.13.11¼
,,	,,	29 September 1840	253. 4. 0¼
,,	,,	25 March 1841	257.19. 5
,,	,,	29 September 1841	319.14. 9
,,	,,	25 March 1842	367.15. 9
,,	,,	29 September 1842	429.11. 1
,,	,,	25 March 1843	338. 8. 4
,,	,,	29 September 1843	386.18.11
,,	,,	25 March 1844	313.13. 3
,,	,,	29 September 1844	297.14.11
,,	,,	25 March 1845	223. 4. 2
,,	,,	29 September 1845	249.17. 4
,,	,,	25 March 1846	239.19. 8¾
,,	,,	29 September 1846	228.10. 2
,,	,,	25 March 1847	237. 4. 4
,,	,,	29 September 1847	206.11. 7

The steep rise which began in the latter part of 1840 coincided with the coming of the railway into full operation, and the fall after 1842 with the opening of the docks.

Borough Rates

These were at first levied for four-monthly periods, but became quarterly after April 1837.

1836 May   –   August   £500
       Sept.   –   Dec.   400
1837 Jan.   –   April   400
       May   –   July   400
       Aug.   –   Oct.   400
       Nov.   –   Jan. 1838   200
1838 Feb.   –   April   550
       May   –   July   550 (now described as a rate of $1\frac{1}{2}d.$ in the £)
       Aug.   –   Oct.   1100 (,,   ,,   ,, $3d.$,,   £)
       Nov.   –   Jan. 1839   455 ($1d.$ in the £)
1839 Feb.   –   April   725 ($2d.$,,   )
       May   –   July   550 ($1\frac{1}{2}d.$,,   )
       Aug.   –   Oct.   916 ($2\frac{1}{2}d.$,,   )
       Nov.   –   Jan. 1840   353 ($1d.$,,   )
1840 Feb.   –   April   725 ($2d.$,,   )
       May   –   July   725 ($2d.$,,   )
       Aug.   –   Oct.   916 ($2\frac{1}{2}d.$,,   )
       Nov.   –   Jan. 1841   725 ($2d.$,,   )
1841 Feb.   –   April   725 ($2d.$,,   )
       May   –   July   916 ($2\frac{1}{2}d.$,,   )
       Aug.   –   Oct.   None levied.
       Nov.   –   Jan. 1842   362.18.4 ($1d.$ in the £)
1842 Feb.   –   April   725   ($2d.$,,   )
       May   –   July   916   ($2\frac{1}{2}d.$,,   )
       Aug.   –   Oct.   725   ($2d.$,,   )
       Nov.   –   Jan. 1843   725   ($2d.$,,   )
1843 Feb.   –   April   725   ($2d.$,,   )
       May   –   July   550   ($1\frac{1}{2}d.$,,   )
       Aug.   –   Oct.   918   ($2\frac{1}{2}d.$,,   )
       Nov.   –   Jan. 1844   551   ($1\frac{1}{2}d.$,,   )
1844 Feb.   –   April   551   ($1\frac{1}{2}d.$,,   )
       May   –   July   917.13.4 ($2\frac{1}{2}d.$,,   )
       Aug.   –   Oct.   917.13.4 ($2\frac{1}{2}d.$,,   )
       Nov.   –   Jan. 1845   551   ($1\frac{1}{2}d.$,,   )

1845	Feb.	–	April	726. 6. 8	(2*d*. in the £)
	May	–	July	363.11. 8	(1*d*. „)
	Aug.	–	Oct.	917.13. 4	(2½*d*. „)
	Nov.	–	Jan. 1846	917.13. 4	(2½*d*. „)
1846	Feb.	–	April	917.13. 4	(2½*d*. „)
	May	–	July	917.13. 4	(2½*d*. „)
	Aug.	–	Oct.	917.13. 4	(2½*d*. „)
	Nov.	–	Jan. 1847	726. 6. 8	(2*d*. „)
1847	Feb.	–	April	726. 6. 8	(2*d*. „)
	May	–	July	917.13. 4	(2½*d*. „)
	Aug.	–	Oct.	775.13.11	(2*d*. „)
	Nov.	–	Jan. 1848	970. 2. 6	(2½*d*. „)

The table shows the increase in the rates from 1844 onwards which caused much criticism and accusations of improvidence from Radicals and others.

BIBLIOGRAPHY

A. MANUSCRIPT SOURCES

Minutes of the Borough Council Cemetery Committee, 1843-7.
Minutes of the Borough Council Finance Committee, 1836-47.
Minutes of the Borough Council Lease Committee, 1838-47.
Minutes of the Borough Council Marsh Improvement Committee, 1844-7.
Minutes of the Borough Council Watch Committee, 1836-47.
Southampton Pavement Commissioners' Minute Books, 1815-44.
Southampton Improvement Commissioners Minutes and Papers, 1844-7.
Southampton Waterworks Commissioners Minute Books, 1815-47.
The Page and Moody Papers.
(All the above are in the Southampton City Archives.)

B. PRINTED SOURCES

The Southampton Guide: editions of 1805, 1819, 1821, 1829, 1832, 1839 and 1847.
Sir H. C. Englefield, *A Walk through Southampton*. Southampton, 1801, 1805 and (with notes by John Bullar) 1841.
John Bullar, *Historical Particulars relating to Southampton*. Southampton, 1820.
John Bullar, *Hints to Assist the Enquiries of Visitors*. Southampton, 1846.
P. Brannon, *The Picture of Southampton*. Southampton, 1849.
R. Mudie, *Southampton and its Neighbourhood*. Southampton, 1843.
W. Ranger, *Report to the General Board of Health on the Sanitary Condition of Southampton*. 1850.
Report of the Royal Commission of Enquiry into the Municipal Corporations, 1835. (Southampton section, printed separately, in Cope Collection in Southampton University Library.)
Southampton Election Petition, 1842: Minutes of Proceedings and Evidence (in City Reference Library and Southampton University Library).
Bye-Laws and Ordinances of Southampton. 1845 (in City Reference Library).
Hampshire Chronicle, 1772-1847.
Southampton Herald, 1822-7.
Hampshire Advertiser, 1827-47.
Hampshire Independent, 1835-47.

C. SECONDARY AUTHORITIES

J. S. Davies, *A History of Southampton*. Southampton, 1883.
J. B. Morgan and Philip Peberdy (eds.), *Collected Essays on Southampton*. Southampton, 1958.

A. Temple Patterson, "The History of Southampton in the Eighteenth and Nineteenth Centuries", in *A Survey of Southampton and its Region* (ed. F. J. Monkhouse). Southampton, 1964.

E. A. Mitchell ("Townsman"), *Occasional Notes*. Southampton, 1938.

C. F. Russell, *A History of King Edward VI's School, Southampton*. Cambridge, 1940.

C. F. Dendy Marshall, *A History of the Southern Railway*. London, 1936.

B. C. Jones, *Crossing the Itchen*. Southampton, 1960.

E. A. Shillington, *The Story of Southampton Harbour*. Southampton, 1947.

S. Stainer, *A History of Above Bar Congregational Church, 1662-1908*. Southampton, 1909.

A Catalogue of Books in the Pitt Collection. Southampton, 1964.

INDEX

LIST OF SUBSCRIBERS TO THE SERIES

INDIVIDUALS

ALEXANDER, Miss M., M.A., Education Office, Civic Centre, Southampton.
ANDERSON, R. C., LITT.D., F.S.A., Gorley Firs, South Gorley, Fordingbridge.
ARNOTT, W. G., Church Street, Woodbridge, Suffolk.

BARBER, Miss K., C/8 Archers, Archers Road, Southampton.
BARNABY, K. C., O.B.E., B.SC., Ferryside, The Green, Hamble, Southampton.
BROMLEY, Professor J. S., M.A., The University, Southampton.

COCKS, W. E. G., 107 St. Mary's Road, Southampton.
CORFIELD, Dr. C., Broadmark Place, Rustington, Sussex.

DE GROUCHY, P. J., M.A., 12 Nutley Close, Goring-by-Sea, Worthing, Sussex.
DIXON, W. S., Flat No. 2, 4 Northlands Road, Southampton.
DOUCH, R., M.A., The University, Southampton.
DOUGLAS, A. E., M.A., The University, Southampton.
DYMOND, Miss D., C.B.E., M.A., 15a Festing Grove, Southsea.

FELSTEAD, Rev. Canon K. W. H., M.SC., St. Michael's Vicarage, Bugle Street, Southampton.
FILBY, P. W., Peabody Institute of the City of Baltimore, Maryland, U.S.A.
FREEMAN, F. L., C.B.E., M.A., LL.D., 59 Brookvale Road, Southampton.

GLEAVE, R. R., Southern Newspapers Ltd., Above Bar, Southampton.
GUTTERIDGE, Col. R. F., T.D., F.R.I.B.A., 31 University Road, Southampton.

HAMMOND, Alderman Mrs. I. D., 217 Winchester Road, Southampton.
HENTON, J. C., 8 Highfield Lodge, Highfield Lane, Southampton.
HOWE, E. J., 2 Blenheim Gardens, Highfield, Southampton.

JACKSON, W., Hartas, Marwell Manor, Fishers Pond, Eastleigh.

MACKEITH, N. W., M.B., B.S., B.SC., 7 Westwood Road, Southampton.
McFARLANE, K. B., M.A., Magdalen College, Oxford.
MERSON, A. L., M.A., The University, Southampton.
MILLIGAN, E. H., B.A., 184 Shinfield Road, Reading, Berkshire.

NUTH, Mrs. L., 3600 Chesterfield Avenue, Baltimore 13, Maryland, U.S.A.

PATTERSON, A. T., M.A., The University, Southampton.
PETREE, J. F., M.I.Mech.E., M.R.I.N.A., 36 Mayfield Road, Sutton, Surrey.
PINHORN, M. A., Bridge Place, Bridge, Nr. Canterbury.

QUINN, Professor D. B., B.A., PH.D., The University, Liverpool.

RABAN, Rev. J. P. C. P., T.D., The Vicarage, Pennington, Nr. Lymington.
RICHARDSON, S., B.A., Howards End, Howards Close, Oakmount Road, Chandler's Ford.
ROTHWELL, Professor H., B.A., PH.D., History Department, The University, Southampton.
RUDDOCK, Miss A. A., B.A., PH.D., Birkbeck College, London, W.C.1.

SANDELL, Miss E. M., 44 Winn Road, Southampton.
SANDELL, R. G., 44 Winn Road, Southampton.
SNELL, L. S., F.S.A., F.R.Hist.S., 7 Eaton Park Road, Palmers Green, London, N.13.
STEAVENSON, A. G., M.B.E. M.A., 7 Henstead Court, Devonshire Road, Southampton.
STEER, Francis W., M.A., F.S.A., 63 Orchard Street, Chichester.

TURNER, Mrs. B. D. M. Carpenter, B.A., 10 The Close, Winchester.

WALLIS, F. A. Emery, Froddington, Craneswater Park, Southsea.
WEBBER, J. G., Fallow Field, Nursling, Southampton.
WELCH, E., M.A., City Archivist, Civic Centre, Southampton.

INSTITUTIONS

ABERYSTWYTH, The National Library of Wales.

BELFAST, The Queen's University Library.
BIRKENHEAD, Central Library.
BIRMINGHAM, Public Library.
,, University Library.
BRISTOL, University Library.
BROCKENHURST, County High School.

CAMBRIDGE, University Library (per G. W. Copp, London, W.C.1).

DUBLIN, Trinity College Library (per G. W. Copp, London, W.C.1).

EAST ANGLIA, University Library.
EDINBURGH, National Library of Scotland (per G. W. Copp, London, W.C.1).
,, University Library.
EXETER, City Library.
,, University Library.

GLASGOW, University Library (per Jackson, Son & Co., Glasgow).

HULL, University Library.
,, Kingston-upon-Hull Central Public Library.

KEELE, University Library.

LEEDS, The Brotherton Library, University of Leeds.
LEICESTER, University Library.
LIVERPOOL, Public Library.
,, University Library.
LONDON, British Library of Political and Economic Science.
,, British Museum, Copyright Office.
,, City of Westminster Public Libraries.
,, College of Arms, Queen Victoria Street.
,, Goldsmith's Librarian, University of London, Senate House, W.C.1.
,, Guildhall Library, E.C.2.
,, Inner Temple Library (per Sweet and Maxwell, Ltd., E.C.4).
,, Institute of Historical Research, Senate House, W.C.1.
,, London Library, St. James's Square, S.W.1.
,, Public Record Office, Chancery Lane, W.C.2.
,, Royal Historical Society, Chelsea, S.W.10.
,, Society of Antiquaries of London, Burlington House, W.1.
LYMINGTON, County Branch Library.

MANCHESTER, Central Library, St. Peter's Square.
,, John Rylands Library.
,, University Library.

NEWCASTLE-UPON-TYNE, University Library, Queen Victoria Road.
NEWPORT, I.O.W., County Seely Library.
NOTTINGHAM, University Library.

OXFORD, Bodleian Library (per G. W. Copp, London, W.C.1).
,, The Queen's College Library.

PORTSMOUTH, Central Public Library.
,, City of Portsmouth Training College.

READING, University Library.

SHEFFIELD, University Library.

SOUTHAMPTON, Central Library.
,, Chamber of Commerce.
,, City Archivist.
,, General Manager and Clerk, Southampton Harbour Board.
,, Glen Eyre Secondary Boys' School.
,, Itchen Grammar School.

Minnesota University (per Stechert-Hafner Inc., London, W.C.2).
Missouri University Library, Columbia (per Stechert-Hafner Inc., London, WC.2.).

New Mexico, University Library.
New York, Columbia University Library (per B. F. Stevens & Brown, Ltd., Godalming, Surrey).
New York State University at Stony Brook (per Blackwells, Oxford).
New York, University Library (per George Harding's Bookshop, London, W.C.1).
New York, Public Library (per B. F. Stevens & Brown, Ltd., Godalming, Surrey).
New York, Vassar College Library, Poughkeepsie (per B. F. Stevens & Brown, Ltd., Godalming, Surrey).

Oregon, University Library.

Princeton, University Library (per E. G. Allen & Son, Ltd., London, W.C.2).

Utah, Genealogical Society, Salt Lake City.

Washington, The Folger Shakespeare Library.
Washington, Library of Congress (per E. G. Allen & Son, Ltd., London, W.C.2).
Wisconsin, University Library (per Blackwell's Exports, Oxford).

Yale, University Library (per E. G. Allen & Son, Ltd., London, W.C.2).